THE
SAVIOR
IN
KIRTLAND

Personal Accounts of
Divine Manifestations

THE
SAVIOR
IN
KIRTLAND

KARL RICKS ANDERSON

DESERET
BOOK

SALT LAKE CITY, UTAH

Library of Congress Cataloging-in-Publication Data

Anderson, Karl R., 1937–   author.
   The Savior in Kirtland : personal accounts of divine manifestations / Karl Ricks Anderson.
      pages   cm
   Includes bibliographical references and index.
   ISBN 978-1-60907-166-0 (paperbound)
1. Jesus Christ—Apparitions and miracles—Ohio—Kirtland.   2. Visions—Ohio—Kirtland.
3. The Church of Jesus Christ of Latter-day Saints—History—19th century.   4. The Church of Jesus Christ of Latter-day Saints—Doctrines.   5. Kirtland Temple.   I. Title.
   BX8643.J4A53 2012
   289.3′771334—dc23   2012019685

Printed in the United States of America
Brigham Young University Press, Provo, UT

10   9   8   7   6   5   4   3   2   1

To Elder Neal A. Maxwell

the remarkable modern Apostle and disciple of the Savior
who gave me the assignment

CONTENTS

Preface

I have devoted more than forty years of my life to working to help fulfill the Lord's promise in Doctrine and Covenants 124:83 that He would "build up Kirtland." My wife, Joyce, and I, along with our small family, were excited to move to Kirtland in 1967 because of its rich Church history. We fell in love with Joseph Smith and the early Saints, whose deep faith and willingness to sacrifice all that they had to establish this last gospel dispensation made them spiritual giants. They left homes, lands, and in many cases families, to obey the Lord's commandment to gather to Kirtland. From there, husbands, fathers, and sons were called to leave Kirtland and go on missions throughout the United States, Canada, and even across the Atlantic—a giant step to reach the entire world with the message of the restored gospel of Jesus Christ. In 1989, I wrote *Joseph Smith's Kirtland* to tell the epic story of these brave men and women whom we venerate.

Since that time, it has become evident to me that as important as their story is, the real and too often overlooked story is that of the Savior and how

He personally and visibly directed His Church and taught His Saints. As I studied more extensively, many before-unnoticed evidences of Christ's leadership came into focus. Indisputable evidences of His divinity and leadership surfaced. It became obvious that early Church members knew and recognized that the Savior was their leader. It became clear that the reason for the Church's phenomenal and highly improbable growth is that Jesus Christ Himself was in charge and in Kirtland He was fulfilling millennia of promises from the Old and New Testaments as well as from the Book of Mormon.

In 1994, I spent a day with Elder Neal A. Maxwell, a latter-day Apostle, and his family in Kirtland. After we had visited together several sacred sites and reviewed much scripture and history, he asked me to write this book. He noted my knowledge and love of Kirtland and added that there was a mother lode of Christology in Kirtland that had never been mined. He asked me to seek out the Christ-centered teachings and evidences of the Savior in Kirtland and write them. Urging patience, inspiration, and thoroughness in research, he suggested that I let it percolate and cautioned that I not be too quick to publish it. (I am not sure he meant for me to take eighteen years—I may yet have to answer for that.) Central to his challenge was this: "Write it on the Christology of Kirtland—what we know that we otherwise would not know, the visions of the universe, and what we gain from the revelations . . . Combine your insights into Christ and your love of Kirtland with the history."

It is my sincere hope that the essence of Elder Maxwell's request has been honored and that he would be happy with the result. In the end, the challenge I faced was how to distill the volumes of scripture, journals, and historical accounts as well as speeches and writings of the Prophet Joseph Smith and his associates. Much more remains yet to be mined. My study of Kirtland has indeed been humbling and life changing, and it promises to be that for all who will seek to find the Savior in Kirtland. It is my desire that members of the Church and others will gain a greater awareness of Kirtland's significance and, more important, the mother lode of Christology that comes to us through this sacred place.

ACKNOWLEDGMENTS

I am deeply indebted to the many who made significant contributions to *The Savior in Kirtland*.

This book would not have been possible without the generous and expert assistance, support and encouragement of Richard Lloyd Anderson. Richard devoted massive amounts of time and offered considerable input. He made himself immediately available day or night. Unselfishly opening his extensive collection of source documents, journals, accounts, and other information, Richard engaged in patient discussion, guidance, consulting, and wise critique. He reviewed drafts, checked sources, made suggestions, and provided invaluable insights. As all who know Richard will attest, he does not seek recognition and will never receive full credit for his influence on so many. As his younger brother, I pay tribute and express my love, brotherhood, and appreciation for his lifelong example.

I am indebted to Carma de Jong Anderson and Tyson Snow for the high quality original drawings that contribute so much to this book. Carma is a recognized artist and the Church's foremost authority on clothing worn by the early Saints. She generously gave a significant number of hours to carefully supervising the development and accuracy of the drawings. Tyson is a remarkable young artist who is endowed with amazing ability as an artist and sculptor. His exceptional capabilities go beyond artistic skills to an ability to place himself in the situation of his subject. He carefully worked and reworked the drawings to ensure historical accuracy and to convey a feeling for the content of each chapter.

Capable editors contributed to the quality of this book. Longtime family friend and able college English professional Maurine Reintjes contributed significantly. Maurine spent seemingly endless hours editing, making suggestions and adding insights to improve clarity and quality. Richard and Beverly Anderson, newfound friends, gave help at a critical juncture. They spent long hours checking and ensuring footnote accuracy. Using backgrounds in English composition and Church history, they further improved the manuscript by adding summary material, produced charts, and offered suggestions.

I express appreciation to Cory Maxwell of Deseret Book Company for his interest, encouragement, and personal direction of the manuscript. Gratitude is also expressed to Suzanne Brady, managing editor at Deseret Book Company, for her personal interest in the manuscript and mastery of Church history, as well as for her competent and careful editing.

Finally, to my wife and long-suffering companion of fifty years, I express my greatest love, appreciation, and thanks. Without Joyce's unfailing support, encouragement, and endurance, this work could never have been accomplished. She patiently worked untold hours, without complaint, typing every word through numerous drafts, proofs, and endless corrections and revisions. She found sources, made suggestions, checked footnotes, filed material and did just about every other mundane duty imaginable in undertaking such a project. Joyce has been part of every major endeavor of my life, including tolerating hundreds of trips through Church history sites, cemeteries, libraries, bookstores etc.

Others also have helped tremendously. Although I would like to acknowledge each and every contribution, my appreciation must of necessity be expressed personally.

INTRODUCTION

Kirtland, known today as "The City of Faith and Beauty," was a largely forgotten place in the history of the Church once the Saints left it in 1838. It appears that after that time, Kirtland simply disappeared from the consciousness of our people.

Once the Saints had departed from their original gathering place in Ohio, the Lord told them, "I, the Lord, have a scourge prepared for the inhabitants [of Kirtland]" (D&C 124:83). Perhaps that scourge also affected the minds of the Latter-day Saints. For many years, people remembered little more of Kirtland than that a temple, no longer owned by the Church, had been built there. Nauvoo was often perceived as the dominant and longest lasting period of early Church history.

In 1979, however, an event occurred in Kirtland that changed all that. On October 14 of that year, President Ezra Taft Benson, a latter-day prophet and at that time president of the Quorum of the Twelve Apostles, stood in Kirtland and said with prophetic authority, "Thus the scourge that was placed upon the people in that prophecy is being lifted today." He prophesied that the Saints could now "look forward to great progress in this part of the Lord's vineyard."[1] Then, with decisive leadership, he provided impetus, support, and direction to the fulfillment of that prophecy until his death.

With the lifting of the scourge, the Lord began the rebuilding of Kirtland in fulfillment of His promise. Part of the Lord's original declaration was this commitment: "Nevertheless, I, the Lord, will build up Kirtland" (D&C 124:83). Certainly, the beautiful and carefully crafted Historic Kirtland Restoration is part of that fulfillment; another important aspect is building up Kirtland in the minds, hearts, and history of His people. Recent efforts at restoration, additional writings, and many more visitors have all worked together to remove the cloak of obscurity from Kirtland. "The City of Faith and Beauty" is now reclaiming its valuable place in the remembrance of the Saints.

---

1. Ezra Taft Benson, address at groundbreaking for the Kirtland Ward meetinghouse, October 14, 1979, Church History Library, The Church of Jesus Christ of Latter-day Saints, Salt Lake City, Utah.

PROLOGUE

In 1820 our Heavenly Father introduced Jesus Christ to the Prophet Joseph Smith with the command, "Hear Him!"[1] From that glorious beginning the Savior has been the center and focus of our religion. In 1831, Christ declared that there would be "no eye that shall not see, neither ear that shall not hear" His voice.[2] Through the following pages of *The Savior in Kirtland,* my hope is that the reader will see the Savior and hear His voice with greater clarity by looking at the Restoration through the lens of Christ. In no other place during the early years of the Restoration was this lens so focused as in Kirtland, Ohio.

Through inspiration, Joseph Smith designated the land of Kirtland as Shinehah.[3] The Lord told Abraham that *Shinehah* meant "the sun."[4] As rays

---

1. Joseph Smith–History 1:17.

2. Doctrine & Covenants 1:2.

3. From the original text of Doctrine & Covenants 82 and 104. Orson Pratt describes the inspired process of substituting names: *The Seer* 2, no. 3 (March 1854): 228.

4. Abraham 3:13.

of the sun give light and life to the world, so also did the rays of gospel light emanating from Kirtland give light and even eternal life to the world's inhabitants. Not only did the sun dawn upon the world from Kirtland but through Elijah it also illuminated the eternal world. The source of that light is Jesus Christ—the light and life of the world. The Lord declared in Kirtland that He is even "the light of the sun, and the power thereof by which it was made" (D&C 88:7).

Kirtland, land of "the sun," was also the land of the Son, our Savior. He prepared the land, gathered His followers, and protected them from the adversary. In Kirtland the Savior promised His Saints, "I will appear unto my servants, and speak unto them with mine own voice."[5] He appeared in vision or spoke to more than twenty-three of His servants there. More first-person words of Christ have gone to the world from Kirtland than from any other location in history. Through His direct voice of revelation, Christ comprehensively taught the world about Himself, His mission of atonement, and the premortal and postmortal worlds. He structured His Church in Kirtland and called its leaders by personal revelation. He taught them in vision as well as through the Spirit. He commanded His poverty-stricken Saints to build His first temple in two thousand years. He showed them the pattern and then gave them the assistance and power to build it. In Kirtland the very heavens thundered many additional witnesses of Christ's visions and voice. He sent angels, heavenly choirs, and divine messengers—who reflected His divinity and direction from heaven above—with keys and authority. Finally, He dispatched His latter-day messengers from Kirtland unto all nations in fulfillment of ancient prophecy. The Savior knew Kirtland well. The story of Kirtland is in reality a story of Christ. Kirtland and Christ can never be separated.

---

5. Doctrine & Covenants 110:8.

CHAPTER 1

The Savior Prepares
"the Ohio"

Thou wast sent forth . . . [to Ohio] to prepare the way before me,
and before Elijah which should come.
—Doctrine & Covenants 35:4

The story of Christ preparing the land of Kirtland is as old as time and
was without doubt foreseen in the heavens long before man appeared upon
the earth. From the beginning, sacred events to transpire in Kirtland were
undoubtedly planned and even announced. Joseph Smith emphasized that
crucial temple work, the keys for which were received in Kirtland, constituted "a voice of gladness for the living and the dead."[1] Christ ordained such
redemptive events "before the world was."[2] Ancient prophets were "fired
with heavenly and joyful anticipations" of these events, which would "bring
about . . . the salvation of the human family."[3] Christ fired with joyful anticipation the soul of the ancient prophet Malachi as He told him of sacred

---

1. Doctrine & Covenants 128:19.

2. Doctrine & Covenants 128:22.

3. Joseph Smith, *History of The Church of Jesus Christ of Latter-day Saints,* ed. B. H. Roberts, 7 vols., 2d
   ed. rev. (Salt Lake City: The Church of Jesus Christ of Latter-day Saints, 1932–51), 4:609–10; "The
   Temple," *Times and Seasons* 3 (May 2, 1842): 776.

events to transpire in the Kirtland Temple.[4] After the Savior's resurrection, He commanded followers on the American continent to "write the words" of prophecy He gave to Malachi regarding events to transpire in Kirtland.[5]

It appears that Christ prepared "the Ohio" for centuries before He gathered His people there. Evidence of this preparation can be found in seventeenth-century England. King Charles II gave the state of Connecticut a thin slice of land that included the land of Kirtland. This thin slice was eventually whittled down to a 120-mile-wide area of land designated as the Connecticut Western Reserve. Settlement was primarily by people from New England. The Western Reserve seems to correspond approximately to the area the Lord called "the Ohio."

A decade after the signing of the Declaration of Independence, America's Congress of the Confederation included Ohio as a part of the Northwest Territory. In what is called the Northwest Ordinance of 1787, Congress inserted two provisions that would have been important to the Lord. They assured religious freedom for all settlers and stated, "Schools and the means of education shall forever be encouraged."[6] Ohio was a desirable place for settlers, as extolled by George Washington: "If I was a young man, just preparing to begin the world or if advanced in life, and had a family to make provision for, I know of no country where I should rather fix my habitation."[7]

From the beginning, Christ prepared an entire land and then selectively peopled it with a remarkable God-fearing frontier folk. The story of Kirtland's preparation reveals their strong moral values, personal trials, incredibly hard work, generosity, and great faith. The story notes their

---

4. Malachi 3–4.

5. 3 Nephi 24–25.

6. *Documents of American History,* ed. Henry Steele Commager and Milton Cantor, 2 vols. (Englewood Cliffs, N.J.: Prentice Hall, 1988), 1:131.

7. *George Washington Writings,* sel. John H. Rhodehamel (New York: Literary Classics of the United States, 1997), 687.

response to the promptings of the Lord to listen, move, nurture, and prepare a frontier land for the advent of the gospel there and the ultimate building of the first temple of God in the Restoration. Kirtland, known intimately to the Lord, was being groomed for a great mission—greater than anything witnessed in two thousand years. The Savior prepared Kirtland and then commanded His Saints to gather there. In the very early days of this land, however, the story began quietly, and its players were few.

Decades before the gospel was brought there, the Lord, as early as 1798, began to nudge key people and their families to "the Ohio." It was no accident that the family of a future member of the First Presidency, Frederick G. Williams, moved there that year. It must also have been in the eternal plan that other families of future greatness would congregate in and around this underdeveloped land of promise. The Snow family, including Lorenzo and Eliza R., came in 1811. A year later the industrious colonizer Isaac Morley with his wife, Lucy, settled on two hundred acres where matters of importance would later occur. In 1814, John and Elsa Johnson (later instrumental in purchasing land for the temple) settled near Kirtland with their two sons, Luke and Lyman, who in time became members of the first Quorum of the Twelve Apostles.

The Lord also planted other future Apostles in Ohio, where He would prepare them to receive His word. He sent Orson Hyde in 1819 and Parley P. Pratt and Lyman Wight in 1826. Future bishops Edward Partridge and Newel K. Whitney arrived in Ohio by 1820 and 1823, respectively. The incredible good that these men were to perform cannot be measured. The Lord not only summoned and prepared His future leaders but also assembled hundreds of other future Church members in the Ohio. Kirtland was ready to receive the gospel and in due time welcome the Prophet of the Restoration, Joseph Smith.

At last, in the late autumn of 1830, the Lord formally began His work in Kirtland by sending four missionaries westward to the Indians—Oliver Cowdery, Peter Whitmer Jr., Ziba Peterson, and Parley P. Pratt—and they stopped there for a short time en route to Missouri. These men contacted a successful preacher named Sidney Rigdon (Parley had known him from earlier years in Ohio), who had many congregations in the area but one specifically located near Kirtland. This Sidney Rigdon, whom the Lord compared to John the Baptist,[8] had a foreordained mission to prepare the people for the coming of Christ and Elijah. He had been carefully groomed, and his works were known. The Ohio was being readied, and Sidney Rigdon was to play an early key role in that preparation.

Preparing the Way

The Savior gave Sidney Rigdon a specific mission to prepare the way for the gospel to be taken to Ohio. In 1830, He told Sidney, "Thou wast sent forth [to Ohio], even as John, to prepare the way before me, and before Elijah which should come, and thou knewest it not."[9] Just as John the Baptist had prepared his people to receive Christ, so Sidney Rigdon was preparing great numbers of people in the Kirtland area to receive Christ's Church. Many of John's followers accepted Christ's message when they heard it. Many of Sidney's followers likewise accepted Christ's latter-day message when it came. Sidney prepared hundreds in Ohio to embrace Christ's restored gospel and to be ready for the Savior's initial appearance in Ohio.

These two forerunners had other similarities. In both cases John the Baptist's and Sidney Rigdon's preaching enabled the Church to take immediate root. Both were fervent and effective preachers. People flocked to each. Just as many people had gone out from Jerusalem and all Judea to hear John's message,[10] so also did large numbers of followers attend Sidney's meetings. Meetings were held outdoors because churches were not "large enough to

---

8. Doctrine & Covenants 35:4.

9. Doctrine & Covenants 35:4; Matthew 3:3.

10. Matthew 3:5–6.

contain the vast assemblies" Sidney attracted.[11] Both preached repentance—
John in the "wilderness" of Judea[12] and Sidney in a developing area still considered something of a wilderness. Neither had authority from God to bestow
the Holy Ghost. Both knew and effectively taught existing Bible scripture.

Just as the Lord had prepared John the Baptist as a youth, so also He
prepared Sidney.[13] Sidney's preparation for some of the Lord's most critical
assignments began step-by-step as a boy. Even as he labored on his father's
farm, he had a passion for learning. He once wrote that he "had an insatiable
thirst for reading."[14] His son John Wickliffe Rigdon described this thirst,
saying,

> Sidney . . . borrowed all the histories he could get and be-
> gan to read them. His parents would not let him have a candle
> to read by night; he therefore gathered hickory bark (there was
> plenty of it around the old farm), and he used to get it and at
> night throw it on the old fireplace and then lie with his face
> and head towards the fire and read history till near morning
> unless his parents got up and drove him to bed before that
> time.[15]

As a youth, Sidney desired a formal education. His son further stated
that Sidney "pleaded with his father and mother to let him go . . . to
school, but they would not consent to let him go, saying . . . he was able

---

11. "History of Joseph Smith," *Times and Seasons* 4 (June 1, 1843): 209–10; *Times and Seasons* 4 (May 15, 1843): 194.

12. Luke 3:3; Matthew 3:1–2.

13. Doctrine & Covenants 84:27–28.

14. Richard S. Van Wagoner, *Sidney Rigdon: A Portrait of Religious Excess* (Provo, Utah: Maxwell Institute, 2002), 5.

15. John Wickliffe Rigdon, "'I Never Knew a Time When I Did Not Know Joseph Smith': A Son's Record of the Life and Testimony of Sidney Rigdon," ed. Karl Keller, *Dialogue* 1, no. 4 (Winter 1966): 20.

to work on the farm and he could not go."[16] Apparently, Sidney spent his time in work and study. It was said of him, "He was never known to play with the boys."[17]

Sidney vowed that despite not being allowed to get a formal education, he would teach himself. One can surmise that the Lord directed Sidney to the scriptures and other studies. In solitude, without interaction with other students, he read and was no doubt tutored by the Spirit. Had he pursued a formal education, he might have been influenced by those already entrenched in scriptural biases. He might also have been enticed to study a profession that could have led him away from his God-given mission to prepare Ohio for the restored Church and to receive personal visitations from Christ and Elijah. Sidney grew up on the family farm, and circumstances, including the death of his father, forced him to remain there for his first twenty-six years.

The Lord endowed Sidney with a photographic memory. Because of his love of learning, eagerness to read, and ability to retain what he read, Sidney became knowledgeable, especially in history, the Bible, and the English language. His son wrote:

> In this way, he became a great historian, the best I ever saw. He seemed to have the history of the world on his tongue's end and he got to be a great biblical scholar as well. He was as familiar with the Bible as a child is with his spelling book. . . . Reading books was the greatest pleasure he could get. He studied English grammar alone and became a very fine grammarian. He was very precise in his language.[18]

---

16. Keller, "Son's Record," 20.

17. Keller, "Son's Record," 20.

18. Keller, "Son's Record," 20.

Twenty-six years of learning in solitude gave Sidney a solid base in the Bible. He was being prepared for his life's mission.

The Key to Sidney's Life

All of his life Sidney was a dedicated student of the Bible. He read it not only by the dim light of the hickory fire because his father refused to give him a candle but also when he apprenticed to become a minister in 1819.[19] In pursuing his self-taught course of learning the Bible, he read and memorized extensive portions of the scriptures.

Sidney truly loved and immersed himself in the Bible. As his son said, "[He] was as familiar with the Bible as a child is with his spelling book" and could recall "everything he read."[20] Sidney described his knowledge of the Bible as "far in advance of all others."[21] His love of the Bible induced him later to affiliate with the Campbellite movement, whose motto was "Where the Scriptures speak, we speak; where the Scriptures are silent, we are silent."[22]

Sidney's grounding in the Bible played a larger role later, not only in preparing people to receive the restored gospel but also in his critical mission as scribe for Joseph's translation of the Bible.

Sidney's Mission to Serve the Lord

Early in life, Sidney was aware of his mission to serve the Lord. Looking back, he wrote that "from his earliest infancy"[23] his "ruling principle" was to

19. F. Mark McKiernan, "The Conversion of Sidney Rigdon to Mormonism," *Dialogue* 5, no. 2 (Summer 1970): 73.

20. Keller, "Son's Record," 20; J. Wickliffe Rigdon, "Life Story of Rigdon," 4, in Van Wagoner, *Sidney Rigdon*, 5n11.

21. Van Wagoner, *Sidney Rigdon*, 8n28.

22. Van Wagoner, *Sidney Rigdon*, 20.

23. Van Wagoner, *Sidney Rigdon*, 6n15.

serve the Lord.[24] Although his call as a forerunner was confirmed after the fact, the Lord must have impressed it upon Sidney's mind early in his youth. He felt his calling strongly enough that he wrote about it as if it were the revealed word of the Lord: "I the Lord called him [Sidney] from his plow as I did Amos."[25] Sidney's son wrote that his father "was of a natural religious turn of mind and he delighted in preaching the gospel."[26] Sidney had a God-given talent for preaching. As his son expressed it, "Nature made him an orator."[27]

In 1819, when Sidney was twenty-six, his career opportunity finally came. He chose to apprentice for a ministerial career with a Baptist minister who lived not far from Sidney's home in western Pennsylvania. On April 1 of the next year, about the same time Joseph Smith received his First Vision, Sidney received his certificate of ordination and became a minister.[28] As he would soon discover, however, rather than having found his calling, he would spend the next six years in broader learning, practice, and preparation for a higher calling.

Key Steps in Sidney's Preparation

During the next six years, Sidney's life revolved around three activities that later had significant bearing on his divinely appointed missions:

1. *He developed an eight-year association with Alexander Campbell.* In 1821, Sidney visited Campbell and was "won over to the reform cause."[29] He

---

24. Sidney wrote late in life that "my fear, saith the Lord" was his ruling principle. He was the scribe for Doctrine & Covenants 76:5, where the terms "saith the Lord" and "fear me" were used in conjunction with "serve me." The phrase "where is my fear? saith the Lord" in Malachi 1:6 points out the relationship of a servant to his master. Sidney felt that his mission was to serve his Master.

25. Van Wagoner, *Sidney Rigdon,* 6n15.

26. Keller, "Son's Record," 20.

27. Keller, "Son's Record," 20.

28. Hans Rollmann, "The Early Baptist Career of Sidney Rigdon in Warren, Ohio," *BYU Studies* 21 (Winter 1981): 47.

29. Rollmann, "Baptist Career of Sidney Rigdon," 49.

even helped pioneer that Reform movement, which sought for a restoration of the gospel. Sidney's son described the Campbellite religion as a simple faith. "There was not much to their confession of faith," he wrote. "It was to believe on the Lord and Savior Jesus Christ, be baptized for the remission of your sins, and take the Bible for your guide was all there was of it. Its simplicity recommended itself to the general public."[30]

The Lord, leading Sidney through his association with Campbell, formulated the basis of his preparing northeastern Ohio for the restored gospel. B. H. Roberts, prominent scholar and an LDS General Authority for fifty-six years, said, "The work of these reformers [Alexander Campbell and Sidney Rigdon] was a preparatory work to the coming forth of the fullness of the gospel, I may say that perhaps more people joined the Church in an early day from [the] 'Disciples' [Campbellites] than from any other denomination whatsoever."[31]

2. *He accepted his first ministerial assignment.* In January 1822, Sidney ascended the pulpit as minister of Pittsburgh's large Baptist church. "Fame and fortune seemed to be within his grasp,"[32] his son said. But Sidney had served only two and a half years when a crisis of conscience arose. Strict Baptist leaders required him to teach the doctrine of infant damnation. Sidney could not do so. He did not believe it to be in the Bible and "would not teach it."[33] Though it meant forsaking the vocation he loved, when something became a matter of conscience, Sidney followed a higher voice. His basic Bible foundation forced him to make what was probably his hardest decision in thirty-one years. Where many might have compromised, Sidney resigned his post to maintain the integrity of his religious beliefs. He left what he felt was his calling, but doing so drew him closer to the Lord. He

---

30. Keller, "Son's Record," 22.

31. B. H. Roberts, *New Witnesses for God,* 3 vols. (Salt Lake City: General Board of the YMMIA, 1911), 3:349–50.

32. Keller, "Son's Record," 21.

33. Keller, "Son's Record," 21.

later wrote that it was done "for conscience sake," and his defining decision came "after . . . deliberation, deep reflection, and solemn prayer to his
Heavenly Father."[34]

In his ministerial assignment, he learned that the Lord had always required His people to make hard decisions, to sacrifice fame and worldly
honor by choosing God over man. He had the integrity to be true to his
conscience, which guided him not to trade his faith and beliefs for fame
and fortune. His agonizing decision foreshadowed a future decision six years
down the road. When the restored Church came to Kirtland, he would listen to a higher voice, and once again Sidney would reject fame and fortune
as he resigned another ministerial post in Mentor, Ohio.

3. *He chose the humble life of a tanner.* After resigning his vocation as a
renowned minister in Pittsburgh, Sidney lost the monetary means to sustain
his family's basic needs. He then decided to apprentice under his brother-in-
law, who knew the tanner's trade. Sidney sold some land and invested money
in a tannery. He said he did it because he had "no way by which to sustain
his family, besides his own industry." He left a life of "wealth, popularity and
honor," opting for a new life of "nothing but poverty and hard labor."[35]

Sidney said his two-year experience as a tanner was a "humble oc-
cupation" that brought "sorrow and humiliation." It was a severe blow
to his pride, he continued, that when past friends saw him "in the garb
suited to the employment of a tanner, there was no longer . . . courtesy and
friendship manifested"; rather, they "looked upon him with coolness and
indifference."[36] Few vocations would have been more humbling to him
than that of a tanner. The experience may have been the Lord's purpose—
to teach humility to Sidney. It came after his formal religious preparation,
which produced remarkable success and popularity. This exercise in humility prepared him for his mission to advance the Savior's last dispensation.

---

34. *Times and Seasons* 4 (May 15, 1843): 193.

35. *Times and Seasons* 4 (May 15, 1843): 193.

36. *Times and Seasons* 4 (May 15, 1843): 193.

Perhaps Sidney's humiliating experiences were the vehicle the Lord used to humble him sufficiently for his mission, which was, in the Savior's words, "to prepare the way before me, and before Elijah."[37] He seemed to struggle with pride. The Lord later said of him, "I, the Lord, am not pleased with my servant Sidney Rigdon; he exalted himself in his heart and received not counsel"; "let him humble himself before me."[38]

After enjoying the fame of a highly acclaimed orator, he was now facing a congregation of smelly animal skins immersed in vats of ammonia and lime. His daily labor was no longer preaching to live audiences but scraping hair from the hides of dead animals. For two years the fine apparel of an orator was replaced by the rough clothes of a tanner.

The Forerunner's Ministry

In December 1825, Sidney took his wife, Phoebe, and their three children and departed on their yet unknown mission to Ohio. They made their new home on land belonging to Phoebe's father in Bainbridge, fifteen miles south of Kirtland. Sidney's family was enthusiastically received. Almost immediately he was invited to preach in Mantua, where he taught the Reformed Baptist, or Campbellite, belief in the Bible to the Snow family, including Lorenzo and Eliza R., who later became prominent Church members.

In June 1826, Sidney preached a funeral service for a Baptist minister in Mentor, barely two miles from Kirtland. The Mentor congregation eventually invited him to fill their ministerial vacancy. Hard work learned on the family farm and in the tannery served Sidney well as he rigorously preached the Campbellite message to surrounding towns such as Kirtland. Like the preaching of John of old, Sidney's message was simple: "repentance and

---

37. Doctrine & Covenants 35:4.

38. Doctrine & Covenants 63:55; 124:103.

baptism, for the remission of sins."[39] He taught the Campbellite message to many families, including those of Edward Partridge, Isaac Morley, Newel K. Whitney, John Murdock, Frederick G. Williams, Orson Hyde, and Lyman Wight. These families later became devout believers and leaders in the restored Church of Jesus Christ.

Sidney traveled far and wide. He was led sixty miles west to prepare the families of Parley P. Pratt, Milo Andrus, and others. He traveled fifty miles east to the Pennsylvania border and fifty miles south to Ohio towns such as Hiram, Nelson, and Mantua. He probably established more than twelve Reformed Baptist congregations in a wide geographic area. He successfully fulfilled his calling to prepare the way for the restored gospel. Sidney's phenomenal work for the Savior is recorded in many journals of those who joined the Church when it came to Kirtland, thus showing a successful fulfillment of this divine work.

Sidney's strict message concerning the Bible appealed to honest seekers of truth whom he was preparing for "one mightier" than he.[40] Edward Partridge wrote that he was attracted because Sidney's message was "nearer right than any other he had heard of."[41] Elizabeth Ann and Newel K. Whitney came to Sidney because his principles "seemed most in accordance with the scriptures [and were] to us the nearest pattern to our Saviour's teachings, until Parley P. Pratt and another elder preached the everlasting gospel in Kirtland."[42]

Orson Hyde wrote simply that he became a convert of Sidney's faith because he was "forcibly struck with the doctrine of immersion or baptism for the remission of sins, and many other important items of doctrine which

---

39. *Times and Seasons* 4 (May 15, 1843): 194.

40. Luke 3:16.

41. Andrew Jenson, *Latter-day Saint Biographical Encyclopedia,* 4 vols. (Salt Lake City: Andrew Jenson History Company, 1901–36; repr., Salt Lake City: Western Epics, 1971), 1:219.

42. Elizabeth Whitney, in Edward W. Tullidge, *The Women of Mormondom* (New York: Tullidge & Crandall, 1877; repr., Salt Lake City: n.p., 1975), 35.

were advocated."[43] Lyman Wight was struck with the same doctrine. He wrote, "I heard Sidney Rigdon preach what was then called the Rigdonite doctrine. After hearing him go through the principle of baptism for the remission of sins I went forward and was baptized by his hands."[44]

John Murdock indicated in his journal, "It caused me to rejoice, believing that I had at last found a people that believed the Scriptures . . . so well agreeing with my feelings, and they professed to be in search of truth as I was, therefore I united with them."[45] John also noted that while he felt that even Sidney had not yet found the fulness of the gospel, "I believe that he . . . [was] honestly seeking for the truth."[46]

One of Sidney's most significant converts to the Campbellites was Parley P. Pratt, later to be one of the first members of the Quorum of the Twelve Apostles in Kirtland. Parley was the man who later taught the restored gospel of Jesus Christ to Sidney, who accepted it and was baptized. Parley said he was initially drawn to Sidney because Sidney taught principles familiar to him, explaining:

> Mr. Sidney Rigdon came into the neighborhood as a preacher . . . and what was my astonishment when I found he preached faith in Jesus Christ, repentance towards God, and baptism for remission of sins, with the promise of the gift of the Holy Ghost to all who would come forward, with all their hearts, and obey this doctrine!
>
> Here was the *ancient gospel* in due form. Here were the very principles that I had discovered years before; but could

43. "History of Orson Hyde," *Millennial Star* 26 (November 19, 1864): 744.

44. *The History of the Reorganized Church of Jesus Christ of Latter Day Saints*, vol. 1 (Independence, Mo.: Herald House, 1951), 151–52.

45. John Murdock, "A Brief Synopsis of the Life of John Murdock: Taken from an Abridged Record of His Journal," 7, in L. Tom Perry Special Collections, Harold B. Lee Library, Brigham Young University, Provo, Utah.

46. Murdock, "Brief Synopsis," 8.

find no one to minister in. But still one great link was wanting to complete the chain of the ancient order of things; and that was, the *authority* to minister in holy things—the apostleship.[47]

The common thread in these accounts is that Sidney Rigdon carried out his interim mission successfully. Sidney "commenced to baptize, and like John of old, there flocked to him people from all the region round about—persons of all ranks and standings in society—the rich, the poor, the noble and the brave, flocked to be baptized of him. . . . He soon had large and flourishing societies throughout that whole region of country."[48]

Four Missionaries Come to Ohio

In November 1830, the Lord dispatched four enthusiastic missionaries—Oliver Cowdery, Parley P. Pratt, Peter Whitmer Jr., and Ziba Peterson. Their mission was to travel to the outer reaches of the United States, the uncivilized Missouri frontier. They were to carry the message of Christ's restored gospel to the Indians. On their way they walked into Sidney Rigdon's life in Mentor. They introduced him to the Church of Christ and gave him a copy of the Book of Mormon. Sidney's five-year mission as a Campbellite minister took an unexpected turn. The four missionaries ignited smoldering religious fervor within and around him. That fire burned brightly and extensively for over seven years in the Kirtland area. After reading the Book of Mormon, followed by prayer and meditation, Sidney became "fully convinced . . . by a revelation from Jesus Christ, which was made known to him in a remarkable manner."[49]

47. Parley P. Pratt, *Autobiography of Parley P. Pratt,* ed. Parley P. Pratt Jr. (Salt Lake City: Deseret Book, 1985), 13.

48. *Times and Seasons* 4 (August 15, 1843): 210.

49. *Times and Seasons* 4 (August 15, 1843): 290.

John Whitmer, the first Church historian, characterized Sidney's revelation as a vision:

> Sidney Rigdon, he having been an instrument in the hands of the Lord of doing much good. He was in search of truth; . . . he obtained a witness from the Lord, of the truth of his work. After several days the Lord heard his cries, and answered his prayers, and by vision showed to him, that this eminated from him [God] and must remain, it being the Fulness of the gospel of Jesus Christ.[50]

Consequently, Sidney submitted himself for baptism in Christ's restored Church. With new spiritual energy, he started on a mission of conversion. He taught and converted people in congregations from at least ten Ohio communities who knew, respected, and believed him. Many people joined the Church because of his influence, prominence, and reputation. Sidney had prepared them to recognize the true gospel of Jesus Christ now found in the newly restored Church. This new convert's missionary efforts were extraordinarily successful, and he had a flood of immediate conversions. In the last two months of 1830, Ohio converts equaled Church membership in New York. Many of the newly converted members in Ohio were promptly ordained to the priesthood.

Parley Pratt described the fertile religious environment that was prepared by Sidney:

> The news of our coming was soon noised abroad. . . . The interest and excitement now became general in Kirtland, and in all the region round about. The people thronged us night and day, insomuch that we had no time for rest and retirement. Meetings were convened in different

---

50. *From Historian to Dissident: The Book of John Whitmer,* ed. Bruce N. Westergren (Salt Lake City: Signature Books, 1995), 3–4.

neighborhoods, and multitudes came together soliciting our attendance; while thousands flocked about us daily; some to be taught, some for curiosity, some to obey the gospel, and some to dispute or resist it.

In two or three weeks from our arrival in the neighborhood with the news, we had baptized one hundred and twenty-seven souls, and this number soon increased to one thousand. The disciples were filled with joy and gladness; . . . faith was strong, joy was great.[51]

Joseph Smith and the Saints in New York, despite being told the field was "white already to harvest,"[52] did not anticipate that the Lord could prepare a harvest field so white or a people so ready to accept Christ's restored gospel. Thus the fertile ground of Ohio emerged as the holy ground of "the Ohio."

Preparing Key Leaders

Sidney Rigdon prepared not only "the Ohio" but also key leaders. Through his influence, a significant core of Church leadership emerged. Sidney reached out, converted, and baptized several prominent citizens who later assumed major leadership roles. Emily Coburn, who moved to Ohio in early 1831, observed that most of the converts had significant status in Kirtland: "They were establishing a Mormon church in that thriving little village. The members now numbered about one hundred persons, the greater part of whom were the brightest and best of the community, merchants, lawyers and doctors."[53]

51. Pratt, *Autobiography*, 36.

52. Doctrine & Covenants 6:3.

53. Emily M. Austin, *Mormonism; or, Life among the Mormons* (Madison, Wis.: M. J. Cantwell Book and Job Printer, 1882), 58–60, in Larry C. Porter, "'Ye Shall Go to the Ohio': Exodus of the New York Saints to Ohio, 1831," in *Ohio*, ed. Milton V. Backman Jr., Regional Studies in Latter-day Saint

The following list identifies those in "the Ohio" who were later called to significant Church offices and made an impact in Church leadership:

- First Presidency: Sidney Rigdon, Frederick G. Williams, and Lorenzo Snow
- Quorum of the Twelve Apostles: Orson Hyde, Parley P. Pratt, Luke S. Johnson, Lyman E. Johnson,[54] and Lyman Wight
- Presiding Bishopric: Edward Partridge, Isaac Morley, Newel K. Whitney, John Corrill, and Titus Billings

In addition to finding and preparing future priesthood leaders, Sidney prepared women for future leadership in the Relief Society. The Lord placed two women in Ohio, where Sidney could find them: Elizabeth Ann Whitney and Eliza R. Snow, who had been staunch members of his Campbellite congregations. Elizabeth later served as counselor to two Relief Society presidents, first Emma Smith and then Eliza Snow. Eliza herself served as president of the Relief Society for twenty-one years.

Sidney Fulfilled His Missions in Kirtland

Sidney excelled in performing the missions given him by the Savior. Before the Kirtland period began, the Lord gave Sidney at least six specific

---

Church History series (Provo, Utah: Department of Church History and Doctrine, Brigham Young University, 1990), 6.

54. Although Luke and Lyman Johnson were not Campbellites or Reformed Baptists, they would have known of Sidney Rigdon and probably heard him preach. The Hiram area, in which they lived, was heavily Campbellite. In 1827, Sidney organized a Campbellite congregation within five miles of their home. The Johnson and Snow families (who were Campbellites) were no doubt friends. Lorenzo Snow formed a close relationship with Luke and Lyman Johnson with whom he "had been intimately acquainted all through [their] boyhood days" (Lorenzo Snow, "Reminiscences of the Prophet Joseph Smith," *[Salt Lake City, Utah] Deseret Evening News,* December 23, 1899, 17). In February 1831, three months after Sidney Rigdon was baptized, Sidney baptized Lyman Johnson.

assignments to which he dedicated his life. Sidney fulfilled them entirely during the Kirtland years as follows:

1. *"Prepare the way before me, and before Elijah."*[55] Sidney labored hard to baptize and prepare the people and the Kirtland Temple for the appearance of the Savior and Elijah. With others, he "wet [the walls of the temple] with . . . tears."[56] When the Savior and Elijah came on April 3, 1836, the people and the temple were prepared.

2. *"Watch over him [Joseph] that his faith fail not."*[57] Few spent as much time with Joseph Smith as Sidney did during the Kirtland years. When Joseph met Sidney, the Lord characterized Joseph as His servant and said, "In weakness have I blessed him."[58] Sidney obviously had no fear of experienced and combative ministers or others who could have tried to intimidate or publicly humiliate Joseph. Sidney was the ideal companion. History shows that Joseph's confidence and faith grew steadily through Sidney's companionship. Seldom has the Lord given anyone the responsibility to "watch over" his prophet.

3. *"Thou shalt write for him; and the scriptures shall be given."*[59] Sidney served as scribe for Joseph from the time they first met. Sidney was at the side of the Prophet as he translated parts of the Bible, including the book of Moses. Speaking of their work together, they recorded, "We were doing the work of translation, which the Lord had appointed unto us," with Joseph as the revelator and Sidney as the scribe.[60] Concerning the translation of sections in the Bible, Joseph once referred to it as "our work."[61] One month before they received the vision recorded in Doctrine and Covenants 76,

55. Doctrine & Covenants 35:4.

56. *History of the Church,* 2:414; *Messenger and Advocate* 2, no. 6 (March 1836): 274.

57. Doctrine & Covenants 35:19.

58. Doctrine & Covenants 35:17.

59. Doctrine & Covenants 35:20.

60. Doctrine & Covenants 76:15.

61. *History of the Church,* 1:211.

the Lord, speaking to both of them, said, "Verily I say unto you my servants, Joseph Smith, Jun., and Sidney Rigdon, saith the Lord, it is expedient to translate again."[62] Although the work of translation was clearly Joseph's assignment, "there must have been frequent periods of discussion about various passages and ideas."[63] Joseph benefited from Sidney's extensive knowledge of and insights into the Bible as well as his writing ability.

4. *"Tarry with him, and he shall journey with you; forsake him not."*[64] In this directive the Lord joined Joseph and Sidney at the hip in missionary work. The two men traveled together extensively as missionary companions. In each of the Prophet's lengthy missionary journeys—seven in all during the Kirtland years—Sidney and Joseph journeyed side by side.

5. *"Thou shalt preach my gospel and call on the holy prophets to prove his [Joseph Smith's] words, as they shall be given him."*[65] Sidney's speaking capability was renowned throughout northeastern Ohio and western Pennsylvania. Joseph Smith and Oliver Cowdery referred to his preaching as forcible, logical, powerful, able, devout, appropriate, and sublime.[66] Probably the best example of his powerful preaching came during the Kirtland Temple dedication. Oliver, the eloquent speaker, used superlative language to shower adulation upon Sidney, who spoke for two and a half hours at the dedication. He wrote that Sidney quoted from scripture and

> drew tears from many eyes. . . .
>
> . . . His whole soul appeared to be fired with his subject.

---

62. Doctrine & Covenants 73:3.

63. Robert J. Matthews, *"A Plainer Translation": Joseph Smith's Translation of the Bible, a History and Commentary* (Provo, Utah: Brigham Young University Press, 1975), 39.

64. Doctrine & Covenants 35:22.

65. Doctrine & Covenants 35:23.

66. *Messenger and Advocate* 2, no. 6 (March 1836): 275; Joseph Smith, *History of The Church of Jesus Christ of Latter-day Saints*, ed. B. H. Roberts, 7 vols., 2d ed. rev. (Salt Lake City: The Church of Jesus Christ of Latter-day Saints, 1932–51), 1:270; 2:414.

Arguments, strong and conclusive seemed almost to vie with each other for utterance....

... To say on this occasion he showed himself master of his subject and did well, would be doing him injustice; to say he acquitted himself with honor or did very well, would be detracting from him real merit; and to say that he did *exceeding* well, would be only halting praise.[67]

6. *"I will ordain you . . . to be a spokesman unto my servant Joseph."*[68] President George Q. Cannon attests to Sidney's success as spokesman for Joseph. He publically recognized and praised Sidney, saying: "Those who knew Sidney Rigdon, know how wonderfully God inspired him, and with what wonderful eloquence he declared the word of God to the people. He was a mighty man in the hands of God, as a spokesman, as long [as] the prophet lived, or up to a short time before his death."[69]

The Lord, through revelation, gave Sidney a significant additional assignment to travel to Missouri to "consecrate and dedicate this land, and the spot for the temple, unto the Lord."[70] Sidney performed this dedication on August 2, 1831, as commanded, and the next day the Prophet Joseph Smith dedicated the temple site in Independence. Sidney stood as Joseph Smith's first counselor, accepting key responsibilities for eleven of the fourteen years Joseph led the Church. It is significant that the Lord directed more revelations in the Doctrine and Covenants to Sidney than to anyone else except Joseph.

---

67. *Messenger and Advocate* 2, no. 6 (March 1836): 275–76.

68. Doctrine & Covenants 100:9.

69. George Q. Cannon, in *Journal of Discourses,* 26 vols. (London: Latter-day Saints' Book Depot, 1854–86), 25:126.

70. Doctrine & Covenants 58:57.

Understanding Sidney Rigdon

Sidney Rigdon paid a heavy price to join the Church. Congregations, communities, and leaders, both religious and otherwise in two states, held him in high regard. Joseph Smith wrote that Sidney "was respected by the entire community, and his name was a tower of strength."[71] The Prophet recognized that Sidney's former congregation had taken good care of the Rigdons and their seven children. He wrote, "His wants were abundantly supplied," adding that his needs were even "anticipated."[72] By joining the Church, Sidney and his family sacrificed all of these benefits. Joseph further characterized Sidney's dilemma as follows: "If he should unite with the Church of Christ, his prospects of wealth and affluence would vanish; his family dependent upon him for support, must necessarily share his humiliation and poverty. He was aware that his character and his reputation must suffer."[73]

Sidney Rigdon joined the Church in Kirtland at considerable sacrifice. Other members of the Church had great status and more material goods than did he and his family, but others had generally left their homes to gather to Ohio or Missouri. Sidney, a leader of great repute, stayed to live among people who knew him and who felt betrayed when he defected from their religion to join the Mormons. They constantly tried to destroy him and brought pressure on him every chance they got. To stop great numbers of Sidney's parishioners from following him into the restored Church, former ministerial colleagues and congregational leaders attempted to defame him and destroy his reputation. By accusing Sidney of collaborating with Joseph Smith to steal a manuscript and publish it as the Book of Mormon, they attempted to destroy the credibility of the Church and of Joseph Smith. They accused Sidney of conniving with Joseph to concoct false revelations

---

71. *Times and Seasons* 4 (September 1, 1843): 305.

72. *Times and Seasons* 4 (September 1, 1843): 305.

73. *Times and Seasons* 4 (September 1, 1843): 305.

and accounts of visions. Because Joseph was not as polished as the seasoned Sidney, they accused Sidney of originating this new church. These false accusations followed Sidney to the grave and beyond. His son John was still attempting to refute them many years after his father had died. Church members must still refute some of the accusations today.[74]

Sidney's son John recalled that the Mentor congregation said that his father "might [have] gone down to the grave as one of the great divines of the age, but now he had gone and thrown it all away and was a-going to follow a fool of a boy who claimed an angel had appeared to him."[75]

During the time he served as a counselor and scribe to Joseph Smith, Sidney was tarred and feathered, beaten, arrested, falsely imprisoned, and suffered debilitating health problems. While being tarred and feathered, he was injured, perhaps irreparably, with a severe brain concussion. He related, "They broke into my house[,] drag[ged] me out of my bed—out of the door my head beating on the floor. [T]hey drag[ge]d me over the wood pile[,] and on they went my head thumping on the frozen ground, after which they threw tar and feathers on me."[76]

John also said, "They . . . pounded him till they thought he was dead."[77] When the mob had finished with Sidney, Joseph Smith also thought his trusted companion was dead. He said that when he visited his friend the next day, he "found him crazy, and his head [was] lacerated . . . exceedingly; . . . and he continued delirious [for] some days."[78]

---

74. One false and implausible accusation was that Sidney Rigdon was the source of the Book of Mormon. According to the Spaulding theory, Rigdon supposedly stole a manuscript from author Solomon Spaulding when Sidney lived in Pittsburgh. The Spaulding manuscript was a story about a fictional band of Romans who became lost at sea and landed in North America. The Spaulding manuscript was found and published in 1885 and bears no resemblance to the Book of Mormon, but some critics still raise this false accusation today.

75. Keller, "Son's Record," 24.

76. Manuscript minutes of April 6, 1844, General Minutes Collection, in Van Wagoner, *Sidney Rigdon*, 115n36.

77. Keller, "Son's Record," 26.

78. *History of the Church*, 1:265.

Sidney might be compared to a military officer who is wounded and physically disabled in battle, never able to achieve battle readiness or greatness again. Effects from the brain concussion, coupled with an earlier concussion, may explain Sidney's on-again, off-again erratic behavior,[79] which was known to many. Regarding Sidney's behavior, Newel K. Whitney, an admirer of Sidney and a convert to his Campbellite congregation, observed, "I was well acquainted with Elder Rigdon a number of years before he came into this church. . . . He was always either in the bottom of the cellar or up in the garret window."[80] Medical authorities have observed similar unexplainable behaviors of patients who have suffered severe head trauma. Could Sidney's medical condition explain his irrational comment, overheard in Liberty Jail, to the effect that Sidney's suffering exceeded Christ's? Could it explain his confrontation with Brigham Young in Nauvoo as Sidney attempted to succeed Joseph Smith after the Martyrdom? We may never understand such actions, but we can appreciate Sidney's earlier devotion and sacrifice. Perhaps he was a casualty in the battle with the adversary. He certainly was a victim of the adversary's attempt to destroy Joseph Smith and thus Christ's restored Church.

Perhaps the saddest time for his former associates in the highest councils of the Church was when they met to put Sidney on trial for his membership in the Church. Brigham Young made it clear to the Church council that he made his judgment out of love and not malice when he said: "I am willing that you should know that my feelings for Sidney Rigdon as a man, as a private citizen, are of the best kind. I have loved that man and always

---

79. When Sidney was seven years old, he was thrown from a horse. His foot caught in a stirrup, and he was dragged some distance before being rescued. His brother Loammi wrote: "He received such a contusion of the brain as ever afterward seriously affected his character, and in some respects his conduct. His mental powers did not seem to be impaired, but the equilibrium of his intellectual exertions seems thereby to have been sadly affected. He still manifested great mental activity and power, but was to an equal degree inclined to run into wild and visionary views on almost every question" (in Van Wagoner, *Sidney Rigdon,* 116–17n43).

80. *Times and Seasons* 5 (October 15, 1844): 686.

had the very best feelings for him; I have stood in defense of his life and his house in Kirtland, and have lain on the floor, night after night, and week after week, to defend him."[81]

It appears that Sidney, to the end of his life, strongly defended the reality of his knowledge that Joseph was a prophet of God. His son John, speaking in a general conference of the Church in 1905, reported that he questioned his father about his feelings toward Joseph Smith and the Church just before his death. The minutes of the conference document John W. Rigdon's remarks:

> His father [Sidney] was emphatic in his claim that Joseph Smith was a Prophet of God, that an angel had delivered to the boy Prophet the Book of Mormon plates, and that, notwithstanding he felt he had been ill-treated by some Church leaders he knew, nevertheless, that the work they represented was in very deed the Gospel of Christ.
>
> The speaker said that his father was present at the meeting held immediately after the death of the Prophet, and that Brigham Young was the chosen successor of the martyred president.[82]

In his biography of his father, John Rigdon wrote more details of this interview held near the end of Sidney's life. John approached his father to ask him for a final affirmation or denial of Joseph Smith and the Book of Mormon. John wrote:

> I went to my father's room; he was there and alone. ... I told him ... you are an old man and you will soon pass away, and I wish to know if Joseph Smith ... obtained that

81. *Times and Seasons* 5 (September 15, 1844): 648.

82. In Conference Report, October 1905, 84.

book [Book of Mormon] in some other way than what he had told you. Give me all you know about it, that I may know the truth. My father . . . looked at me a moment, raised his hand above his head and slowly said, with tears glistening in his eyes: "My son, I can swear before high heaven that what I have told you about the origin of that book [Book of Mormon] is true. . . . " He also said to me . . . that 'Mormonism' was true; that Joseph Smith was a Prophet, and this world would find it out some day.[83]

Despite Sidney's fall from leadership, one fact is clear. In Kirtland he was devoted to Joseph. During the Kirtland years, he proved himself to be an indispensable strength and support to God's chosen prophet. During the 1830s, Sidney was one of the great leaders of the Church, without whom the Church could not have been firmly established. Sidney stood by Joseph when other Church leaders forsook him during Kirtland's dark days of financial disaster and persecution. By the end of the Kirtland period, Sidney had wonderfully fulfilled all of his God-given missions. The Kirtland years were indeed Sidney's significant years.

83. John W. Rigdon, "Life of Sidney Rigdon," 185–95, in *History of the Church,* 1:123n.

CHAPTER 2

THE LORD GATHERS HIS PEOPLE

In obedience to the commandment . . .
I . . . began to make preparations to go to Ohio. . . .
We bade adieu to all we held dear on this earth.

—NEWEL KNIGHT

As 1831 opened on the Church, members found themselves in two geographic locations about four hundred miles apart. In and around Kirtland, more than two hundred newly baptized Saints eagerly awaited the Lord's instructions. Church members in western New York, where the Lord had established His Church nine months before, were scattered in a radius of one hundred miles around Fayette. The Lord had already told his prophet that it was time for the Saints to leave New York.

In three revelations the Savior directed the New York Saints to move to Ohio.[1] In the first, given to Joseph Smith in December 1830, He said, "A commandment I give unto the church, that it is expedient in me that they should assemble together at the Ohio."[2] Joseph Smith announced the news at a January 2, 1831, conference at the Peter Whitmer farm in Fayette.

---

1. Doctrine & Covenants 37:3; 38:32; 39:15.

2. Doctrine & Covenants 37:3.

Newel Knight, a faithful member from the Colesville Branch, said, "We were instructed as a people, to begin the gathering of Israel."[3] It was shocking news to people who, through hard labor, had settled in New York, developed farms, built businesses, and raised families. Church members, most of whom had been baptized less than a year before, had not bargained to pull up stakes so soon and move to another new frontier.

The Lord knew this entailed significant sacrifices, and this displacement was only the beginning of what would become a pattern of sacrifice and movement for years to come. In the next revelation, given January 2, 1831, Christ offered His Saints "riches" in exchange for their sacrifice. He explained that "the will of the Father" was to give them "the riches of eternity," which would make them "the richest of all people."[4] To obtain these riches, however, they must first obey "the commandment [to] go to the Ohio."[5] This commandment was difficult to obey because it necessitated immediate response. No doubt, their quandary was what to do with their homes, farms, and property. The Savior gave them three options: sell them, rent them, or leave them, whichever "seemeth them good."[6]

As might be expected, some initially resisted. John Whitmer, the Church historian, said: "After the Lord had manifested the above words [to move to Ohio], through Joseph the Seer, there were some divisions among the congregation, some would not receive the above as the word of the Lord: but [held] that Joseph had invented it himself to deceive the people that in the end he might get gain. Now this was because, their hearts were not right in the sight of the Lord, for they wanted to serve God and man; but our Savior has declared that it was impossible to do so."[7]

---

3. "Newel Knight's Journal," in *Scraps of Biography* in *Classic Experiences and Adventures* (Salt Lake City: Bookcraft, 1969), 68.

4. Doctrine & Covenants 38:39.

5. Doctrine & Covenants 38:32.

6. Doctrine & Covenants 38:37.

7. *From Historian to Dissident: The Book of John Whitmer,* ed. Bruce N. Westergren (Salt Lake City: Signature Books, 1995), 12.

Some members weeded themselves out. The sacrifice was greater than their faith, as John Whitmer indicates: "It is hard for those who receive the fulness of the gospel, and came into the new and everlasting covenant [to] get clear of the traditions of their forefathers: and are [slow] to be made to believe the commandments that came forth in these last days for the upbuilding of the kingdom of God, and the salvation of those who believe."[8]

But to the faithful, even though they struggled, the course was clear.

The Lord Sends Leaders to "the Ohio"

The first person to be sent to "the Ohio" was John Whitmer. John explained that his call came from the Lord, who "manifested Himself to Joseph." The summons directed that John's leadership would strengthen the newly baptized Saints. John says, "The Lord . . . gave commandment for me . . . to go to the Ohio, and carry the commandments and revelations with me, to comfort and strengthen my brethren in that land."[9] He left immediately and arrived in Kirtland by January 15, 1831.

Sidney Rigdon, who had participated as a forerunner in the conversion of most of the Ohio Saints, taught them the gospel, and saw them baptized, wrote a letter of introduction so they would warmly welcome John. Emphasizing that the Lord directed this transfer, Sidney wrote:

> The Lord has declared unto us that you pray unto him that Joseph Smith and myself go speedily unto you; but at present it is not expedient for him to send us. He has required of us, therefore, to send unto you our beloved brother John, and with him the revelations which he [the Lord] has given

8. Westergren, *Historian to Dissident*, 8.

9. Westergren, *Historian to Dissident*, 13.

unto us, by which you will see the reason why we cannot come at this time.[10]

Within weeks the Lord directed Joseph Smith and his wife, Emma, to go to Kirtland and leave New York permanently. Their obedience was remarkable, and they promptly loaded up all their earthly possessions and left in a horse-drawn sled. This move entailed traveling more than two hundred miles by sleigh in the middle of a cold and snowy winter. Emma was then six months pregnant with twins. The Lord had inspired Joseph to make this journey, revealing to him that Newel K. Whitney was praying and petitioning the Lord to send Joseph. When Joseph arrived at the Whitney store in Kirtland, he walked up to Brother Whitney, whom he had never met, shook his hand and, without introduction, greeted him by saying: "Newel K. Whitney, thou art the man. . . . I am Joseph, the Prophet. You have prayed me here. Now, what do you want of me?"[11]

One account indicates that Joseph Knight Sr. accompanied Joseph and Emma from western New York. As a result of the revelation given to the Church to "go to the Ohio"[12] and because a mob was encroaching upon him, Knight had been preparing to leave his farm in Colesville. He left within hours after being invited to make the arduous and cold journey with Joseph and Emma. He recorded, "I Loaded up what I Could Cary and went away that nite. . . . I also took my wife and Daughter for we war[e] [were] calcalating to go soon for we a litle Before had a revelation to go to ohio."[13]

Joseph Knight Jr. recounted that this invitation came with a price to

---

10. E. D. Howe, *Mormonism Unvailed* (Painesville: E. D. Howe, 1834), 110–11, in Larry C. Porter, "'Ye Shall Go to the Ohio': Exodus of the New York Saints to Ohio, 1831," in *Ohio,* ed. Milton V. Backman Jr., Regional Studies in Latter-day Saint Church History series (Provo, Utah: Department of Church History and Doctrine, Brigham Young University, 1990), 1.

11. Orson F. Whitney, in Conference Report, April 1912, 50; Elizabeth Whitney, "Autobiography," *Woman's Exponent* 7 (August 15, 1878): 51.

12. Doctrine & Covenants 38:32.

13. Dean C. Jessee, "Joseph Knight's Recollection of Early Mormon History," *BYU Studies* 17, no 1 (Autumn 1976): 38; original spelling and punctuation retained.

him personally: "My Father . . . and Joseph . . . started in the Winter with my sleigh, which cost me fifty dollars."[14]

The Saints Begin to Sell Their Property

These earliest members of the restored Church placed their lives and everything they owned on their faith that Christ truly led them. Many Church members put their land up for sale without delay. Freeborn Demill closed the sale on thirty-six acres of his property on March 9, 1831.[15] Aaron Culver recorded his sale of one hundred acres on the same date.[16] Peter Whitmer Sr. and his wife, Mary, finalized the deed on their one-hundred-acre lot in Fayette on April 1, 1831.[17]

Having to sell immediately created a buyer's market. Newel Knight said, "As might be expected, we were obliged to make great sacrifices of our property."[18] Newel's brother, Joseph Knight Jr., said, "The rest of us said [stayed] till Spring and sold what property we could."[19]

The Knight family, from Colesville, New York, exhibited exemplary willingness to obey the Lord. Joseph Knight Sr., known as "Father" Knight to the Saints, lived a comfortable life operating a farm and gristmill on the Susquehanna River. He did not submit himself for baptism until the Lord told him in a revelation that it was his "duty."[20] Four years earlier he had befriended Joseph Smith at a pivotal point in the Prophet's life. Father

---

14. "Joseph Knight's Incidents of History from 1827–1844," comp. Thomas Bullock from loose sheets in Joseph Knight Jr.'s possession, August 16, 1862, Church History Library, The Church of Jesus Christ of Latter-day Saints, Salt Lake City, Utah, in Porter, "'Ye Shall Go to the Ohio,'" 3.

15. Deed Book 13, p. 298, Broome County Courthouse, Binghamton, New York, in Porter, "'Ye Shall Go to the Ohio,'" 6–7.

16. Deed Book 14, p. 299, in Porter, "'Ye Shall Go to the Ohio,'" 7.

17. Deed Book W., p. 318, located in Seneca County Courthouse, Waterloo, New York, in Porter, "'Ye Shall Go to the Ohio,'" 13.

18. "Newel Knight's Journal," 68.

19. "Joseph Knight's Incidents of History from 1827–1844," in Porter, "'Ye Shall Go to the Ohio,'" 3.

20. Doctrine & Covenants 23:6–7.

Knight gave twenty-year-old Joseph much-needed employment and even let him take "a horse and Cutter" to court Emma.[21] As Joseph was translating the Book of Mormon, Knight gave him "some few things out of the Store[:] apair of shoes and three Dollars in money to help him a litle."[22] He also gave Joseph and Oliver Cowdery food and necessary paper so they could continue translating.

Brother Knight said:

> Joseph . . . Came up to see me if I Could help him to some provisons, [they] having no way to Buy any. . . . and I Bought a Barral of Mackrel and some lined paper for writing. And . . . some nine or ten Bushels of grain and five or six Bushels [of] taters [potatoes] and a pound of tea, and I went Down to see him and they ware [were] in want. . . . And they ware [were] glad for they ware [were] out.[23]

Many Leave Their Property

Following Christ's revelatory instruction to leave "farms that cannot be sold,"[24] many of the Saints did just that. They simply gathered what they could take with them and pointed themselves toward Kirtland. As they left, Joseph and Emma Smith became perhaps the first persons to place their property on the altar of faith. In January 1831 they left thirteen acres of land and a home in Harmony, Pennsylvania, which would not be sold until June 28, 1833.[25]

Unable to sell his farm on short notice, Joseph Knight Sr. hired an

21. Jessee, "Joseph Knight's Recollection," 32.

22. Jessee, "Joseph Knight's Recollection," 36; original spelling retained.

23. Jessee, "Joseph Knight's Recollection," 36; original spelling retained.

24. Doctrine & Covenants 38:37.

25. Deed Book no. 9, p. 290, Susquehanna County Courthouse, Montrose, Pennsylvania, in Porter, "'Ye Shall Go to the Ohio,'" 2–3.

attorney to dispose of his property and embarked, not knowing what would happen. His attorney placed this advertisement in a local newspaper after Father Knight had gone:

> FOR SALE, THE farm lately occupied by Joseph Knight, situate[d] in the town of Colesville, near the Colesville Bridge—bounded on one side by the Susquehanna River, and containing about one hundred and forty two acres. On said Farm are two Dwelling Houses, a good Barn, and a fine Orchard. The terms of sale will be liberal—Apply to Wm M. Waterman.[26]

Newel, Father Knight's thirty-year-old son, never questioned the counsel to move but picked up immediately and left for Ohio. His property didn't close until after he had moved. He described his feelings as he walked away, sacrificing everything in leaving:

> In obedience to the commandment which had been given, I, together with the Colesville Branch, began to make preparations to go to Ohio. . . .
> . . . We bade adieu to all we held dear on this earth.[27]

Some New Yorkers felt that their Mormon neighbors were deceived. Martin Harris, thought to be one such person, was admired as well as pitied. An editorial in the *Wayne Sentinel,* published in Palmyra, reported the departure of Martin and the Saints bound for Kirtland:

> Several families, numbering about fifty souls, took up their line of march from this town [Palmyra] this week

---

26. *Broome [County, N. Y.] Republican,* May 5, 1831, 3. Microfilm copy located in the Binghamton Free Library, Binghamton, N.Y., in Porter, "'Ye Shall Go to the Ohio,'" 7.

27. "Newel Knight's Journal," 68–69.

for the 'promised land,' among whom was MARTIN HARRIS, one of the ORIGINAL believers in the 'BOOK OF MORMON.' Mr. Harris was among the early settlers of this town, and has ever borne the character of an honorable and upright man, and an obliging and benevolent neighbor. He had a respectable fortune—and he has left a large circle of acquaintances and friends to pity his delusion.[28]

Persecution Centers in Colesville

Some skeptics, not motivated by respect, sought to add greater hardship to the already burdened Saints. Newel Knight, a future Church leader and son of Joseph Knight, discovered this firsthand. Newel, designated to lead the Colesville Saints to Ohio, departed with his group. After they had left, troublemakers under guise of the law needlessly brought him back for a court proceeding. He wrote:

> We had proceeded but a few days on our journey, when I was subepnaed as a witness, and had to go to Colesville. On arriving there it was very evident that this plan had been adopted by our enemies to add a little more to the persecutions already heaped upon us. The whole company declined traveling until I should return.[29]

Persecution set in solidly at Colesville and became the Saints' lot for most of their early history. Nonetheless, the Lord had raised up and directed good men in the Colesville area to protect and assist Joseph Smith and the Saints for some time, even before the command came to go to Ohio. One of

28. *Wayne [County, N. Y.] Sentinel*, May 27, 1831, in Porter, "'Ye Shall Go to the Ohio,'" 19.
29. "Newel Knight's Journal," 69.

those men, a respected attorney named John S. Reid, was asked by Father Knight to defend Joseph in Broome County, New York, in 1830. Reid, not a Church member, later stated: "A peculiar impression or thought struck my mind, that I must go and defend him, for he was the Lord's anointed. I did not know what it meant, but thought I must go and clear the Lord's anointed."[30]

After Reid helped Joseph escape a mob of three hundred people, he testified of the power that finally helped Joseph and the Colesville Saints to depart: "I am well aware that we were assisted by some higher power than man; . . . I cannot tell how we succeeded in getting him away. I take no glory to myself, it was the Lord's work."[31]

Despite the ongoing harassment, the Lord blessed His departing Saints. Newel Knight records one incident in which the Lord caused a miraculous healing of his aunt:

> Soon after I left, my aunt, Electa Peck, fell and broke her shoulder in a most shocking manner; a surgeon was called to relieve her sufferings, which were very great. My aunt dreamed that I returned and laid my hands upon her, prayed for her, and she was made whole, and pursued her journey with the company. She related this dream to the surgeon who replied, "If you are able to travel in many weeks it will be a miracle, and I will be a Mormon too."
>
> I arrived at the place, where the company had stopped, late in the evening; but, on learning of the accident, I went to see my aunt, and immediately on my entering the room she said, "O, Brother Newel, if you will lay your hands upon me, I shall be well and able to go on the journey with you." I stepped up to the bed, and, in the name of the Lord

---

30. *Times and Seasons* 5 (June 1, 1844): 551.

31. *Times and Seasons* 5 (June 1, 1844): 551.

Jesus Christ, rebuked the pain with which she was suffering, and commanded her to be made whole; and it was done; for the next morning she arose, dressed herself, and pursued the journey with us.[32]

The Exodus to Ohio

These displaced Saints trusted implicitly in God. With an unshakable faith, they loaded their earthly goods on wagons or canal boats, knowing they were God's latter-day Israel. John Whitmer described the spirit that drove their exodus from New York: "The Lord had manifested his will to his people. Therefore they made preperations to Journey to the Ohio, with their wives, and children and all that they possessed, to obey the commandment of the Lord."[33]

These Saints obediently walked away from comfortable situations, friends, and, in many cases, parents, brothers and sisters, or grown children. An especially poignant story is told of Betsy Peck and her fiancé, Cornelius. The Saints' exodus ended their engagement. Hezekiah Peck, Betsy's father, forbade their marriage unless Cornelius joined the Church and went with them. Cornelius refused to do either. Seventy-two years later, Cornelius's niece, Harriet Shay, vividly recalled his heartbreak as Betsy left him behind: "That day was made impression to me as I witnessed the sorrow of Uncle Cornelius who was at our house when the wagon train went by."[34]

Local people remembered watching the Mormons leave and take all they possessed. One said, "The train consisted of three baggage and eleven passenger-wagons."[35] Harriet Shay wrote: "I distinctly remember seeing the

---

32. "Newel Knight's Journal," 69.

33. Westergren, *Historian to Dissident,* 12–13; original spelling retained.

34. Jacob Morris Papers, no. 1656, Olin Research Library, Cornell University, Ithaca, New York., in Porter, "'Ye Shall Go to the Ohio,'" 8–9.

35. Frederick G. Mather, "The Early Days of Mormonism," *Lippincott's Magazine* 36 (August 1880): 204, in Porter, "'Ye Shall Go to the Ohio,'" 8.

followers of Joseph Smith, Jr., of Mormon fame, go by my fathers, George Clappers, house on the east side of the Susquehanna River. . . .

"To the best of my recollection there were eight (8) or ten (10) wagons. They were covered like western emigrant wagons, and were drawn by oxen."[36]

Joseph Hervy described these departing Saints walking beside their wagons: "My memory is that some twenty or thirty women, girls, men and boys, on foot and in two old-fashioned western emigrant wagons comprised the emigrating party."[37]

As with ancient Israel's exodus, the journey to Kirtland was full of challenges. It was made difficult by inclement weather, imperfect construction of the fairly new Erie Canal in New York, and blocks of ice in Lake Erie that delayed the Saints' departure from Buffalo. The Saints also experienced sickness and food shortages. The body of the Saints came in three separate groups, leaving in April or early May 1831. Newel Knight led almost seventy Saints from Colesville, New York. Martin Harris reportedly headed the group of about fifty Saints from the Manchester and Palmyra area. Thomas Marsh and Lucy Mack Smith, the Prophet's mother, shepherded about eighty Saints from Fayette. The Lord watched over each of these groups as they journeyed.

The travel of the group from Fayette is best documented in the detailed account left by Lucy Mack Smith. They took the first leg of their journey from New York to Kirtland on the Erie Canal, the waterway connecting Buffalo on the west and the Hudson River on the east. The Saints boarded a barge, which would have been pulled by horses or draft animals walking on a towpath along the bank. As they started, Lucy reminded the group, as she would later do at each juncture of their trip, that the Lord watched over them:

> I then called the brethren and sisters together, and re-
> minded them that we were traveling by the commandment of

---

36. Jacob Morris Papers, in Porter, "'Ye Shall Go to the Ohio,'" 8–9.

37. Statement of Joseph Hervy, *Oneonta [N. Y.] Herald*, January 18, 1900, Jacob Morris Papers, in Porter, "'Ye Shall Go to the Ohio,'" 9.

the Lord, as much as Father Lehi was, when he left Jerusalem; and, if faithful, we had the same reasons to expect the blessings of God. I then desired them to be solemn, and to lift their hearts to God continually in prayer, that we might be prospered.[38]

As they began their journey, Lucy was stunned to realize that there were "twenty grown persons [and] thirty children, who were almost destitute of food." She observed: "This was unaccountable to me at first, but I afterwards learned that they had converted their substance into clothing, expecting that those who were in better circumstances would support them, as well as defray their traveling expense; those, however, from whom they expected the most assistance, disappointed them."[39]

The Lord assisted Lucy's group through the help of a stranger as they were departing for Kirtland. She relates how "one Esquire Chamberlain came on board, and asked me, if I had what money I wanted to make my family comfortable. I replied, that I had an abundance for myself and children, but he might, perhaps, find some on board, who stood in need of assistance. 'Well,' said he, 'here is a little money, and you can deal it out as you like,' and, handing me seventeen dollars, he left the boat."[40]

The most frightening experience on the canal occurred when the canal's sidewall gave way, spilling essential water out of the canal and thus preventing further travel. The prospect for rebuilding the sidewall quickly looked bleak. The group lacked food for an extended delay, and a delay posed problems about rendezvousing with two other groups—one of which had already arrived in Buffalo. Lucy again provided reassurance that the Lord led them:

---

38. Lucy Mack Smith, *History of Joseph Smith by His Mother,* ed. Preston Nibley (Salt Lake City: Bookcraft, 1958), 196.

39. Smith, *History of Joseph Smith,* 197.

40. Smith, *History of Joseph Smith,* 196.

"No, no," said I, "you will not starve, brethren, nor anything of that sort; only do be patient and stop your murmur-
ing. I have no doubt but the hand of the Lord is over us for
good; perhaps it is best for us to be here a short time. It is
quite probable that the boats cannot leave Buffalo harbor on
account of the ice; if so, the town must inevitably be crowded
with families, in which case it would be next to impossible for
us to get into a comfortable house. Are we not in far better
circumstances in our present situation?"[41]

The canal was repaired with unexpected speed, bringing the Mormon
emigrants to Buffalo five days after leaving the Fayette area. Lodging was des-
perately needed for sisters whose children became sick. Lucy was successful
in finding the necessary quarters for the women and their sick children. She
boldly spoke to a landlady, who listened to her gospel teaching and then gave
lodging to the mothers and sick children. Having no means arranged to sail
on Lake Erie, Lucy now needed to find transportation to Kirtland for her
stranded travelers. While she was forced to bargain for scarce transportation,
another miracle came to her aid. She located a captain of a ship, Captain Blake,
who by chance had earlier captained a ship owned by her brother, Stephen
Mack. Captain Blake offered the stranded company deck passage on his ship
to Fairport Harbor, Ohio, just twelve miles from Kirtland. Lucy's group, feeling blessed and grateful, resumed their trip from Buffalo.

The Lord's Assistance on Lake Erie

The Lord assisted the Fayette Saints to leave Buffalo by responding
dramatically to their prayers and granting them yet another miracle. The
Buffalo harbor, on the east end of Lake Erie, filled with chunks of ice in late
spring because of winds and water current. Captains, anxious to navigate

---

41. Smith, *History of Joseph Smith*, 198.

the lake, waited for the ice chunks to melt and break up so they could launch. On the day the Fayette Saints were to depart, Captain Blake asked Lucy to have her group board the vessel so that if the ice parted, he could start at a moment's notice. He dispatched one of his crew to measure the ice, which he reported to be twenty feet. The crew member said they wouldn't be able to leave for two more weeks. At that point, Lucy described a promise and a prophecy she had made. The Fayette group realized the prophesied fulfillment:

> I said, "Now, brethren and sisters, if you will all of you raise your desires to heaven, that the ice may be broken up, and we be set at liberty, as sure as the Lord lives, it will be done." At that instant a noise was heard, like bursting thunder. The captain cried, "Every man to his post." The ice parted, leaving barely a passage for the boat, and so narrow that as the boat passed through, the buckets of the waterwheel were torn off with a crash, which, joined to the word of command from the captain, the hoarse answering of the sailors, the noise of the ice, and the cries and confusion of the spectators, presented a scene truly terrible. We had barely passed through the avenue when the ice closed together again, and the Colesville brethren were left in Buffalo, unable to follow us.
>
> As we were leaving the harbor, one of the bystanders exclaimed, "There goes the 'Mormon' company! That boat is sunk in the water nine inches deeper than ever it was before, and, mark it, she will sink—there is nothing surer." In fact, they were so sure of it that they went straight to the office and had it published that we were sunk, so that when we arrived at Fairport we read in the papers the news of our own death.
>
> After our miraculous escape from the wharf at Buffalo, we called our company together and had a prayer meeting in which

we offered up our thanks to God for his mercy, which he had manifested towards us in our deliverance.[42]

Although the 150-mile voyage on Lake Erie was faster, more comfortable, and less strenuous than travel by foot or in wagons, Newel Knight said it was still difficult. He and his group of Colesville Saints followed Mother Smith's company aboard a slower sloop.[43] Newel said: "When we set sail on the lake, the winds continued boisterous, and the vessel was tossed about in such a manner that nearly all the company were sea-sick, which made it rather a disagreeable voyage. We arrived safely, however, at our destination."[44] Lucy comforted those of her company who were seasick by paying the ship's cook twenty-five cents for "some hot water for the sick folks."[45] William Smith described his two-day voyage as being "long and tedious." He reported that they faced "many storms, cold winds and rains."[46]

Like the group from Fayette, Martin Harris's group also probably came by Lake Erie, landed at Fairport Harbor, Ohio, and then journeyed twelve miles southwest to Kirtland. The Colesville Saints, however, trekked southeast about twenty miles to Thompson, Ohio.

In gathering His Saints to Ohio, the Lord was not just moving them from one place to another. He was developing a people with steadfast faith—a people who would be strong enough to sacrifice worldly enticements for "the riches of eternity."[47]

---

42. Smith, *History of Joseph Smith*, 204–5.

43. A sloop is "a vessel with one mast, the main-sail of which is attached to a gaff above, to a boom below, and to the mast on its foremost edge. . . . Sloops are of various sizes, from the size of a boat to that of more than 100 tons burthen" (Noah Webster, *American Dictionary of the English Language* [1828; repr., San Francisco: Foundation for American Christian Education, 1980], s.v. "sloop").

44. "Newel Knight's Journal," 69.

45. Smith, *History of Joseph Smith*, 205.

46. William Smith, *William Smith on Mormonism: A True Account of the Origin of the Book of Mormon* (Lamoni, Iowa: Herald Steam Book and Job Office, 1883), 19.

47. Doctrine & Covenants 38:39.

CHAPTER 3

CHRIST TEACHES AND MAGNIFIES HIS PROPHET

I did call upon [Joseph Smith] by mine angels, my ministering
servants, and by mine own voice out of the heavens.
—DOCTRINE & COVENANTS 136:37

That the Lord would identify Joseph Smith as His chosen prophet of the latter days was foreseen by ancient prophets. In the premortal existence the Lord ordained this man of humble circumstances.[1] He taught Joseph personally. He provided intense instruction. He directed his ancient prophets from past dispensations of His Church to teach and to confer the Lord's priesthood upon the fledgling prophet. The Lord said, "I did call upon [Joseph Smith] by mine angels, my ministering servants, and by mine own voice out of the heavens."[2]

As a young boy untainted by the ways of the world, Joseph Smith sought spiritual learning from on high. He preferred to get his spiritual education directly from the scriptures and the Lord rather than from ministers and churches of the day. He once told his mother, Lucy Mack Smith: "Mother,

---

1. Joseph Smith, *History of The Church of Jesus Christ of Latter-day Saints,* ed. B. H. Roberts, 7 vols., 2d ed. rev. (Salt Lake City: The Church of Jesus Christ of Latter-day Saints, 1932–51), 6:364.

2. Doctrine & Covenants 136:37.

I do not wish to prevent your going to meeting, or any of the rest of the family's; or your joining any church you please; but, do not ask me to join them. I can take my Bible, and go into the woods, and learn more in two hours, than you can learn at meeting in two years, if you should go all the time."[3]

Two historians and authors who have written about Joseph Smith conclude, "His knowledge of the Bible and his biblical style of writing suggest that much of his early education came from that source."[4]

Lucy said that Joseph was "much less inclined to the perusal of books than any of the rest of the children, but far more given to meditation and deep study."[5] As Joseph matured, he not only immersed himself more deeply in the Bible but also continually sought heavenly instruction. It seems this desire was a driving force throughout his short life of thirty-eight and a half years: "The best way to obtain truth and wisdom is not to ask it from books, but to go to God in prayer, and obtain divine teaching. . . .

"There is never a time when the spirit is too old to approach God."[6]

The Lord provided Joseph with stellar secular training in Kirtland. He furnished Joseph with access to prominent men such as Sidney Rigdon, the renowned experienced minister; Orson Hyde, of superior intellect and master of languages in his later life; and Joshua Seixas, noted professor of Hebrew. The Kirtland period is marked by formal schooling, and Joseph was a star pupil. The Lord constantly challenged Joseph to gain education in Kirtland. He told him, "The glory of God is intelligence."[7] He directed Joseph to "study and learn, and become acquainted with all good books,

---

3. Lucy Mack Smith, *History of Joseph Smith by His Mother*, ed. Preston Nibley (Salt Lake City: Book-craft, 1958), 90.

4. Richard L. Bushman and Dean C. Jessee, "Joseph Smith: The Prophet," in *Encyclopedia of Mormonism*, ed. Daniel H. Ludlow et al., 4 vols. (New York: Macmillan, 1992), 3:1333.

5. Smith, *History of Joseph Smith*, 82.

6. Minutes of general conference, October 2, 1841, in *History of the Church*, 4:425.

7. Doctrine & Covenants 93:36.

and with languages, tongues and people."[8] In response, Joseph organized schools: the School of the Prophets, the School of the Elders, the School of Mine Apostles, the Hebrew School, and the Kirtland High School.

The ancient prophet Joseph of Egypt, son of Jacob, prophesied of Joseph Smith's significance as a latter-day prophet. He identified Joseph by name.[9] He then prophesied that the Lord would make a spokesman and a scribe for Joseph, who would supplement his deficiencies in speaking and writing: "A choice seer will I raise up. . . . And out of weakness he shall be made strong. . . . And the Lord said . . . I will make for him a spokesman. And I, behold, I will give unto him that he shall write the writing of [Joseph Smith]."[10]

In the Kirtland area the Lord raised up Sidney Rigdon, a man well-versed in the Bible and a renowned orator, who as directed by the Spirit and the Prophet would write and speak for Joseph.[11] Early leaders and members of the Church were aware of Joseph's weaknesses in language, education, and book learning. For example, in November 1831, a group of the Prophet's closest confidants met in John Johnson's home in Hiram, Ohio, and suggested that someone with better language skills be used to compose words of revelation.[12] Before moving to Kirtland, Emma Smith, who perhaps knew Joseph's weaknesses best, described his limited language abilities:

> Joseph Smith . . . could neither write nor dictate a coherent and well-worded letter, let alone dictate a book like the Book of Mormon. . . .
>
> . . . I am satisfied that no man could have dictated the writing of the manuscripts unless he was inspired; for, when acting as his scribe, [he] would dictate to me hour after hour;

---

8. Doctrine & Covenants 90:15.

9. 2 Nephi 3:15.

10. 2 Nephi 3:7, 13, 18.

11. Doctrine & Covenants 35:20, 23; 100:9–11.

12. See Doctrine & Covenants 67:5.

and when returning after meals, or after interruptions, he could at once begin where he had left off. . . . This was a usual thing for him to do. It would have been improbable that a learned man could do this; and, for one so ignorant and unlearned as he was, it was simply impossible.[13]

Joseph Smith had little formal schooling. He states that his family's poverty required that he work to provide meager necessities of frontier life, which had limited his educational attainment:

> My Father Joseph Smith Siegnior moved to Palmyra Ontario County in the State of New York and being in indigent circumstances were obliged to labour hard for the support of a large Family having nine chilldren and as it required the exertions of all that were able to render any assistance for the support of the Family therefore we were deprived of the bennifit of an education[;] suffice it to say I was mearly instructtid in reading and writing and the ground <rules> of Arithmatic which const[it]uted my whole literary acquirements.[14]

During the early 1830s, Wilford Woodruff, Joseph's companion during the march of Zion's Camp and later the fourth president of the Church, characterized Joseph as "illiterate" while most of the revelations in the Doctrine and Covenants were given during this period of time: "When Joseph Smith received these revelations he was an illiterate boy, like David among the sheep. . . .

13. "Last Testimony of Sister Emma," *Saints' Herald* 26 (October 1879): 290.

14. Karen Lynn Davidson, David J. Whittaker, Mark Ashurst-McGee, and Richard L. Jensen, eds., *Histories, 1832–1844*, vol. 1 of the Histories series of *The Joseph Smith Papers*, edited by Dean C. Jessee, Ronald K. Esplin, and Richard Lyman Bushman (Salt Lake City: Church Historian's Press, 2012), 1:11.

" . . . He, although an illiterate youth, presented to the world the Gospel of Jesus Christ in its fulness, plainness and simplicity, as taught by its Author and his Apostles."[15]

The ancient prophet Joseph prophesied that Joseph Smith would "be made strong."[16] By the end of Joseph's life, the Lord had molded him into a strong leader and a mature prophet. In 1844 a Nauvoo visitor described Joseph's superior education, well-rounded knowledge, and language capabilities:

> I have been conversant with the great men of the age; and, last of all I feel that I have met with the greatest, in the presence of your esteemed Prophet, General Joseph Smith. . . . I have found him as familiar in the cabinet of nations as with his Bible and in the knowledge of that book I have not met with his equal in Europe or America. . . .
>
> The General appears perfectly at home on every subject, and his familiarity with many languages affords him ample means to become informed concerning all nations and principles, which . . . must secure to his interest the affections of every intelligent and virtuous man. . . . I am astonished that so little is known abroad concerning him. . . .
>
> . . . He dives into every subject, and it seems as though the world was not large enough to satisfy his capacious soul, and from his conversation one might suppose him as well acquainted with other worlds as this.[17]

In 1844, after a personal interview with Joseph, Josiah Quincy, graduate of Harvard University and a prominent citizen and later mayor of Boston, commented: "Born in the lowest ranks of poverty, without

---

15. Wilford Woodruff, in *Journal of Discourses*, 26 vols. (London: Latter-day Saints' Book Depot, 1854–86), 16:265–66.

16. 2 Nephi 3:13.

17. *History of the Church*, 6:269; *Times and Seasons* 5 (April 15, 1844): 501.

book-learning and with the homeliest of all human names, [Joseph Smith] had made himself at the age of thirty-nine a power upon earth. Of the multitudinous family of Smith . . . none had so won human hearts and shaped human lives as this Joseph. His influence . . . is potent today, and the end is not yet."[18]

How did Joseph grow from educational inadequacy to attain respected educational and spiritual stature? It is evident that the Lord tutored Joseph, his willing and devoted prophet. Wilford Woodruff understood, saying,

> How could he, an illiterate boy, do that which the whole of the learning of the Christian world for seventeen centuries failed to do? Because he was moved upon by the power of God, he was instructed by those men who, when in the flesh, had preached the same gospel themselves, and in doing this he fulfilled that which Father Adam, Enoch, Moses, Elias, Isaiah, Jeremiah and Jesus and his Apostles all prophesied about.[19]

The Savior Taught Joseph "by Mine Angels"

The Lord Himself acknowledged that He sent angels to teach Joseph Smith. He said, "I did call upon [Joseph Smith] by mine angels, my ministering servants."[20] Early leaders and members who knew the Prophet were aware of angels often teaching and giving Joseph knowledge of things not known to him. John Taylor, a strong and dedicated Canadian convert who later became Church president, testified:

> When Joseph Smith was raised up as a Prophet of God, Mormon, Moroni, Nephi . . . and Peter and John and others

---

18. Josiah Quincy, *Figures of the Past from the Leaves of Old Journals* (Boston, 1883): 399–400.

19. Wilford Woodruff, in *Journal of Discourses*, 16:266–67.

20. Doctrine & Covenants 136:37.

... came to him and communicated to him certain principles pertaining to the Gospel of the Son of God. ... He was indebted to God. ... Who in this generation knew anything about Temples and their uses until Joseph revealed it? Nobody. Who knew anything about baptism for the dead until then? Nobody. Who knew anything about the past or the future?[21]

Associates of Joseph Smith were amazed by the great number of ancient prophets who appeared to Joseph. John Taylor spoke of Joseph's familiarity with prophets and angels who personally appeared and spoke with him. He said that Joseph Smith was placed "in communication with the Lord, and ... with the ancient apostles and prophets; such men, for instance, as Abraham, Isaac, Jacob, Noah, Adam, Seth, Enoch, and Jesus and the Father, and the apostles that lived on this continent as well as those who lived on the Asiatic continent. He seemed to be as familiar with these people as we are with one another."[22]

Wilford Woodruff described the constant visitations, saying, "[Joseph Smith] was taught for years by visions and revelations, and by holy angels sent from God out of heaven to teach and instruct him and prepare him to lay the foundation of this Church."[23] During Joseph's life, he saw or communicated with more than forty-seven angels: Elias (Gabriel, Noah), Raphael, Moses, Enoch, Isaac, Enos, Twelve ancient Apostles, Seth, Mahalaleel, Alvin Smith, Adam (Michael), Eve, Elijah, Jacob, Methusaleh, Twelve Nephite Apostles, Jared, Cainan, John the Baptist, Paul, Abraham, Zelph the Lamanite, Nephi, Mormon, and Moroni.[24]

---

21. Taylor, in *Journal of Discourses*, 17:374–75.

22. Taylor, in *Journal of Discourses*, 21:94.

23. Woodruff, in *Journal of Discourses*, 16:265.

24. Taylor, in *Journal of Discourses*, 17:374; 21:94; Extracts from William Clayton's Private Book, January 5, 1841 (Tuesday), in *The Words of Joseph Smith,* comp. and ed. Andrew F. Ehat and Lyndon W. Cook (Provo, Utah: Brigham Young University Religious Studies Center, 1980), 59; Zebedee

In addition, Joseph Smith saw and on occasion communed with large groups of angels. For example, Joseph recorded the following encounters in the Kirtland Temple:

- "We all communed with the h[e]avenly host's [of holy angels]."[25]

- "Angels ministered unto them [many of my brethren], as well as my self."[26]

- "Angels mingled . . . their voices with ours. . . . their presence was in our midst, and unseasing prases swelled our bosoms for the space of half an hour."[27]

- "I beheld the Temple was filled with angels, which fact I declared to the congregation."[28]

Joseph and others described some of the angels they saw:

Paul the Apostle[29]: "[Paul] is about 5 foot high; very dark hair; dark

---

Coltrin, in *Salt Lake School of the Prophets Minute Book, 1883* (Salt Lake City: Pioneer Press, 1992), 64; Wilford Woodruff, *Wilford Woodruff's Journal, 1833–1898*, ed. Scott G. Kenney, typescript, 9 vols. (Midvale, Utah: Signature Books, 1983–85), 1:10; Doctrine & Covenants 13; 107:53; 110; 128:19–21; 137:5. Oliver Cowdery recorded in the Patriarchal Blessing Book that Joseph "pronounced a blessing upon his father." That blessing was given "by vision and the spirit of prophecy" (Joseph Fielding Smith, *Church History and Modern Revelation*, 2 vols. [Salt Lake City: Deseret Book, 1953], 1:472, 473). In the blessing he related part of his vision, naming "Adam, Seth, Enos, Cainan, Mahalaleel, Jared, Enoch, and Methuselah" (see D&C 107:53).

25. Dean C. Jessee, Mark Ashurst-McGee, and Richard L. Jensen, eds., *Journals, 1832–1839*, vol. 1 of the Journals series of *The Joseph Smith Papers,* edited by Dean C. Jessee, Ronald K. Esplin, and Richard Lyman Bushman (Salt Lake City: Church Historian's Press, 2008), 1:170.

26. Jessee, Ashurst-McGee, and Jensen, *Journals,* 1:170.

27. Jessee, Ashurst-McGee, and Jensen, *Journals,* 1:172.

28. *History of the Church,* 2:428.

29. An ancient apocryphal description of Paul existed at Joseph Smith's time and could have been read by Joseph ("Acts of Paul and Thecla," *The Apocryphal New Testament,* ed. William Hone [London: Ludgate Hill, 1820], 100). Because of this, some scholars are hesitant to attribute Joseph's description of Paul to revelation or vision. A detailed comparison of the ancient description and Joseph's statement overwhelmingly lead one to conclude that Joseph's description did not come

complexion; dark skin; large Roman nose; sharp face; small black eyes, penetrating as eternity; round shoulders; a whining voice, except when elevated and then it almost resembles the roaring of a Lion. He was a good orator."[30]

Peter, the chief Apostle: "He was a very tall personage, black eyes, white hair, and stoop shouldered; his garment was whole, extending to near his ankles; on his feet he had sandals."[31]

Adam and Seth, the oldest prophets: "My brother Alvin . . . was a very handsome man, surpassed by none but Adam and Seth, and of great strength."[32]

Moroni, the last Book of Mormon prophet: "The stature of [Moroni] was a little above the common size of men in this age; his garment was perfectly white, and had the appearance of being without seam."[33]

---

from the apocryphal source, however. The apocryphal document describes nine characteristics of Paul; Joseph describes twelve. Richard Lloyd Anderson, an authority on Paul, wrote, "The profiles overlap in only two respects: the ancient 'crooked nose' compares to Joseph Smith's 'large Roman nose,' and the ancient 'low stature' compares to Joseph Smith's 'about 5 foot high.'

"These two points of resemblance are important, for Joseph Smith adds a specific detail to each. Much apocryphal literature is boring because it narrates in generalities. Granted, a creative historical forger might give particulars; but in real life, vagueness generally reflects lack of firsthand observation, and pictorial sharpness comes from having been personally on the scene. Joseph Smith's description of Paul is stunning for that reason—it includes exact measurements, complexion, shapes, even sounds. The modern Prophet comments with the precision of one who has seen and heard. . . .

" . . . The significance is that the prophet of the last dispensation knew so well the great apostle to the Gentiles" (*Understanding Paul* [Salt Lake City: Deseret Book, 1983], 400–401).

30. Ehat and Cook, *Words of Joseph Smith*, 59.

31. Heber C. Kimball, in Orson F. Whitney, *Life of Heber C. Kimball* (Salt Lake City: Bookcraft, 1945), 91. Although Heber C. Kimball describes Peter as he appeared in the Kirtland Temple, Joseph Smith was present and identified Peter in the meeting where Peter was seen (Lyndon W. Cook, "The Apostle Peter and the Kirtland Temple," *BYU Studies* 15, no. 4 (Summer 1975): 551.

32. *History of the Church*, 5:247; Andrew H. Hedges, Alex D. Smith, and Richard Lloyd Anderson, eds., *Journals, December 1841–April 1843*, vol. 2 of the Journals series of *The Joseph Smith Papers*, edited by Dean C. Jessee, Ronald K. Esplin, and Richard Lyman Bushman (Salt Lake City: Church Historian's Press, 2011), 2:242.

33. *Messenger and Advocate* 1, no. 5 (February 1835): 79.

Adam and Eve, our first parents: "Their heads were white as snow, and their faces shone with immortal youth. They were the two most beautiful and perfect specimens of mankind I ever saw. . . . Adam was a large broad shouldered man, and Eve, as a woman, was as large in proportion."[34]

Nephite prophet, possibly Moroni: "When I was returning to Fayette, with Joseph and Oliver . . . a very pleasant, nice-looking old man suddenly appeared by the side of our wagon and saluted us with, 'good morning, it is very warm,' at the same time wiping his face or forehead with his hand. . . . I invited him to ride. . . . But he said very pleasantly, 'No, I am going to Cumorah.' . . . We all gazed at him and at each other, and . . . the old man instantly disappeared. . . .

" . . . He was, I should think, about 5 feet 8 or 9 inches tall and heavy set, about such a man as James Vancleave there, but heavier; his face was as large, he was dressed in a suit of brown woolen clothes, his hair and beard were white, like Brother Pratt's, but his beard was not so heavy. I also remember that he had on his back a sort of knapsack with something in [it], shaped like a book. It was the messenger who had the plates, who had taken them from Joseph just prior to our starting from Harmony."[35]

Joseph saw more than forty-seven angels, but some of them made repeated visits. For example, the angel Moroni instructed Joseph Smith at least twenty-two times. Joseph often encountered skeptics who did not believe that angels appeared to him. In frustration, he once told a congregation, "I have it from God, and get over it if you can."[36]

---

34. Zebedee Coltrin, address at a meeting of high priests in Spanish Fork, Utah, February 5, 1878, in *They Knew the Prophet,* comp. Hyrum L. Andrus and Helen Mae Andrus (Salt Lake City: Bookcraft, 1974), 28; paragraphing altered. This account comes from a vision in New Portage, Ohio (now Barberton), that was seen by Joseph Smith, Oliver Cowdery and Zebedee Coltrin.

35. Orson Pratt and Joseph F. Smith, interview with David Whitmer, in *Millennial Star* 40 (December 9, 1878): 772.

36. *History of the Church,* 6:475.

The Savior Taught Joseph "by Mine Own Voice Out of the Heavens"

Joseph Smith often received instruction through the Lord's own "voice out of the heavens."[37] He described how consistently the voice of the Lord came to him as the Church evolved from its beginnings in New York to his martyrdom in Illinois: "What do we hear? . . . The voice of God in the chamber of old Father Whitmer, in Fayette, Seneca county, and at sundry times, and in divers places through all the travels and tribulations of this Church of Jesus Christ of Latter-day Saints!"[38]

In Pennsylvania, the Lord spoke to Joseph Smith and Oliver Cowdery when they received the Aaronic Priesthood. Oliver Cowdery described how, after he and Joseph had gone into the woods to pray on the banks of the Susquehanna River, they were overwhelmed with joy, wonder, and amazement upon hearing the Savior's voice: "On a sudden, as from the midst of eternity, the voice of the Redeemer spake peace to us, while the vail was parted and the angel of God came down clothed with glory, and delivered the anxiously looked for message, and the keys of the gospel of repentance."[39]

In the Sacred Grove, Joseph conversed directly with Deity, who introduced Themselves and called Joseph by name. Joseph said, "I asked the Personages . . . which of all the sects was right . . . and which I should join. . . . I was answered that I must join none of them . . . but to continue as I was until further directed."[40]

At the secluded Johnson farm in the forested area of Hiram, Ohio, the Lord spoke to Joseph and Sidney Rigdon directly in the vision recorded as Doctrine and Covenants 76. They wrote, "We bear record . . . of Jesus Christ [who is the Son,] whom we saw and with whom we conversed in the

---

37. Doctrine & Covenants 136:37.

38. Doctrine & Covenants 128:20–21.

39. *Messenger and Advocate* 1, no. 1 (October 1834): 15.

40. Joseph Smith–History 1:18, 19, 26.

heavenly vision."[41] They referred specifically to hearing the Lord's voice at least fifteen times during one vision alone.

In the sacred atmosphere of Joseph's upper office at the Kirtland Temple in 1836, he recorded that the Lord spoke to him and instructed him: "[I] marveled how it was that [Alvin] had obtained an inheritance in [the Celestial] kingdom, seeing that he . . . had not been baptized. . . . Thus came the voice of the Lord unto me, saying: All who have died without a knowledge of this gospel, who would have received it if they had been permitted to tarry, shall be heirs of the celestial kingdom of God."[42]

The following scriptures exemplify that the Lord called upon Joseph Smith:

- "Listen to the voice of Jesus Christ, your Redeemer."[43]
- "I prophesy . . . that the commencement of the [Civil War] difficulties . . . will be in South Carolina. . . . This a voice declared to me, while I was praying earnestly."[44]
- "I was once praying very earnestly . . . when I heard a voice repeat the following: Joseph, my son . . . let this suffice, and trouble me no more on this matter."[45]

The Savior Taught Joseph through Countless Visions

One historical researcher found evidence of seventy-six visions the Lord gave Joseph Smith during his lifetime.[46] William Taylor, a confidant of the Prophet, described how familiar Joseph was with the other side of

---

41. Doctrine & Covenants 76:14.

42. Doctrine & Covenants 137:6–7.

43. Doctrine & Covenants 29:1.

44. Doctrine & Covenants 130:12–13.

45. Doctrine & Covenants 130:14–15.

46. Alexander L. Baugh, "Parting the Veil: Joseph Smith's Seventy-Six Documented Visionary

the veil. "He seemed to be just as familiar with the spirit world, and as well acquainted with the other side, as he was here."[47]

Apparently, one of Joseph's greatest frustrations was teaching the Saints of the overpowering knowledge and understanding he had learned through his visions. "It is my meditation all the day . . . to know how I shall make the Saints of God comprehend the visions that roll like an overflowing surge before my mind."[48]

It is fascinating to comprehend the depth and breadth, the specificity and plainness of the visions the Lord gave to Joseph. In one vision, possibly given in 1832 at Hiram, Ohio, Joseph described the reality of the resurrection: "So plain was the vision I actually saw men, before they had ascended from the tomb, as though they were getting up slowly, they took each other by the hand & it was my father & my son. my mother & my daughter, my brother & my sister."[49]

Joseph and Sidney saw in vision the phenomenal growth of the Church, as recorded by Sidney in 1844: "We knew fourteen years ago that the Church would become as large as it is today. . . . We saw by vision the Church of God, a thousand times larger. . . . All the members [at that time] met in conference in a room twenty feet square."[50]

Joseph expanded on this vision when the priesthood gathered in a log schoolhouse in Kirtland. Wilford Woodruff remembered that "Joseph Smith was full of revelation. He foresaw this people, and this work until it was wound up."[51] Joseph continued to prophesy of the amazing growth of the Church: "It is only a little handfull of Priesthood you see here tonight,

---

Experiences," in *Opening the Heavens: Accounts of Divine Manifestations, 1820–1844*, ed. John W. Welch and Erick B. Carlson (Provo, Utah: Brigham Young University Press, 2005), 265.

47. William Taylor, *Young Woman's Journal* 17 (1906): 548.

48. *History of the Church*, 5:362.

49. Joseph Smith Diary, by Willard Richards, April 16, 1843 (Sunday morning), in Ehat and Cook, *Words of Joseph Smith*, 195.

50. *History of the Church*, 6:289.

51. Wilford Woodruff, in Conference Report, April 1898, 58.

but this Church will fill North and South America—it will fill the world. ... This people will go into the Rocky Mountains; they will there build temples to the Most High. They will raise up a posterity there."[52]

In vision the Savior instilled an understanding of the Church's future in the Prophet Joseph Smith. Joseph, in turn, instilled it in prospective missionaries and future leaders who had not been in the Church even a year. By the power of the Spirit, these men knew the divine nature of the work, but they had little comprehension that the Church would become a worldwide organization. How hard it must have been for the "whole of the priesthood" assembled in that little log schoolhouse in Kirtland to understand what the Lord would do with His Church. In retrospect, the accurate unfolding of this vision is stunning. Joseph prophesied that the Church, before expanding to all continents, would first fill North and South America. At the beginning of the twenty-first century, North and South America accounted for 83 percent of Church membership.

The Savior Taught Joseph as a Translator, Revelator, and Seer

The Lord gave Joseph Smith key assignments. He said, "I give unto you my servant Joseph ... to be a *translator, a revelator, a seer.*"[53] It is staggering to consider the instruction and learning that the Lord gave Joseph as he fulfilled these three roles:

1. *Translator.* The Lord inspired Joseph to translate more than 545 pages over an eight-year period. This includes 531 pages in the Book of Mormon, translated from ancient gold plates. Joseph translated them in about sixty-five working days. (This page count doesn't include the lost 116 pages.) In addition, he translated or dictated by revelation the book of Abraham from the papyrus scrolls, which represents 14 pages in about eight days.

---

52. Wilford Woodruff, in Conference Report, April 1898, 57.

53. Doctrine & Covenants 124:125; emphasis added.

The Lord taught Joseph effectively through the translating process. For example, Emma Smith related how the Lord expanded Joseph's mind: "One time while he was translating he stopped suddenly, pale as a sheet, and said, 'Emma, did Jerusalem have walls around it?' When I answered, 'Yes,' he replied, 'Oh! I was afraid I had been deceived.' He had such a limited knowledge of history at the time that he did not even know that Jerusalem was surrounded by walls."[54]

David Whitmer added that Joseph "stopped until they got a Bible & showed him where the fact was recorded—Smith not believing it was a walled city."[55]

Joseph learned more of the nature of God as he translated the book of Abraham in Kirtland. He wrote, "I want to reason a little on this subject [of God]. I learned it by translating the papyrus which is now in my house."[56]

2. *Revelator.* The Lord revealed more than 494 pages of scripture to Joseph Smith, mostly during the Kirtland years. This page count includes the Doctrine and Covenants, which consists of 281 pages. (This estimate does not include significant revelations that have not been formally canonized.) Joseph Smith's translation of the Bible (JST) contains 3,410 verses that Joseph modified from the King James Version of the Bible. If printed on successive pages, these changed verses would equal 213 pages. The book of Moses (received as part of the Joseph Smith Translation) represents 27 pages that Joseph dictated by revelation in less than a month.

3. *Seer.* In his role as a seer, Joseph foresaw the Civil War and future wars. He learned principles of astronomy and saw beyond what was recorded and later printed. Joseph sometimes received even more than he desired. For example, Jedediah M. Grant, father of Heber J. Grant, the seventh president

---

54. Edmund C. Briggs, "A Visit to Nauvoo in 1856," *Journal of History* 9 (January 1916): 454, in Stephen D. Ricks, "Death Knell or Tinkling Cymbals?" *FARMS Review* 4, no. 1 (1992): 240.

55. M. J. Hubble interview, November 13, 1886, University of Missouri Library, Columbia, Missouri; published by Stanley Kimball in "Missouri Mormon Manuscripts: Sources in Selected Societies," *BYU Studies* 14, no. 4 (Summer 1974): 486.

56. *History of the Church,* 6:476.

of the Church, related that Joseph once had a vision of wars that would come to pass. He perhaps saw this vision in the Whitney store on December 25, 1832. Jedediah said Joseph could not endure the whole vision:

> The Prophet . . . told several of us of the night the visions of heaven were opened to him, in which he saw the American continent drenched in blood. . . . He also saw the father shed the blood of the son, and the son the blood of the father . . . and natural affection forsook the hearts of the wicked. . . . The Prophet gazed upon the scene his vision presented, until his heart sickened, and he besought the Lord to close it up again.[57]

Advanced principles of astronomy were revealed to Joseph as he translated the papyrus scrolls. We are left to wonder just what he saw. He said, "This afternoon I labored on the Egyptian alphabet [and] the principles of astronomy as understood by Father Abraham and the ancients unfolded to our understanding."[58]

As used in ancient times, the Urim and Thummim was a tool of translation and learning. Lorenzo Brown, a friend of the Prophet, remembered that Joseph told him that he read the Bible and saw actual biblical scenes revealed through the Urim and Thummim. "After I got through translating the Book of Mormon, I took up the Bible to read with the Urim and Thummim," Brown reported Joseph as saying. "I read the first chapter of Genesis and I saw the things as they were done. I turned over the next and the next, and the whole passed before me like a grand panorama; and so on chapter after chapter until I read the whole of it. I saw it all!"[59]

---

57. Jedediah M. Grant, in *Journal of Discourses,* 2:147.

58. *History of the Church,* 2:286; Jessee, Ashurst-McGee, and Jensen, *Journals,* 1:67.

59. Related by Lorenzo Brown in 1880, "Sayings of Joseph, by Those Who Heard Him at Different Times," Papers of Joseph Smith Jr., Church History Library, The Church of Jesus Christ of Latter-day Saints, Salt Lake City, in Robert J. Matthews, *"A Plainer Translation": Joseph Smith's Translation of the Bible, a History and Commentary* (Provo, Utah: Brigham Young University Press, 1975): 25.

The Lord Taught Joseph Knowledge Beyond
That of Experts of His Day

Beginning in Fayette, New York, and continuing to Hiram and Kirtland, Ohio, the Lord gave Joseph an understanding especially about astronomy that went far beyond the knowledge of scholars of Joseph's day. In 1830, Joseph began learning knowledge of the heavens through translating and receiving revelation. At that time scholars were quoting Galileo, who died in 1642. Galileo documented many thousands of previously invisible stars that make up part of the Milky Way galaxy. Frederick William Herschel was one of the leading authorities of Joseph Smith's time. He died in 1822, shortly after the First Vision. Herschel had examined every star in the standard star charts and by 1802 had counted more than ninety thousand stars in the Milky Way. Seemingly, that was the state of knowledge of our galaxy in the early nineteenth century.

Consider how a number of scientific authorities of that day would have scoffed and jeered at Joseph Smith's knowledge of astronomy. In his role as translator, revelator, seer, and prophet, Joseph received the following statements from the Lord:

- "And were it possible that man could number the particles of the earth, yea, millions of earths like this, it would not be a beginning to the number of thy creations; and thy curtains are stretched out still."[60]
- "For behold, there are many worlds that have passed away by the word of my power."[61]

---

60. Moses 7:30.

61. Moses 1:35.

- "And as one earth shall pass away, and the heavens thereof even so shall another come."[62]
- "God spake unto Moses, saying: The heavens, they are many, and they cannot be numbered unto man; but they are numbered unto me, for they are mine."[63]

There is no doubt that Joseph's advanced knowledge of astronomy met with ridicule in 1830. But the previous statements prove that the Lord revealed facts about astronomy to His prophet. Consider how outrageous just one of Joseph's statements to the world seemed at that time: "Millions of earths like this . . . would not be a beginning to the number of thy creations."[64]

Robert M. Hazen, a noted twentieth-century professor trained at MIT and Harvard and who has written numerous scientific books, confirms the Lord's statement as to the vastness and expansiveness of the universe: "Looking outward to space, we observe tens of billions of stars in each of tens of billions of galaxies—perhaps a trillion solar systems exist for every human. There is so much left to discover. . . .

" . . . Each galaxy holds tens to hundreds of billions of stars in a region that may exceed a 100,000 light years in diameter."[65]

During a relatively short period, twenty-four years from his First Vision in the Sacred Grove until his death in Carthage Jail, Joseph was lifted, supported, and tutored by Christ. Joseph intimately knew, communed with, and loved the Savior. He desired to be with the Savior. The Savior loved Joseph. He used the endearing word *friends* fourteen times in addressing Joseph and his companions in revelations. In one revelation, the Savior clearly defined His relationship, both formal and informal. He told Joseph

---

62. Moses 1:38.

63. Moses 1:37.

64. Moses 7:30.

65. Robert M. Hazen, "The New Alchemy," *Technology Review,* November/December 1994, 24.

and other leaders that in front of the world He called them servants, but on a personal level they were His friends. In Kirtland, the Savior gave Joseph this assurance, "I say unto my servant Joseph Smith, Jun., or in other words, I will call you friends, for you are my friends, and ye shall have an inheritance with me."[66]

Joseph, as student and humble disciple, returned the title of *friend* to the Savior, who was his teacher and mentor. He expressed his desire to be with Christ forever in this heartfelt statement: "God is my friend in him I shall find comfort. . . . I desire to be with Christ."[67]

---

66. Doctrine & Covenants 93:45.

67. Joseph Smith to Emma, June 6, 1832, Greenville, Indiana, in *Personal Writings of Joseph Smith*, comp. Dean C. Jessee, rev. ed. (Salt Lake City: Deseret Book, 2002), 264–65.

CHAPTER 4

CHRIST PROTECTS HIS SAINTS
FROM THE ADVERSARY

In Kirtland, the very forces of the Almighty came to be locked in conflict with the
forces of evil in a manner reminiscent of what occurred in the great war in heaven.
—PRESIDENT GORDON B. HINCKLEY

During the Kirtland years the adversary not only continued his opposition to Joseph Smith and the Church as he had done in New York but
intensified it. Satan has always furiously opposed Christ's Church and His
prophets. Joseph Smith and God's latter-day kingdom were no exception.
President Gordon B. Hinckley acknowledged Satan's influence in Kirtland
and noted that it began in the premortal existence. At the dedication of
Kirtland historic sites in 2003, he said:

> In Kirtland, the very forces of the Almighty came to be
> locked in conflict with the forces of evil in a manner remi-
> niscent of what occurred in the great war in heaven when
> the Son of the Morning was cast out and became Satan, the
> devil.

> Kirtland became the sifting ground where the faithful
> were winnowed as grain from the chaff.[1]

Satan tried to thwart Joseph Smith even in his early years. Joseph described this opposition, saying, "It seems as though the adversary was aware, at a very early period of my life, that I was destined to prove a disturber and an annoyer of his kingdom; else why should the powers of darkness combine against me? Why the opposition and persecution that arose against me, almost in my infancy?"[2]

The Savior warned Joseph Smith of Satan's power and of his intention to destroy Joseph and the work of God. At the Morley farm in Kirtland, the Lord told Joseph, "Satan hath sought to . . . overthrow you."[3] He later said, "Satan seeketh to destroy [you]."[4] In Hiram, Ohio, Joseph clearly saw in vision that Satan's goal was "to take the kingdom of our God and his Christ."[5] The Savior made Joseph aware that Satan was waging a war against Christ. Joseph and the Saints were caught in the middle of that war. Joseph saw that Satan introduced "warfare in heav'n . . . rebell'd against Jesus, and sought for his pow'r."[6] Joseph understood that "the devil's for war,—and yet will encompass the saints round about."[7]

The Lord assured and comforted Joseph that with His ultimate power He would protect His latter-day servants. Through Joseph, He promised:

---

1. Gordon B. Hinckley, Kirtland historic sites dedicatory prayer, May 18, 2003, in "Dedicatory Prayer: Remembering Those Who Walked Pioneer Paths," *Church News* (Salt Lake City, Utah), May 24, 2003, 5.

2. Joseph Smith–History 1:20.

3. Doctrine & Covenants 50:3.

4. Doctrine & Covenants 132:57.

5. Doctrine & Covenants 76:28.

6. *Times and Seasons* 4 (February 1, 1843): 83 [v. 21].

7. *Times and Seasons* 4 (February 1, 1843): 83 [v. 23].

- "Do not fear, for I the Lord am with you, and will stand by you."[8]
- "I will go before you and be your rearward."[9]
- "God . . . shall subdue all enemies."[10]
- "There is no weapon that is formed against you shall prosper."[11]

The Lord plainly assured Joseph that Satan would be bound and ultimately defeated:

- "In mine own due time . . . Satan shall be bound."[12]
- "Satan shall be bound, that he shall have no place in the hearts of the children of men."[13]
- "In that day Satan shall not have power to tempt any man."[14]
- "Satan shall be bound, that old serpent, who is called the devil."[15]
- "And Michael . . . shall gather together his armies, even the hosts of heaven. And the devil shall gather together his armies; even the hosts of hell, and shall come up to battle against Michael and his armies. And then cometh the battle of the great God; and the devil and his armies shall be cast away into their own place, that they shall not have power over the saints any more at all.

8. Doctrine & Covenants 68:6.

9. Doctrine & Covenants 49:27.

10. Doctrine & Covenants 76:61.

11. Doctrine & Covenants 71:9.

12. Doctrine & Covenants 43:29–31.

13. Doctrine & Covenants 45:55.

14. Doctrine & Covenants 101:28.

15. Doctrine & Covenants 88:110.

> For Michael shall fight their battles, and shall overcome
> him who seeketh the throne of him who sitteth upon
> the throne, even the Lamb."[16]

It is obvious, by looking back on Joseph Smith's life, that the Lord protected him until his mission was completed. It is also obvious that Satan wanted to overthrow and destroy Joseph by ending his life. Joseph knew he would become a martyr. The Lord hinted as much to Joseph in 1829, when He promised Joseph that he would have eternal life, "even if you should be slain."[17] After the tarring and feathering in 1832, it was obvious to Joseph that he would have "been slain" had the Lord not intervened. No doubt Joseph sensed his ultimate fate. He wrote of his commitment to his calling and to the Savior and finished by writing: "I have given . . . my life into his hands. . . . I Count not my life dear to me only to do his will."[18]

At the end of the Kirtland period, the Lord intervened and warned Joseph to immediately leave Kirtland. As death threatened Joseph, the Lord assured him that He would protect him for at least five years.[19] Lucy Mack Smith, the Prophet's mother, said, "The persecution finally became so violent that Joseph regarded it as unsafe to remain any longer in Kirtland." She wrote of her son's final instructions to the brethren in Kirtland:

> One evening, before finishing his preparations for the
> contemplated journey (to Missouri), he sat in council with the
> brethren at our house. After giving them directions as to what
> he desired them to do, while he was absent from them, and,
> as he was about leaving the room, he said, "Well, brethren, I

---

16. Doctrine & Covenants 88:112–15.

17. Doctrine & Covenants 5:22.

18. Joseph Smith to Emma Smith, June 6, 1832, in *Personal Writings of Joseph Smith*, comp. and ed. Dean C. Jessee, rev. ed. (Salt Lake City: Deseret Book, 2002), 264–65.

19. Lucy Mack Smith, *History of Joseph Smith by His Mother*, ed. Preston Nibley (Salt Lake City: Bookcraft, 1958), 248.

do not recollect anything more, but one thing, brethren, is certain, I shall see you again, let what will happen, for I have a promise of life five years, and *they cannot kill me until that time is expired.*"[20]

The Savior Counters Satan's Deceptions

Within weeks of their arrival in Kirtland, members of the Church faced confusing manifestations from the adversary. These manifestations would have led many astray had the Lord not given them instruction about how to detect and overcome the evil one. Parley P. Pratt described what happened:

> As I went forth among the different branches, some very strange spiritual operations were manifested, which were disgusting, rather than edifying. Some persons would seem to swoon away, and make unseemly gestures, and be drawn or disfigured in their countenances. Others would fall into ecstacies, and be drawn into contortions, cramp, fits, etc. Others would seem to have visions and revelations, which were not edifying, and which were not congenial to the doctrine and spirit of the gospel. In short, a false and lying spirit seemed to be creeping into the Church. . . .
>
> Feeling our weakness and inexperience, and lest we should err in judgment concerning these spiritual phenomena, myself, John Murdock, and several other Elders, went to Joseph Smith, and asked him to inquire of the Lord concerning these spirits or manifestations.

---

20. Smith, *History of Joseph Smith,* 247–48; emphasis added.

After we had joined in prayer in his translating room, he dictated [a revelation] in our presence.[21]

In the revelation the Lord defined that light, truth, and edification are of the Lord and that darkness and "that which doth not edify" comes from Satan.[22] The Lord then admonished the Church to "chase darkness [Satan] from among you."[23] As a result, elders carried the warning by visiting branches of the Church and "rebuking the wrong spirits which had crept in among them."[24]

Satan's Opposition at the First Ohio Conference

The adversary threatened and tried to intimidate Christ's leaders at the first conference of the Church in Ohio, held at the Morley farm in early June 1831, by evoking a startling manifestation of his power. This was one of the great conferences of the Church. The first high priests of the dispensation were chosen and ordained. Transcendent spiritual experiences were granted to the brethren, which included a vision of God the Father and His Son, Jesus Christ. The Lord called twenty-eight missionaries by name (the largest missionary group to date) and instructed them to travel to Missouri, where Sidney Rigdon was directed to dedicate "this land, and the spot for the temple" in Independence.[25]

Lyman Wight described the spiritual nature of the conference: "I . . . saw the visible manifestations of the power of God as plain as could have been on the day of pentecost. . . . The spirit of God was made manifest to

21. Parley P. Pratt, *Autobiography of Parley P. Pratt*, ed. Parley P. Pratt Jr. (Salt Lake City: Deseret Book, 1985), 48.

22. Doctrine & Covenants 50:23–25.

23. Doctrine & Covenants 50:25.

24. Pratt, Autobiography, 51.

25. Doctrine & Covenants 58:57; see also vv. 50–56.

the heeling of the sick, cast<ing> out devils, speaking in unknown tongues, discerning of spirits and prophesying with mighty power."[26]

Joseph Smith promised, "Some should see their Savior, face to face."[27] John Whitmer, Church historian, recorded, "The glory of the Lord shone around."[28]

These actions threatened the adversary. Satan did not want high priests ordained or a temple begun. As he did in the Sacred Grove, the adversary tried to block these events. He entered the meeting. He bound two of the brethren. He possessed others and threw them around. John Whitmer said, "The devil took a notion to make known his power. He bound Harvey Whitlock and John Murdock so that they could not speak, and others were affected."[29]

Philo Dibble described an exhibition of the adversary's fury and power, saying,

> I saw a man came flying through the window from out-side. He was straight as a man's arm as he sailed into the room over two rows of seats filled with men, and fell on the floor between the seats and was pulled out by the brethren. . . . He weighed over two hundred pounds. This I saw with my own eyes and know it is all true, and bear testimony to it.[30]

---

26. Lyman Wight to Wilford Woodruff, August 24, 1857, in Church History Library, The Church of Jesus Christ of Latter-day Saints, Salt Lake City, Utah, 5–6; hereafter cited as Church History Library; also available online at http://saintswithouthalos.com/m/310604-m.phtml.

27. Ezra Booth to Ira Eddy, October 31, 1831, "Mormonism—No. IV," *[Ravenna] Ohio Star* 2 (November 3, 1831): 3.

28. *From Historian to Dissident: The Book of John Whitmer,* ed. Bruce N. Westergren (Salt Lake City: Signature Books, 1995), 69.

29. John Whitmer, in Joseph Smith, *History of The Church of Jesus Christ of Latter-day Saints,* ed. B. H. Roberts, 7 vols., 2d ed. rev. (Salt Lake City: The Church of Jesus Christ of Latter-day Saints, 1932–51), 1:175n†.

30. Philo Dibble, in "Recollections of the Prophet Joseph Smith," *Juvenile Instructor* 27 (May 15, 1892): 303.

Levi Hancock expressed his terror: "I was so scared I would not stir without his [Joseph Smith's] liberty for all the world."[31] Learning to control Satan's power, Joseph, in the name of Jesus Christ, cast out the adversary from the meeting, and the ordinations then proceeded smoothly. John Whitmer recalled, "The Lord showed to Joseph, the seer, the design of the thing; he commanded the devil in the name of Christ, and he departed, to our joy and comfort."[32]

Zebedee Coltrin, an eyewitness to Satan's departure, gave this description:

> During the meeting the power of darkness were made manifest in a remarkable degree. . . . Joseph . . . rebuked the spirit . . . from the house upon which the spirit left . . . and went outside, among the crowd of men standing near the door, and made a swath among them several feet wide, throwing them violently to the ground. Joseph said this was a fulfillment of the scriptures where it says the man of sin should be revealed.[33]

Satan Rages with Tar and Feathers

The adversary seemingly followed Joseph and Emma as they moved from place to place. In September 1831, they relocated from Kirtland to

---

31. Levi Hancock, "The Life of Levi Hancock," in Levi Hancock, Autobiography, copied by Clara E. H. Lloyd, typescript, 33, L. Tom Perry Special Collections, Harold B. Lee Library, Brigham Young University, Provo, Utah; hereafter cited as BYU Special Collections.

32. John Whitmer, in *History of the Church,* 1:175n†.

33. Minutes of a high priests meeting held at Spanish Fork, Utah, February 5, 1878, Church History Library, in Calvin Robert Stephens, "The Life and Contributions of Zebedee Coltrin" (master's thesis, Brigham Young University, 1974), 13–14.

Hiram, Ohio, a day's journey away. They lived for one year with John and Elsa Johnson, who loved them dearly.

Satan raged there one night, forever altering the lives of Joseph and Emma. On the night of March 24, 1832, Joseph's life was almost taken. A mob of about forty men gathered outside the Johnson home. Twelve of the group dragged Joseph Smith, kicking and struggling, out of his bedroom into the freezing darkness of the night. The mob threatened several times to kill him. Emma, convinced that they would kill him, screamed, "Murder."[34] No doubt it was to get the attention of their hosts, the Johnson family, who were sleeping.

Joseph pleaded with the mob not to kill him. The mob responded by saying, in effect, that only God could spare him because "we'll show ye no mercy."[35] Someone in the mob seized Joseph by his throat until he lost consciousness. Then they beat him, scratched him with sharp fingernails, and tore off all of his clothes except his shirt collar. Some tried to force a tar-paddle into his mouth as well as a vial of nitric acid, which he broke with his teeth, cutting his lip and burning his mouth. According to Joseph's son, Joseph III, they hauled "him over the frozen ground, pounding, scratching, and otherwise maltreating him. . . .

" . . . Some held him, others beat him."[36] They applied tar and then the added humiliation of feathers from a pillow taken by one of the mob. Joseph then began to pray. At this point, according to George A. Smith, the mob "heard an alarm which made them think they were about to be surprised, and left suddenly."[37] Joseph came to and slowly found his way back to the Johnson home. Emma opened the door and fainted, thinking the tar was

---

34. Joseph describes the events of this night in his history (*History of the Church,* 1:261–65).

35. *History of the Church,* 1:262.

36. Joseph Smith III, "Biography of Emma Smith, Prepared 1892–1893 for Recollections of the Pioneers of Lee County," typescript, 4, Community of Christ Archives, Independence, Mo.

37. George A. Smith, in *Journal of Discourses,* 26 vols. (London: Latter-day Saints' Book Depot, 1854–86), 11:5.

blood. Joseph III wrote, "A number of his immediate neighbors had gathered [at the house], roused by the cries of his wife. He presented a ghastly appearance."[38]

Joseph bore the effects of this satanic deed throughout his life as a constant reminder of the hatred of Satan. The mob had pulled a clump of hair out of his head by the roots, leaving his scalp bare.[39] Afterward, Joseph combed his hair in a different way to hide the bare spot. He spoke with a lisp for several years, until in Nauvoo, Alexander Neibaur fixed the tooth. The mob apparently broke several of his ribs as well. Two and a half years later, Joseph described this injury to his side in a letter to William, his younger brother, after William physically attacked him:

> You were too quick for me, and having once fallen into the hands of a mob, and been wounded in my side, . . . my side gave way. . . . [W]ith a lame side . . . I returned home, not able to sit down or rise up without help. . . .
> . . . I am older than you and have endured more suffering, having been marred by mobs . . . persecutions and injuries . . . all serve to debilitate my body; and it may be that I cannot boast of being stronger than you.[40]

The full extent of Joseph's injuries that night is shown by a little-known account recorded by Joseph III, who must have heard the details from one or both of his parents. Joseph was so near dying that he had a near-death experience. He was "beaten into insensibility . . . and left for dead." Joseph III related that Joseph's "spirit seemed to leave his body, and that during

---

38. Smith, "Biography of Emma Smith," 4.

39. Hancock, Autobiography, typescript, 50.

40. *History of the Church*, 2:341–42; Karen Lynn Davidson, David J. Whittaker, Mark Ashurst-McGee, and Richard L. Jensen, eds., *Histories, 1832–1844*, vol. 1 of the Histories series of *The Joseph Smith Papers*, edited by Dean C. Jessee, Ronald K. Esplin, and Richard Lyman Bushman (Salt Lake City: Church Historian's Press, 2012), 1:156.

the period of insensibility he consciously stood over his own body, feeling no pain, but seeing and hearing all that transpired."[41] After the tarring and feathering, Joseph "found himself scarcely able to move, but managed to clear the tar from his mouth and nostrils so that he could breathe more freely, and then dragged himself back to his home."[42]

To add to the tragedy, Joseph and Emma's almost ten-month-old ad-opted son, Joseph, who was sick with measles, became "chilled from the cold draft, rapidly grew worse and died the next week."[43] As bad as the mob-bing was for Joseph, it was terrifying for Emma, who was pregnant with Joseph III. This same son later said, "It was some time before Mrs. Smith recovered from the shock and exposure of that terrible night."[44] Emma's oldest grandson, Frederick Alexander Smith, said that Emma "made very little reference to any persecutions. [But he] Heard her tell about the mob in Hiram, O[hio]. She [was in] terror, prayed, [and] never expected to see him [Joseph] again."[45] She also made reference to Joseph's "skinned [and] bruised [body]."[46] This frightening experience, in which the Lord interceded and preserved Joseph's life, was both a great sacrifice and valuable training for them. The probable heaven-sent alarm stopped the mob action and sent them scurrying away. Had the mob not been frightened by the sound of the alarm, they might have killed Joseph outright.

Satan Unveils His Wrath to Missionaries

After missionaries to Missouri participated in ceremonies of dedicating the land and laying the cornerstone of the temple, they commenced their return

41. Joseph Smith III, in *Recollections of the Pioneers of Lee County [Illinois]* (Dixon, Ill.: Inez A. Kennedy, 1893), 98.

42. Smith, "Biography of Emma Smith," 4.

43. Smith, "Biography of Emma Smith," 5.

44. Smith, "Biography of Emma Smith," 5.

45. Buddy Youngreen, *Reflections of Emma: Joseph Smith's Wife* (Orem, Utah: Grandin Book, 1982), 93.

46. Youngreen, *Reflections of Emma,* 103.

to Kirtland. Satan made his power manifest to them while they were traveling in their canoes on the Missouri River. Joseph Smith describes their return trip:

> Nothing very important occurred till the third day, when many of the dangers so common upon the western waters, manifested themselves; and after we had encamped upon the bank of the river, at McIlwaine's Bend, Brother Phelps, in open vision by daylight, saw the destroyer in his most horrible power, ride upon the face of the waters; others heard the noise, but saw not the vision.[47]

This must have been a terrifying experience for this small group. Providing protection, the Lord gave Joseph Smith a revelation in which He warned the brethren to be careful when traveling on water because "the destroyer rideth upon the face thereof."[48] The Lord reassured the Saints of His protection, saying, "Nevertheless, all flesh is in mine hand, and he that is faithful among you shall not perish by the waters."[49]

"Bells of Hell Toll"

Perhaps at no other time in Kirtland did the adversary rage in opposition as often and as long as he did during the two and a half years it took to build the Kirtland Temple. Brigham Young, who had primary responsibility for building the temple, remembered Satan's constant opposition. He later reminisced: "Some say, . . . 'we never began to build a temple without the bells of hell beginning to ring.' I want to hear them ring again. . . .

" . . . We completed a temple in Kirtland and in Nauvoo; and did not

---

47. *History of the Church*, 1:202–3.

48. Doctrine & Covenants 61:19.

49. Doctrine & Covenants 61:6.

the bells of hell toll all the time we were building them? They did, every week and every day."[50]

The harsh reality is that the Church experienced continual opposition while building the temple. The adversary incited rampant persecution and mob violence. Heber C. Kimball spoke from firsthand experience when he said, "While we were building the Temple, in Kirtland . . . we were persecuted . . . there were mobs gathering all around us to destroy us, and prevent us from building the Temple."[51] He added, "Our enemies were raging and threatening destruction upon us, and we had to guard ourselves night after night, and for weeks were not permitted to take off our clothes, and were obliged to lay with our fire locks in our arms."[52]

Joel Hills Johnson said there were "thousands of enemies who were holding their secret meetings to devise a plan to thwart and overthrow all our arrangements. We were obliged to keep night watchers to prevent being mobbed, and our workers being overthrown."[53]

As construction of the temple began, Joseph Smith, writing to William Phelps in August 1833, foresaw "all Hell" being marshaled to stop the temple from being built. Joseph said:

> We <are> no safer here in Kirtland then you are in Zion[;] the cloud is gethering around us with great fury and . . . all hell and the comb[ined] powrs of Earth are Marsheling their forces to overthrow us and we like the children of Is<s>arel with the red Sea before . . . them and

---

50. Brigham Young, *Discourses of Brigham Young,* sel. John A. Widtsoe (Salt Lake City: Deseret Book, 1973), 410.

51. *Times and Seasons* 6 (July 15, 1845): 972.

52. *Times and Seasons* 6 (January 15, 1845): 771.

53. "Joel Hills Johnson, 1802–1882," typescript, Church History Library; and BYU Special Collections; available online at www.boap.org/LDS/Early-Saints/JHJohnson.html.

the Egyptions ready to fall upon them to distroy them and no arm could diliver but the arm of God.[54]

Four months later conditions hadn't improved. The Prophet wrote, "The inhabitants of this county threaten our destruction."[55] The following month a mob assembled near Kirtland with a cannon. The Prophet recalled this night, saying:

> The threats of the mob about Kirtland through the fall and winter had been such as to cause the brethren to be constantly on the lookout, and those who labored on the temple were engaged at night watching to protect the walls they had laid during the day, from threatened violence. On the morning of the 8th of January, about 1 o'clock, the inhabitants of Kirtland were alarmed by the firing of about thirteen rounds of cannon, by the mob, on the hill about half a mile northwest of the village.[56]

One year later Satan still persisted. In his journal, Benjamin Johnson describes opposition and persecution: "Up to this period from our commencement to settle at Kirtland, there had been by our enemies one continual persecution of the Prophet and contempt for the Saints and their religion. And such was their opposition and hatred towards the Temple during its construction, that it had to be guarded, not only by night but also by day; and the laborers upon its walls, while with one hand they held the hammer or trowel were always ready with the other to grasp the sword."[57]

---

54. Joseph Smith to William W. Phelps and others, August 18, 1833, in Jessee, *Personal Writings*, 309.

55. *History of the Church*, 1:450.

56. *History of the Church*, 2:2.

57. Benjamin F. Johnson, *My Life's Review* (Independence, Mo.: Zion's Printing & Publishing Co., 1947), 24.

Bells Ring Loudest July 23, 1833

The bells of hell perhaps rang loudest on July 23, 1833. As the Saints in Kirtland experienced an apex of rejoicing while laying the cornerstones of their temple, the Saints in Missouri experienced an apex of disaster when they were forced at gunpoint to vacate their homes and property and to leave Jackson County. According to the official report, "Early in the morning of the 23rd of July, the mob again assembled, armed with weapons of war, and bearing a red flag; whereupon the Elders, led by the Spirit of God, and in order to save time, and stop the effusion of blood, entered into a treaty with the mob."[58]

Prior to the signing of the treaty, the older Missouri settlers banded together and demanded that the Mormons leave Jackson County. Local authorities banned the Church's newspaper, ordered that the printing office discontinue operations, and mandated that businesses operated by Mormons close immediately. When the Saints refused to accede to such unthinkable demands, mobs began harassing and plundering their property in an effort to drive them from Missouri. One mob member boasted that 203 Mormon homes had been burned.[59] From July through November, mobs vandalized or destroyed such buildings as the home of W. W. Phelps, which housed the printing press; A. Sidney Gilbert's home; and a dozen homes near the Big Blue River, which were pounded with stones and clubs.

A treaty was forced upon the Saints whereby they essentially agreed to leave the county in stages. All the Saints were to be gone within eight months. The Saints also agreed "to stop any more of their sect from moving to this county." In addition, Church members agreed that the Church newspaper, *The Evening and the Morning Star*, would not again "be published

---

58. *History of the Church*, 1:394.

59. *History of the Church*, 3:427.

nor a press set up by any of the society in this county." The mob agreed only "to use all their influence to prevent any violence being used."[60]

Forced to surrender their arms, these desolate people were defenseless. It was a matter of leave and live or stay and die. A letter from W. W. Phelps shows the dire condition of the Saints as they were forced to leave Jackson County. He wrote: "The condition of the scattered Saints is lamentable, and affords a gloomy prospect. . . . But, brethren, if the Lord will, I should like to know what the honest in heart shall do? Our clothes are worn out; we want the necessaries of life, and shall we lease, buy, or otherwise obtain land where we are, to till, that we may raise enough to eat?"[61]

In retribution for the Saints laying the temple cornerstone in Kirtland, Ohio, Satan directed his fury against the Church in Missouri. The price of laying the cornerstone for the Kirtland Temple on July 23, 1833, began to be exacted that very day from the Saints in Jackson County, Missouri, who would soon be driven from their homes and other property. Certainly, the bells of hell tolled loudly that day.

The Temple Completed and Satan Bound

Satan intensified his attacks in Kirtland as the temple neared completion. Joseph Smith bluntly stated in January 1836, "The devil has made a violent attack. . . . the powers of earth and hell seem combined to overthrow us and the Church."[62]

The Lord temporarily halted Satan's interference, however. Journal accounts certify that the Lord sent heavenly hosts to protect the Saints and His temple so that His purposes could be fulfilled. Less than three

---

60. *History of the Church*, 1:394–95.

61. *History of the Church*, 1:457.

62. *History of the Church*, 2:352; Dean C. Jessee, Mark Ashurst-McGee, and Richard L. Jensen, eds., *Journals, 1832–1839*, vol. 1 of the Journals series of *The Joseph Smith Papers*, edited by Dean C. Jessee, Ronald K. Esplin, and Richard Lyman Bushman (Salt Lake City: Church Historian's Press, 2008), 1:140.

months before the temple dedication, the Prophet confirmed that unseen forces protected the Saints. Roger Orton, a member of the First Quorum of the Seventy, saw angels protecting them. Joseph Smith recorded the event, writing, "Roger Orton saw a mighty angel riding upon a horse of fire, with a flaming sword in his hand, followed by five others, encircle the house, and protect the Saints, even the Lord's anointed, from the power of Satan and a host of evil spirits, which were striving to disturb the Saints."[63]

William Smith, the Prophet's brother and one of the Twelve, "saw the heavens opened, and the Lord's host protecting the Lord's anointed."[64]

Truman O. Angell, a construction worker, saw two angels guard the Kirtland Temple. One evening at the time the temple was dedicated, he walked with Brigham Young toward the temple from the west. He expressed his certain testimony, saying:

> When about ten rods distant we looked up and saw two Personages; before each window, leaving and approaching each other like guards would do. This continued until quite dark. As they were walking back and forth, one turned his face to me for an instant; but while they walked to and fro, only a side view was visible. I have no doubt that the house was guarded, as I have had no other way to account for it.[65]

Daniel Tyler, a missionary and workman on the temple, said: "All felt that they had a foretaste of heaven. In fact, there were several weeks in

---

63. *History of the Church*, 2:386–87; Jessee, Ashurst-McGee, and Jensen, *Journals,* 1:174.

64. *History of the Church*, 2:387; Jessee, Ashurst-McGee, and Jensen, *Journals,* 1:174.

65. "Truman Angell Autobiography," in *Our Pioneer Heritage,* comp. Kate B. Carter, 20 vols. (Salt Lake City: Daughters of Utah Pioneers, 1958–77), 10:202–3.

which we were not tempted of the devil; and we wondered whether the millennium had commenced."[66]

The Prophet announced to the brethren in the temple: "Brethren, for some time Satan has not had power to tempt you. Some have thought that there would be no more temptation. But the opposite will come; and unless you draw near to the Lord you will be overcome and apostatize."[67]

Angels did their job. The temple was protected against Satan and his hosts. Sacred ordinances were given. Long-awaited keys were restored. But the respite from the adversary soon ended.

Christ Protects the First Missionaries to England

Perhaps there is no more dramatic evidence of Satan's continuing war against the Savior and the Church than occurred with the first missionaries sent from Kirtland to England. It was daybreak on Sunday, July 30, 1837, the day on which the first baptisms were to be performed in England. Satan was desperate and angry. Legions of evil spirits appeared in Heber C. Kimball's bedroom with the intention of killing him and the other missionaries. The Lord, however, delivered His servants. Heber described the awful battle as follows:

> I was struck with great force by some invisible power, and fell senseless on the floor. . . . my agony was so great I could not endure it, and I arose, bowed my knees and prayed. I . . . could distinctly see the evil spirits. . . . We gazed upon them about an hour and a half. . . . we saw the devils coming in legions, with their leaders, . . . like armies rushing to battle. . . . who were angry and desperate; and I shall never forget the vindictive malignity depicted on their

---

66. Daniel Tyler, "Incidents of Experience," in *Scraps of Biography* in *Classic Experiences and Adventures* (Salt Lake City: Bookcraft, 1969), 32.

67. Tyler, "Incidents of Experience," 33.

countenances . . . any attempt to paint the scene which then presented itself . . . would be vain. I perspired exceedingly, my clothes becoming as wet as if I had been taken out of the river. I felt excessive pain. . . . I learned the power of the adversary, his enmity against the servants of God, and got some understanding of the invisible world. . . . However, the Lord delivered us from them, and blessed us exceedingly that day. . . .

Notwithstanding the weakness of my body . . . I had the pleasure, about 9 A.M., of baptizing nine individuals.[68]

Orson Hyde, who was with Heber C. Kimball, contended with the devils until only one remained. He recounted, "I replied to him thus: ' . . . you are a liar from the beginning! In the name of Jesus Christ, depart!' He immediately left, and the room was clear. That closed the scene of devils for that time."[69] Heber later asked Joseph Smith the meaning of this evil onslaught. He wondered if they might have done something wrong to cause it, but the Prophet reassured him:

"No, Brother Heber, . . . at that time you were nigh unto the Lord; there was only a veil between you and Him, but you could not see Him. When I heard of it, it gave me great joy, for I then knew that the work of God had taken root in that land. It was this that caused the devil to make a struggle to kill you."

Joseph then related some of his own experience, in many contests he had had with the evil one, and said: "The nearer a person approaches the Lord, a greater power will be

---

68. Heber C. Kimball, in Orson F. Whitney, *Life of Heber C. Kimball* (Salt Lake City: Bookcraft, 1945), 130–31, 135.

69. Orson Hyde, in Whitney, *Life of Heber C. Kimball*, 131.

manifested by the adversary to prevent the accomplishment of His purposes."[70]

The Adversary's Final Efforts in Kirtland

After the temple dedication, the adversary resumed his attacks on the Saints. Joseph saw a dark time ahead for the Saints. He knew that this coming period would be a refiner's fire for the Church. It was a test. He knew some would fail it. He made an inspired prophecy: "Satan's kingdom [will] be laid in ruins, with all his black designs; and the Saints will come forth like gold seven times tried in the fire, being made perfect through sufferings and temptations, and that the blessings of heaven and earth will be multiplied upon their heads."[71]

In the Church's last two years in Kirtland, one form of persecution followed another until the forces of evil drove the Saints out of the city. The bank failed. Townspeople broke into homes of the Saints, many of whom feared for their lives. As the Kirtland era closed, the Lord "warned" Joseph "by the Spirit" to leave and masked his identity as he did so.[72] About two months later the Lord sent "a messenger . . . very large . . . dressed in a white robe down to his ankles" to provide divine assurance to the main body of Saints before they departed.[73] This messenger came in answer to prayers of Zerah Pulsipher and other Church leaders as they prayed in the temple that the Lord would open the way for the remaining Saints to leave Kirtland.

Satan inflicted deep wounds upon the Church. Some of the most faithful faltered. The Lord allowed Satan to sift the Saints and winnow the wheat from the chaff. The Church was wounded severely and many persons apostatized, including, eventually, five Apostles—Thomas B. Marsh, William E. McLellin,

---

70. Joseph Smith, in Whitney, *Life of Heber C. Kimball*, 132.

71. *History of the Church*, 2:353; Jessee, Ashurst-McGee, and Jensen, *Journals*, 1:141.

72. Smith, *History of Joseph Smith*, 248.

73. Zerah Pulsipher, "Autobiography 1789–1872" (ca. 1803–62), typescript, BYU Special Collections.

Luke Johnson, Lyman Johnson and John Boynton.[74] Those who overcame the forces of Satan not only survived but also became more stalwart and faithful. The adversary had inadvertently made them stronger, with a definite resolve to become faithful members and leaders. They were now prepared by those excruciating trials to face and conquer even more stringent tests in Missouri, in Nauvoo, and in crossing the plains. The Lord may have hidden His face for a time and shed tears over those who fell by the wayside, but He nevertheless ensured the continuation and growth of the Church. By allowing His Saints to be "seven times tried in the fire, being made perfect through sufferings, and temptations," His kingdom was launched.[75]

Some Leaders Fell

The Lord fulfilled His promises to protect His Saints, but many gave in to the adversary and succumbed to his subversive temptations and trials. They did not understand what Joseph tried to teach in 1836: "The powers of darkness . . . cast a gloomy shade . . . which prevents . . . seeing things as they realy are."[76] They did not understand that ultimate exaltation requires consistent trust, obedience to God's commandments, and faith in the Lord to follow and support the Prophet. They did not understand that they were rightly placed in the continuing battle between Christ and Satan. They did not understand that enduring such trials and persecutions induced by Satan were necessary for growth and glory. Joseph tried to teach them, but all did not endure. Wilford Woodruff, one who did, focused on the simple revealed principle that light and truth overcome darkness and evil. After hearing Joseph teach, Wilford said: "Light, principle & virtue . . . came forth out of the heart & mouth of the Prophet JOSEPH . . . such evidences . . . ought to drive into oblivion every particle of unbelief & dubiety from the mind of

---

74. Except for Thomas B. Marsh, all left the Church before July 1838 when the Kirtland Camp, the main body of Saints, left Kirtland. Marsh was excommunicated eight months later.

75. *History of the Church*, 2:353; Jessee, Ashurst-McGee, and Jensen, *Journals*, 1:141.

76. *History of the Church*, 2:352; Jessee, Ashurst-McGee, and Jensen, *Journals*, 1:140.

the hearers, for such language sentiment principle & spirit cannot flow from darkness. Joseph Smith jr is a prophet of God."[77]

Those who fell away were warned that Satan would fight for their souls. Four years earlier, Joseph had seen Satan making war with the Saints. In 1832, Joseph saw in vision that "Satan, that old serpent, even the devil . . . maketh war with the saints of God, and encompasseth them round about."[78]

Joseph also saw those with whom Satan made war and overcame.[79] He saw that they would have misery and suffering.[80] At the demise of the Church in Kirtland, he proclaimed, "If I obtain the glory which I have in view I expect to wade through much tribulation."[81]

Noteworthy lessons can be learned from those of prominence who did not remain true to their earlier convictions. They suffered misery because they didn't recognize the adversary's influence until they fell. Some examples are Lyman Johnson, Harvey Whitlock, and Thomas B. Marsh. Lyman Johnson, the first Apostle to be called in this dispensation, related his feelings to a meeting of the Quorum of the Twelve in Nauvoo:

> If I could believe "Mormonism" as I did when I traveled
> with you and preached, if I possessed the world I would give it.
> I would give anything. I would suffer my right hand to be cut
> off, if I could believe it again. Then I was full of joy and glad-
> ness. My dreams were pleasant. When I awoke in the morning
> my spirit was cheerful. I was happy by day and by night, full of
> peace and joy and thanksgiving. But now it is darkness, pain,

---

77. Dean C. Jessee, "The Kirtland Diary of Wilford Woodruff," *BYU Studies* 12, no. 4 (1972): 390–91.

78. Doctrine & Covenants 76:28–29.

79. Doctrine & Covenants 76:30.

80. Joseph Smith, "A Vision" (poem), *Times and Seasons* 4 (February 1, 1843): 83–85 [v. 24]; Doctrine & Covenants 76:36.

81. In David Osborn, "Recollections," *Juvenile Instructor* 27, no. 6 (March 15, 1892): 173.

sorrow, misery in the extreme. I have never since seen a happy moment.[82]

Harvey Whitlock, a priesthood leader who saw a vision of the Father and the Son at the first conference of the Church in Kirtland, wrote in a letter to Joseph Smith, saying:

> When I consider the happy times, and peaceful moments, and pleasant seasons I have enjoyed with you and this people, contrasted with my now degraded state; together with the high and important station I have held before God, and the abyss into which I have fallen—it is a subject that swells my heart too big for utterance, and I am overwhelmed with feelings that language cannot express. . . .
>
> . . . I have fallen from that princely station whereunto our God has called me. . . .
>
> . . . I have sealed my own doom, and pronounced my own sentence. . . . [F]ollow not my example, but steer . . . onward in spite of all the combined powers of earth and hell, for [I] know that one misstep here is only retrievable by a thousand groans and tears before God.[83]

Thomas B. Marsh, president of the Quorum of the Twelve Apostles in Kirtland, allowed negative feelings toward Joseph Smith, which lasted eighteen years, to start his fall. This period, which he described as "grooping in darkness," reached a low point with the death of his wife.[84] Finally, in May

---

82. Brigham Young, in *Journal of Discourses,* 19:41.

83. *History of the Church,* 2:313–14; Davidson, Whittaker, Ashurst-McGee, and Jensen, *Histories,* 1:126–27.

84. Lyndon W. Cook, "'I Have Sinned against Heaven, and Am Unworthy of Your Confidence, but I Cannot Live without a Reconciliation': Thomas B. Marsh Returns to the Church," *BYU Studies* 20, no. 4 (Summer 1980): 397.

1857 he concluded, "I see, the Lord could get along very well without me and He has lost nothing by my falling out of the ranks; But O what have I lost?! Riches Greater Riches than all this world or many planets like this could afford."[85]

At a meeting with Church members in Salt Lake City later that year, Thomas explained that he had been mad at Joseph. He said he "talked with Brother Brigham and Brother Heber, and I wanted them to be mad like myself; and I saw they were not mad, and I got madder still because they were not."[86] With a repentant spirit, he described how the adversary had led him away, telling the congregation:

> Many have said to me, "How is it that a man like you ... should fall away?" I told them ...
>
> ... Let no one feel too secure: for, before you think of it, your steps will slide. You will not then think nor feel for a moment as you did before you lost the Spirit of Christ; for when men apostatize, they are left to grovel in the dark. I ... lost the Spirit of the Lord out of my heart. ...
>
> ... And then, when the Devil began to lead me, it was easy for the carnal mind to rise up, which is anger, jealousy, and wrath. I could feel it within me; I felt angry and wrathful; and the Spirit of the Lord being gone, as the Scriptures say, I was blinded. ...
>
> ... If you do not want to suffer in body and mind, as I have done ... nip that spirit in the bud; for it is misery and affliction in this world, and destruction in the world to come.[87]

---

85. Cook, "I Have Sinned," 398.

86. Thomas B. Marsh, in *Journal of Discourses*, 5:207.

87. Marsh, in *Journal of Discourses*, 5:206–7.

Surely the battle, begun in the heavens before this world, did in fact increase throughout the Kirtland era and beyond. Nevertheless, those steadfast Saints who recognized the hand of the Lord through it all remained true to their faith, became stronger through the adversity, and forged ahead in His divine work.

CHAPTER 5

CHRIST TEACHES OF HIMSELF

I am he who was lifted up. I am Jesus that was crucified.
I am the Son of God.
—DOCTRINE & COVENANTS 45:52

Nothing is more central to Kirtland than Christ's personal instruction concerning His own divine nature, Atonement, and Resurrection. He taught plainly and completely that the eternal plan of salvation is centered in Him. His revelations focus on Himself, His roles and missions, and the redemption of mankind. This Christ-centered teaching could be referred to as the Christology of Kirtland. Christ dictated more revelations and caused the initial printing of more of His words during the Kirtland period than at any other time in Church history.[1] The totality of words referring to the Savior establish a word

---

1. Christ's instruction during the Kirtland period as referenced in this chapter includes the following categories of revelation: (1) *Revelations or instruction.* These include revelations received in Kirtland, Hiram, Thompson, and Amherst, Ohio. They also include revelations received by Joseph Smith while on missions from Kirtland in New York, Massachusetts, and Missouri. (2) *First printing of revelations.* These include revelations received before 1831 in New York and Pennsylvania and published in *The Evening and the Morning Star,* the Book of Commandments, or the first edition of the Doctrine & Covenants in 1835. (3) *Revealed changes and additions to the Bible.* These were given to Joseph Smith as he translated the Bible in Kirtland. (4) *The book of Moses.* Joseph received chapters 1–7 in the seven months before moving to Kirtland, but they were not generally made available to

print, showing that in modern revelation the Savior speaks with authority and describes His powers. Christ's latter-day instruction was recorded as it came to Joseph Smith. The Savior either identified Himself as the source, or He spoke in first-person language in almost every revelation. These revelations come to us as they were given in the English language.[2] Christ made it clear that the revelations came from Himself. He testified, "I, Jesus Christ, your Lord and your God, have spoken it. These words are not of men nor of man, but of me."[3] It could be said of Joseph Smith in Kirtland as it was said of Moses: the Lord spoke with him "face to face, as a man speaketh unto his friend."[4]

Christ Teaches through Testimonies of Deity

One remarkable and timeless aspect of the Savior's teaching was His consistent identification and testimony of Himself. Christ often testified to the reality of His own existence and divinity. Following are just some of His many first-person testimonies that went to the world from Kirtland:

- "I was in the beginning with the Father, and am the Firstborn."[5]
- "I am Jesus Christ, the Savior of the world."[6]

---

the Church until the Kirtland period. When John Whitmer moved to Kirtland in January 1831, it was publicly acknowledged that he brought a manuscript of the book of Moses with him, and its general contents were made public. Portions of seven chapters of the book of Moses were printed or referenced during the Kirtland period in *The Evening and the Morning Star, Messenger and Advocate,* or *Lectures on Theology.* Chapter 8 was translated in Kirtland. (5) *The book of Abraham.* The ancient papyrus containing this record was acquired and translated mainly in Kirtland.

2. All other scripture in the standard works was originally recorded in some language other than English, and thus, what we read in ancient scripture is all translated information. Because these words were spoken in English, our record of them reduces misunderstandings caused by translation and corroborates the accuracy of other translated words of Jesus Christ.

3. Doctrine & Covenants 18:33–34.

4. Exodus 33:11; Doctrine & Covenants 76:14; 110:1–10; 137.

5. Doctrine & Covenants 93:21.

6. Doctrine & Covenants 43:34.

- "I am he who was lifted up. I am Jesus that was crucified."[7]
- "I am Jesus Christ, the Son of God."[8]
- "I am from above. . . . I am over all, and in all, and through all."[9]
- "I am Alpha and Omega, even Jesus Christ."[10]
- "I am the Lord of Hosts."[11]
- "I the Lord . . . even Jesus Christ . . . am the Son of the living God."[12]
- "I am the true light . . . I am in the Father, and the Father in me."[13]
- "I was in the world . . . and dwelt among the sons of men."[14]
- "I am he who liveth, I am he who was slain; I am your advocate with the Father."[15]
- "I am the Lord of glory I was crucifyed for the world."[16]

Also remarkable is that God the Father apparently desired that His own first-person testimony of Jesus Christ be repeatedly recorded. Heavenly Father's own words testified to Christ's existence and divinity time and time again.[17] Following are just some of the Father's many words of testimony regarding the Son:

---

7. Doctrine & Covenants 45:52.

8. Doctrine & Covenants 52:44.

9. Doctrine & Covenants 63:59.

10. Doctrine & Covenants 63:60.

11. Doctrine & Covenants 64:24.

12. Doctrine & Covenants 68:6.

13. Doctrine & Covenants 93:2–3.

14. Doctrine & Covenants 93:4.

15. Doctrine & Covenants 110:4.

16. Karen Lynn Davidson, David J. Whittaker, Mark Ashurst-McGee, and Richard L. Jensen, eds., *Histories, 1832–1844,* vol. 1 of the Histories series of *The Joseph Smith Papers,* edited by Dean C. Jessee, Ronald K. Esplin, and Richard Lyman Bushman (Salt Lake City: Church Historian's Press, 2012), 1:13.

17. God the Father did not speak directly to Joseph Smith in any of the visions Joseph saw of Him in

- "The Son . . . is mine Only Begotten."[18]
- "I . . . God . . . have sent mine Only Begotten Son into the world for the redemption of the world."[19]
- "Mine Only Begotten . . . was with me from the beginning."[20]
- "My Beloved Son . . . was my Beloved and Chosen from the beginning."[21]
- "Jesus Christ [is] the only name which shall be given under heaven, whereby salvation shall come unto the children of men."[22]
- "Mine Only Begotten is and shall be the Savior."[23]

In reading the Savior's revelations, we could easily conclude that both the Savior and the Father wanted the Latter-day Saints to know of Christ's divinity and to have confidence that He had power and ability to fulfill His promises to them. For example, when the Lord commanded the Saints in New York to sell, rent, or even leave their farms behind and go to the unknown world of Kirtland, He first assured them of His leadership and divine nature. He preceded the

---

Kirtland, but Joseph recorded the Father's first-person words on occasion, such as in Doctrine & Covenants 29 and 49, as well as repeatedly in the book of Moses. President Joseph Fielding Smith explained: "In giving revelations our Savior speaks at times for himself; at other times for the Father, and in the Father's name, as though he were the Father, and yet it is Jesus Christ, our Redeemer who gives the message. So, we see, in Doctrine & Covenants 29:1, that he introduces himself as 'Jesus Christ, your Redeemer,' but in the closing part of the revelation he speaks for the Father, and in the Father's name as though he were the Father, and yet it is still Jesus who is speaking, for the Father has put his name on him for that purpose" (*Doctrines of Salvation,* comp. Bruce R. McConkie, 3 vols. [Salt Lake City: Bookcraft, 1954–56], 1:27–28). Therefore, on account of President Smith's declaration, these words are included in this chapter as words that Christ taught.

18. Moses 1:33.

19. Doctrine & Covenants 49:5.

20. Moses 2:26.

21. Moses 4:2.

22. Moses 6:52.

23. Moses 1:6.

command to move to Ohio by making sure His Saints understood who is-sued the edict. He identified Himself to them as "the Lord your God, even Jesus Christ . . . which knoweth all things . . . I am the same which spake, and the world was made, and all things came by me. . . . I am in your midst and ye cannot see me. . . . I will . . . watch over you."[24] Knowing that Jesus Christ, their Lord and God, led them and would watch over them would certainly have given the early Saints faith and confidence to obey His command.

The Savior Taught of Himself through His Names and Titles

The Savior taught volumes about Himself through the use of descriptive names and titles. He identified Himself by more than one hundred different names or titles in Kirtland. Most of these identify an aspect of His divine mission or at least one of His attributes that typify something about Him. Each name also teaches something about Him. Each gives a little different insight into Him. Each increases our confidence in Him. Many refer to His power and ability to lead and save mankind. The Savior used many names over and over. As an example of this, He used the title "I the Lord" 123 times in the canonized revelations published in Kirtland. The following list identifies 101 names the Savior used to identify Himself in revelations printed or received in Kirtland.[25]

- Advocate with the father[26]
- Almighty[27]
- Alpha and Omega[28]

---

24. Doctrine & Covenants 38:1–3, 7, 21.

25. Not all of the variations of the Savior's names and titles appear in the list. In most cases multiple references exist for each name or title; however, only one reference is cited in the list.

26. Doctrine & Covenants 45:3.

27. Doctrine & Covenants 84:96.

28. Doctrine & Covenants 45:7.

- Alphus[29]
- Beginning and the end[30]
- Beloved Son[31]
- Bridegroom[32]
- Christ[33]
- Christ the Lamb[34]
- Creator of the first day[35]
- Creator of the heavens and the earth[36]
- Creator of worlds[37]
- Endless[38]
- The first and the last[39]
- Firstborn[40]
- Glorious Majesty on high[41]
- God[42]
- God of Enoch[43]
- God the Lord[44]
- Good shepherd[45]

---

29. Doctrine & Covenants 95:17.

30. Doctrine & Covenants 45:7.

31. Doctrine & Covenants 93:15.

32. Doctrine & Covenants 133:10.

33. Doctrine & Covenants 68:25.

34. Doctrine & Covenants 76:85.

35. Doctrine & Covenants 95:7.

36. Doctrine & Covenants 14:9.

37. Doctrine & Covenants 76:24.

38. Doctrine & Covenants 19:10.

39. Doctrine & Covenants 110:4.

40. Doctrine & Covenants 93:21.

41. Doctrine & Covenants 20:16.

42. Doctrine & Covenants 1:24.

43. Doctrine & Covenants 45:11.

44. Doctrine & Covenants 1:20.

45. Doctrine & Covenants 50:44.

- Great I Am[46]
- Greatest of all[47]
- He who liveth[48]
- He who spake in righteousness[49]
- He who was lifted up[50]
- He who was slain[51]
- He who has all power[52]
- He who is from all eternity to all eternity[53]
- He who is from everlasting to everlasting[54]
- He who sitteth upon the throne[55]
- Holy One[56]
- Holy One of Zion[57]
- I am[58]
- Jehovah[59]
- Jesus[60]
- Jesus Christ the Son of the living God[61]
- Jesus Christ your Lord[62]

---

46. Doctrine & Covenants 38:1.

47. Doctrine & Covenants 19:18.

48. Doctrine & Covenants 110:4.

49. Doctrine & Covenants 133:47.

50. Doctrine & Covenants 45:52.

51. Doctrine & Covenants 110:4.

52. Doctrine & Covenants 61:1.

53. Doctrine & Covenants 39:1.

54. Doctrine & Covenants 61:1.

55. Doctrine & Covenants 88:115.

56. Doctrine & Covenants 78:16.

57. Doctrine & Covenants 78:15.

58. Doctrine & Covenants 50:45.

59. Doctrine & Covenants 109:68.

60. Doctrine & Covenants 45:52.

61. Doctrine & Covenants 42:1.

62. Doctrine & Covenants 95:17.

- Jesus Christ, the Son of God[63]
- Jesus that was crucified[64]
- Judge of all[65]
- King[66]
- King of kings[67]
- King of Zion[68]
- The Lamb[69]
- Lamb of God[70]
- Lamb, who was slain[71]
- Law by which all things are governed[72]
- Lawgiver[73]
- Life of men[74]
- Life of the world[75]
- Light[76]
- Light of men[77]
- Light of the moon[78]
- Light of the stars[79]

---

63. Doctrine & Covenants 52:44.

64. Doctrine & Covenants 45:52.

65. Doctrine & Covenants 76:68.

66. Doctrine & Covenants 45:59.

67. JST, Psalm 24:9.

68. Moses 7:53.

69. Doctrine & Covenants 76:85.

70. Doctrine & Covenants 88:106.

71. Doctrine & Covenants 76:39.

72. Doctrine & Covenants 88:13.

73. Doctrine & Covenants 64:13.

74. Doctrine & Covenants 93:9.

75. Doctrine & Covenants 45:7.

76. Doctrine & Covenants 93:9.

77. Doctrine & Covenants 93:9.

78. Doctrine & Covenants 88:8.

79. Doctrine & Covenants 88:9.

- Light of the sun[80]
- The light and the life of the world[81]
- Light of truth[82]
- Light that shineth in darkness[83]
- Light which cannot be hid in darkness[84]
- Light which is in all things[85]
- Light which shineth[86]
- The living God[87]
- Lord[88]
- Lord God[89]
- Lord Jesus[90]
- Lord Jesus Christ[91]
- Lord of Hosts[92]
- Lord of Sabaoth[93]
- Lord of the whole earth[94]
- Master[95]
- Mediator[96]

---

80. Doctrine & Covenants 88:7.

81. Doctrine & Covenants 45:7.

82. Doctrine & Covenants 88:6.

83. Doctrine & Covenants 45:7.

84. Doctrine & Covenants 14:9.

85. Doctrine & Covenants 88:13.

86. Doctrine & Covenants 88:11.

87. Doctrine & Covenants 50:1.

88. Doctrine & Covenants 66:1.

89. Doctrine & Covenants 49:7.

90. Doctrine & Covenants 49:12.

91. Doctrine & Covenants 21:1.

92. Doctrine & Covenants 1:33.

93. Doctrine & Covenants 88:2.

94. Doctrine & Covenants 55:1.

95. Doctrine & Covenants 104:86.

96. Doctrine & Covenants 76:69.

- Messenger of salvation[97]
- Messiah[98]
- Mighty One of Israel[99]
- Mighty to save[100]
- Omegus[101]
- Only Begotten of the Father[102]
- Only Begotten Son[103]
- Redeemer[104]
- Redeemer of the world[105]
- Righteous Judge[106]
- The Rock of Heaven[107]
- Savior[108]
- Savior of the world[109]
- The Son[110]
- Son Ahman[111]
- Son of God[112]
- Son of Man[113]

---

97. Doctrine & Covenants 93:8.

98. Doctrine & Covenants 109:67.

99. Doctrine & Covenants 36:1.

100. Doctrine & Covenants 133:47.

101. Doctrine & Covenants 95:17.

102. Doctrine & Covenants 93:11.

103. Doctrine & Covenants 76:25.

104. Doctrine & Covenants 66:13.

105. Doctrine & Covenants 93:9.

106. Moses 6:57.

107. Moses 7:53.

108. Doctrine & Covenants 76:1.

109. Doctrine & Covenants 1:20.

110. Doctrine & Covenants 42:17.

111. Doctrine & Covenants 78:20.

112. Doctrine & Covenants 45:52.

113. Doctrine & Covenants 49:6.

- Son of thy bosom[114]
- Spirit of truth[115]
- Stone of Israel[116]
- The Lord your Redeemer[117]
- The same which knoweth all things[118]
- The same which spake, and the world was made[119]
- True light[120]
- The Word[121]
- Your Lord and your God[122]
- Your Maker[123]
- Your ruler[124]

The Savior Taught of Himself through Short Declarations

Revelations received or printed in the Kirtland period are generally Christ centered. In them Christ teaches of Himself. His teaching goes beyond just the names He used for Himself. In them He affirms His divinity clearly and without equivocation. In them He reveals a personal touch often overlooked by casual readers. In them He gives critical assurances needed by His followers. He comforts His Saints and reassures them of His friendship and companionship. He asks questions. He responds to His Saints and even

---

114. Doctrine & Covenants 109:4.

115. Doctrine & Covenants 93:9.

116. Doctrine & Covenants 50:44.

117. Doctrine & Covenants 66:1.

118. Doctrine & Covenants 38:2.

119. Doctrine & Covenants 38:3.

120. Doctrine & Covenants 88:50.

121. Doctrine & Covenants 93:8.

122. Doctrine & Covenants 75:1.

123. Doctrine & Covenants 30:2.

124. Doctrine & Covenants 41:4.

counsels with them. The following statements by Jesus Christ reveal further insights into His divine nature and His roles:

- "I am pure."[125]
- "I am no respecter of persons."[126]
- "I am endless."[127]
- I dwell "on high."[128]
- "I . . . rule in the heavens above."[129]
- I fulfill what I have promised.[130]
- "I am able to make you holy."[131]
- "[I] knoweth . . . how to succor them who are tempted."[132]
- "I . . . cannot lie."[133]
- "I do [the Father's] will."[134]
- "My words are sure and shall not fail."[135]
- "Be still and know that I am God."[136]
- "[Your] prayers I have heard."[137]
- "[Your] hearts I know."[138]

125. Doctrine & Covenants 35:21.

126. Doctrine & Covenants 1:35.

127. Doctrine & Covenants 19:10.

128. Doctrine & Covenants 1:1.

129. Doctrine & Covenants 60:4.

130. Doctrine & Covenants 58:31.

131. Doctrine & Covenants 60:7.

132. Doctrine & Covenants 62:1.

133. Doctrine & Covenants 62:6.

134. Doctrine & Covenants 19:24.

135. Doctrine & Covenants 64:31.

136. Doctrine & Covenants 101:16.

137. Doctrine & Covenants 67:1.

138. Doctrine & Covenants 67:1.

- "[Your] desires have come up before me."[139]
- "I, the Lord, am merciful."[140]
- "I, the Lord, am . . . gracious."[141]
- "I, the Lord, . . . delight to honor those who serve me."[142]
- "I will lead you along."[143]
- "[The Lord] is full of mercy, justice, grace and truth, and peace."[144]
- "[The Lord] comprehendeth all things."[145]
- "My grace is sufficient for you."[146]
- "You shall have peace in me."[147]
- "The Lord your God [is] the same today as yesterday, and forever."[148]
- "My soul delighteth in the song of the heart."[149]
- "I will be merciful unto you."[150]
- "Fear not . . . for you are mine."[151]
- "I am the good shepherd."[152]
- "I have not forsaken you."[153]
- "I will have compassion upon you."[154]

---

139. Doctrine & Covenants 67:1.

140. Doctrine & Covenants 70:18.

141. Doctrine & Covenants 76:5.

142. Doctrine & Covenants 76:5.

143. Doctrine & Covenants 78:18.

144. Doctrine & Covenants 84:102.

145. Doctrine & Covenants 88:41.

146. Doctrine & Covenants 17:8.

147. Doctrine & Covenants 19:23.

148. Doctrine & Covenants 35:1.

149. Doctrine & Covenants 25:12.

150. Doctrine & Covenants 50:16.

151. Doctrine & Covenants 50:41.

152. Doctrine & Covenants 50:44.

153. Doctrine & Covenants 61:36.

154. Doctrine & Covenants 64:2.

- "Be of good cheer, and do not fear."[155]
- "I the Lord am with you, and will stand by you."[156]
- "I will go before your face. I will be on your right hand and on your left."[157]
- "My Spirit shall be in your hearts, and mine angels round about you, to bear you up."[158]
- "Draw near unto me and I will draw near unto you."[159]
- "I, the Lord, show mercy unto all the meek."[160]
- "I am with you even unto the end."[161]
- "[Fear not] what man can do, for I am with you."[162]
- "I will be your king and watch over you."[163]
- "I rule in . . . all wisdom and prudence."[164]
- "The Lord . . . knoweth all things."[165]
- "In me there is all power."[166]
- "I the Lord cannot look upon sin with the least degree of allowance."[167]
- "I will fight your battles."[168]

155. Doctrine & Covenants 68:6.

156. Doctrine & Covenants 68:6.

157. Doctrine & Covenants 84:88.

158. Doctrine & Covenants 84:88.

159. Doctrine & Covenants 88:63.

160. Doctrine & Covenants 97:2.

161. Doctrine & Covenants 100:12.

162. Doctrine & Covenants 30:11.

163. Doctrine & Covenants 38:21.

164. Abraham 3:21.

165. Doctrine & Covenants 38:1–2.

166. Doctrine & Covenants 100:1.

167. Doctrine & Covenants 1:31.

168. Doctrine & Covenants 105:14.

Christ Taught of His Loving, Kind, Compassionate Nature

Through His many interactions with Joseph Smith, Christ revealed His love, kindness, and compassion. He clearly expressed His love to His Saints. To Oliver Cowdery, He said, "I will encircle thee in the arms of my love."[169] He told Joseph, "I have loved you."[170] He explained how His love for mankind motivated the Atonement. He said, "Jesus Christ your Redeemer . . . so loved the world that he gave his own life."[171]

Christ frequently referred to the early Saints as friends. In ten separate revelations He called them "my friends."[172] He explained the reason He called them servants throughout His revelations: "I called you servants for the world's sake, and ye are their servants for my sake."[173] He assured them, however, that they meant more to Him than servants. He said, "I will call you friends, for you are my friends, and ye shall have an inheritance with me."[174]

Christ agonized and even wept as His Saints struggled. As Missouri persecutions became intense, He soulfully revealed, "My bowels are filled with compassion towards them."[175] Christ also revealed His compassionate nature to Joseph Smith as he translated the Bible. Joseph was given an insight not found in the original text. As people crowded to be near the Savior after His miraculous feeding of the five thousand near the Sea of Galilee, the Savior struggled to be alone. But despite His personal need for privacy, Christ yielded to the people. Joseph wrote that Christ "entered into an house, and would that no man should come unto him. But he could not deny them; for he had compassion upon all men."[176]

---

169. Doctrine & Covenants 6:20.

170. Doctrine & Covenants 95:1.

171. Doctrine & Covenants 34:1–3.

172. Doctrine & Covenants 84:77; 88:3; 93:45, 51; 94:1; 97:1; 98:1; 100:1; 103:1; 104:1; 105:26.

173. Doctrine & Covenants 93:46.

174. Doctrine & Covenants 93:45.

175. Doctrine & Covenants 101:9.

176. JST, Mark 7:22–23.

In an 1836 vision Joseph Smith saw the Savior brought to tears by the suffering of His latter-day Apostles. Joseph said he saw the Apostles "much fatigued, with their clothes tattered and feet swollen, with their eyes cast downward, [and Jesus] looked upon them and wept."[177] Christ urged His Saints to show this same kind of compassion. Speaking of death, which often lurked nearby during the early days of the Restoration, Christ instructed the Church to "weep for the loss of them that die."[178] Jesus followed the pattern of His Father, who wept as He saw the wickedness of His children. It was revealed to Joseph Smith that Enoch talked with God and saw him weep.[179] Enoch asked God, "How is it thou canst weep?"[180] Looking down on His disobedient children in ancient times, God replied, "Unto thy brethren have I . . . given commandment, that they should love one another, . . . but behold, they are without affection, and they hate their own blood."[181]

Christ taught of His tenderness and kindness toward each for whom He suffered in completing the Atonement. He said that His redeemed "shall mention the loving kindness of their Lord, and all that he has bestowed upon them according to his goodness, and according to his loving kindness, forever and ever."[182] Showing great empathy, He revealed "in all their afflictions he was afflicted."[183] He assured them that He "saved them . . . and . . . redeemed them" and then described that He "bore them, and carried them" because of

---

177. Joseph Smith, *History of The Church of Jesus Christ of Latter-day Saints*, ed. B. H. Roberts, 7 vols., 2d ed. rev. (Salt Lake City: The Church of Jesus Christ of Latter-day Saints, 1932–51), 2:381; Dean C. Jessee, Mark R. Ashurst-McGee, and Richard L. Jensen, eds., *Journals, 1832–1839*, vol. 1 of the Journals series of *The Joseph Smith Papers*, edited by Dean C. Jesse, Ronald K. Esplin, and Richard Lyman Bushman (Salt Lake City: Church Historian's Press, 2008), 1:168.

178. Doctrine & Covenants 42:45.

179. Moses 7:29.

180. Moses 7:31.

181. Moses 7:33.

182. Doctrine & Covenants 133:52.

183. Doctrine & Covenants 133:53.

His "love, and . . . pity" for them.[184] Christ's suffering in Gethsemane and on the cross is beyond comprehension. He said the sufferings He endured were "sore—how sore you know not, how exquisite you know not, yea, how hard to bear you know not."[185] He further explained that His "suffering caused myself, even God, the greatest of all, to tremble because of pain, and to bleed at every pore, and to suffer both body and spirit."[186]

Christ showed concern for families who were often left destitute as missionaries and leaders traveled on official assignment. He directed missionaries to "obtain places for your families."[187] He directed Church members "to support the families of those who are called."[188] When missionaries were given money, He told them to "send it" to their "families."[189] He also comforted missionaries who worried about their families. He once assured a concerned Joseph Smith and Sidney Rigdon as they traveled in western New York State and Canada, saying, "Your families are well; they are in mine hands."[190]

Christ Revealed Insights into His Divinity

During the Kirtland period Christ clarified many points of doctrine and provided insights into His divine nature and atonement that are not taught as comprehensively in other scripture. Four of those points of doctrine follow.

Christ Taught of His Submission to the Father

In all of His revelations published in the Kirtland period, Christ exemplified submissiveness to His Father's will. Throughout His latter-day teaching,

---

184. Doctrine & Covenants 133:53.

185. Doctrine & Covenants 19:15.

186. Doctrine & Covenants 19:18.

187. Doctrine & Covenants 75:25.

188. Doctrine & Covenants 75:24.

189. Doctrine & Covenants 84:103.

190. Doctrine & Covenants 100:1.

Christ's life shines as an example of strict obedience in carrying out the will of the Father. Christ taught that in the premortal existence He began His mission, from which there was no turning back, with this pledge: "Father, thy will be done, and the glory be thine forever."[191] The Savior told Joseph Smith, "I came by the will of the Father, and I do his will."[192] Of His agony in Gethsemane when His suffering reached beyond what mortals could bear, He cried out His intense reluctance: "[I] would that I might not drink the bitter cup, and shrink."[193] Despite this momentary hesitancy, however, He declared dutifully, "Nevertheless . . . I partook and finished my preparations."[194]

Throughout His revelations, Christ taught the early Saints of His submissiveness, meekness, and obedience. In teaching about Himself, could He have been providing the role model for the Saints in their arduous trials that lay ahead? In this early 1830 setting, could He have been tutoring a young latter-day prophet in how to approach his ultimate sacrifice fourteen years hence? Could He have been preparing His latter-day Saints for their own sacrifices of great magnitude, even for some to give their lives? The Savior's life stood as an example of His submission to His Father's will. In a triumphant declaration of ultimate submission, Christ conceded, "I . . . accomplished and finished the will of him whose I am, even the Father."[195] The Savior taught His latter-day Saints to show this same submissiveness to the Father. In the Kirtland Temple dedicatory prayer, the Savior inspired Joseph Smith to pray: "Help thy servants to say, with thy grace assisting them: Thy will be done, O Lord, and not ours."[196]

---

191. Moses 4:2.

192. Doctrine & Covenants 19:24.

193. Doctrine & Covenants 19:18.

194. Doctrine & Covenants 19:19.

195. Doctrine & Covenants 19:2.

196. Doctrine & Covenants 109:44.

Christ Defined What It Means to Be the Advocate with the Father

In Kirtland, Christ taught that He is our advocate with the Father. That title has been used only one other time in scripture.[197] Christ explained that as our advocate, He represents "even as many as have believed in my name."[198] He explained that His blood, which He shed, enables Him to successfully represent and plead for us before the Father. He said, "By the virtue of the blood which I have spilt, have I pleaded before the Father for them."[199] As He stands before God, He fully knows our weaknesses and sins. He said, "Jesus Christ, your advocate . . . knoweth the weakness of man."[200] He will say to His Father, "Behold the sufferings and death of him who did no sin, in whom thou wast well pleased; behold the blood of thy Son which was shed, the blood of him whom thou gavest that thyself might be glorified; wherefore, Father, spare these my brethren that believe on my name, that they may come unto me and have everlasting life."[201]

Christ assures us of the positive result of His pleading. He told the Saints, "Lift up your hearts and be glad, for I am . . . your advocate with the Father; and it is his good will to give you the kingdom."[202] In addition to being their advocate, He assured the Saints that He was also ordained to be their Mediator with God. Christ told Joseph Smith and Sidney Rigdon in their 1832 vision, "Just men [are] made perfect through Jesus the mediator . . . who wrought out this perfect atonement through the shedding of his own blood."[203] Christ also taught in Kirtland that He ransomed mankind.

---

197. 1 John 2:1.

198. Doctrine & Covenants 38:4.

199. Doctrine & Covenants 38:4.

200. Doctrine & Covenants 62:1.

201. Doctrine & Covenants 45:4–5.

202. Doctrine & Covenants 29:5.

203. Doctrine & Covenants 76:69.

In translating the book of Matthew, Joseph Smith was inspired to write that the sacramental bread is taken "in remembrance of my body which I give a ransom for you."[204]

Christ Remembered the Loneliness of His Atonement

Christ also taught deeper insights into how alone He felt as He completed the Atonement. He said that at His glorified coming, an angel will declare for all to hear, "The Lamb of God hath overcome and trodden the wine-press alone."[205] Joseph Smith was told not only that the angel would speak of His aloneness but also that the Savior would remember and declare for all to hear, "I have trodden the wine-press alone . . . and none were with me."[206] He will also proclaim, "When I came unto mine own, no man among you received me. . . . When I called again there was none of you to answer."[207]

Christ Taught of His Willingness to Forgive Sin

Christ underscored His total forgiveness based upon the sinner's repentance. He clearly explained, "I, the Lord, forgive sins unto those who confess their sins before me and ask forgiveness, who have not sinned unto death."[208] Christ also demonstrated the extent of His forgiveness as He said, "He who has repented of his sins, the same is forgiven, and I, the Lord, remember them no more."[209] The Savior indicated that mercy also plays a role. He said, "I . . . am merciful unto those who confess their sins with humble hearts."[210] He also explained that His own suffering enabled Him to forgive. He said,

204. JST, Matthew 26:22.

205. Doctrine & Covenants 88:106.

206. Doctrine & Covenants 133:50.

207. Doctrine & Covenants 133:66–67.

208. Doctrine & Covenants 64:7.

209. Doctrine & Covenants 58:42.

210. Doctrine & Covenants 61:2.

"I, God, have suffered these things for all, that they might not suffer if they would repent."[211]

The Savior Teaches His Mission of Redemption

The Savior's central message in Kirtland heralded His atonement for mankind. He reinforced, expanded, and clarified earlier teachings and introduced new principles and insights into His redemptive mission, declaring it to be "glad tidings": "This is the gospel, the glad tidings . . . that he came into the world, even Jesus, to be crucified for the world, and to bear the sins of the world, and to sanctify the world, and to cleanse it from all unrighteousness; that through him all might be saved."[212]

The Prophet Joseph clearly understood the Savior's central message of "glad tidings" by the end of the Kirtland period. Joseph answered a frequently asked question concerning the Church's basic tenets by emphatically stating, "The fundamental principles of our religion are the testimony of the Apostles and Prophets, concerning Jesus Christ, that He died, was buried, and rose again the third day, and ascended into heaven; and all other things which pertain to our religion are only appendages to it."[213]

Joseph's understanding of Christ's mission of redemption came directly from the Savior Himself, who simply stated, "I am . . . the Redeemer of the world."[214] In the words of God the Father, Christ's atonement and redemption constitute "the plan of salvation."[215] The Savior repeatedly and comprehensively taught God's plan of salvation through revelations He gave in Kirtland. The following summary cites at least one statement of Deity for each selected element of the plan:

---

211. Doctrine & Covenants 19:16.

212. Doctrine & Covenants 76:40–42.

213. *Joseph Smith,* Teachings of Presidents of the Church series (Salt Lake City: The Church of Jesus Christ of Latter-day Saints, 2007), 49; Joseph Smith, *Elders' Journal* 1, no. 3 (July 1838): 44.

214. Doctrine & Covenants 19:1.

215. Moses 6:62.

- *Christ was the firstborn of the heavenly spirits.* Christ said, "I was in the beginning with the Father, and am the Firstborn."[216]

- *Christ volunteered to become the Redeemer and was chosen over Satan, who also volunteered.* Satan said, "Send me, . . . and I will redeem all mankind, that one soul shall not be lost."[217] Satan wanted to destroy man's moral agency and to usurp the power and glory of God.[218] Christ volunteered by saying, "Send me."[219] He was chosen because He responded, "Father, thy will be done, and the glory be thine forever."[220]

- *Christ, under the direction of the Father, cast out Satan and his followers from heaven.* Christ removed Satan, as stated in the words of the Father: "By the power of mine Only Begotten, I caused that he should be cast down."[221] Christ said Satan "was thrust down from the presence of God and the Son."[222] Satan's followers were cast out with him. The Savior also said, "A third part of the hosts of heaven turned he away from me because of their agency; and they were thrust down, and thus came the devil and his angels."[223]

- *Christ was designated to be the only Savior and Redeemer.* The words of the Father testify, "Jesus Christ [is] the only

---

216. Doctrine & Covenants 93:21.

217. Moses 4:1.

218. Moses 4:3.

219. Abraham 3:27.

220. Moses 4:2.

221. Moses 4:3.

222. Doctrine & Covenants 76:25.

223. Doctrine & Covenants 29:36–37.

name . . . whereby salvation shall come."[224] Joseph was told, "The Lord is God, and beside him there is no Savior."[225]

- *Christ was the Creator.* Jesus said, "By the power of my Spirit created I . . . all things both spiritual and temporal."[226] He also said, "I . . . spake, and the world was made, and all things came by me."[227] Joseph Smith learned that Christ's creations extended to creatures in the animal world, such as "beasts, . . . creeping things, and . . . fowls of the air."[228] In addition, Christ created other worlds. Joseph was told, "By him, and through him, and of him, the worlds are and were created."[229] The Father confirmed the extent of the Son's creations: "Worlds without number have I created . . . and by the Son I created them."[230]

- *Christ is the Savior of other worlds.* Joseph Smith was told in an 1832 vision that the inhabitants of all the worlds "that career in the heavens so broad . . . Are sav'd by the very same Saviour of ours . . . by the very same truths, and the very same pow'rs.[231]

- *Christ assisted the Father in giving Adam and Eve moral agency to choose whether to eat the forbidden fruit.* Christ's assistance in man's creation is confirmed in the words of the Father: "I, God, said unto mine Only Begotten . . .

---

224. Moses 6:52.

225. Doctrine & Covenants 76:1.

226. Doctrine & Covenants 29:31.

227. Doctrine & Covenants 38:3.

228. Doctrine & Covenants 77:2.

229. Doctrine & Covenants 76:24.

230. Moses 1:33.

231. *Times and Seasons* 4 (February 1, 1843): 83 [vv. 19–20].

Let us make man in our image, after our likeness; and it was so."[232] Adam and Eve became "the first flesh upon the earth."[233] "The Lord said . . . I gave unto them their knowledge, in the day I created them; and in the Garden of Eden, gave I unto man his agency."[234] The Lord forbade them to eat or even touch the fruit of the tree planted in the midst of the Garden of Eden.[235] Satan tempted Adam and Eve, and they "partook of the forbidden fruit and transgressed the commandment."[236] In eating of the fruit, Adam and Eve "became spiritually dead, which is the first death."[237]

- *The Son assisted the Father by sending Adam and Eve from the Garden of Eden after their transgression.* The Lord cast Adam and Eve out of the garden because they partook of the forbidden fruit and introduced spiritual death into the world.[238] Joseph was told, "I, the Lord God, caused that he [Adam] should be cast out from the Garden of Eden . . . because of his transgression, wherein he became spiritually dead, which is the first death, even that same death which is the last death . . . which shall be pronounced upon the wicked when I shall say: Depart, ye cursed."[239]

- *Christ taught Adam that His atoning sacrifice provided the way to redeem him and his posterity from their fallen state.*

---

232. Moses 2:26; JST, Genesis 1:27.

233. Moses 3:7.

234. Moses 7:32.

235. Moses 4:9.

236. Doctrine & Covenants 29:40.

237. Doctrine & Covenants 29:41.

238. Doctrine & Covenants 29:40–41; Moses 4:12, 29, 31.

239. Doctrine & Covenants 29:41.

Christ said, "I am the Only Begotten of the Father . . . as thou hast fallen thou mayest be redeemed, and all mankind, even as many as will."[240] Christ taught Joseph Smith that He redeemed all men from the fall of Adam and returned them to an innocent state. He said, "Every spirit of man was innocent in the beginning; and God having redeemed man from the fall, men became again, in their infant state, innocent before God."[241]

- *God commanded Adam to teach his children of Jesus Christ and the plan of salvation.*[242] The Father's words summarize the plan of salvation: "By reason of transgression cometh the fall, which fall bringeth death, . . . so ye must be born again into the kingdom of heaven, of water, and of the Spirit, and be cleansed by blood, even the blood of mine Only Begotten; that ye might be sanctified from all sin, and enjoy the words of eternal life in this world, and eternal life in the world to come, even immortal glory. . . .

"This is the plan of salvation unto all men, through the blood of mine Only Begotten, who shall come in the meridian of time."[243]

Joseph Smith learned that Adam, upon hearing the plan, asked the Lord, "Why is it that men must repent and be baptized in water?"[244] The Lord replied: "I have forgiven thee thy transgression in the Garden of Eden. Hence came the saying abroad among the people, that the

240. Moses 5:9.

241. Doctrine & Covenants 93:38.

242. Moses 6:58.

243. Moses 6:59, 62.

244. Moses 6:53.

Son of God hath atoned for original guilt, wherein the sins of the parents cannot be answered upon the heads of the children, for they are whole from the foundation of the world."[245] Those words and the following verse give an added dimension to the Savior's atonement: "Little children are redeemed from the foundation of the world through mine Only Begotten."[246]

- *Christ became mortal by choice and was born in the meridian of time.* He said, "I . . . made flesh my tabernacle, and dwelt among the sons of men."[247] He gave the relative time period of his mortal life to Joseph Smith: "I . . . came in the meridian of time."[248]

- *Christ was sent to earth by the Father to be His Only Begotten.* Although Christ often identified himself as the "Only Begotten Son," more significantly God the Father did the same in these words: "I . . . God . . . sent mine Only Begotten Son into the world."[249] The Father's witness that Christ is "mine Only Begotten" was given to Joseph Smith nineteen times in scripture initially printed or otherwise made available in Kirtland.[250]

- *Christ progressed and set an example of obedience.* Jesus did not receive "of the fulness at first, but continued from grace to grace, until he received a fulness."[251] Joseph Smith

---

245. Moses 6:53–54.

246. Doctrine & Covenants 29:46.

247. Doctrine & Covenants 93:4.

248. Doctrine & Covenants 39:1, 3.

249. Doctrine & Covenants 49:5.

250. Doctrine & Covenants 29:42, 46; 49:5; Moses 1:6; 16, 17, 32, 33; 2:1, 26, 27; 3:18; 4:1, 3, 28; 6:52, 59, 62; 7:62.

251. Doctrine & Covenants 93:13.

was taught that Christ submitted himself for baptism to John the Baptist, "and the Holy Ghost descended upon him in the form of a dove, and sat upon him, and there came a voice out of heaven saying: This is my beloved Son."[252] Jesus "suffered temptations but gave no heed unto them."[253] He did not commit any sin. Christ said that he will say to God, "Father, behold the sufferings and death of him who did no sin."[254]

- *Jesus carried out His perfect atonement—He was crucified, died, and rose from the dead.* To redeem all mankind from the Fall, it was necessary for Christ to come to earth and complete the "perfect atonement."[255] He volunteered to suffer, take upon Himself our sins, give His life by the shedding of blood, and thus overcome physical death and bring to pass the resurrection of all men.[256] Joseph Smith and Oliver Cowdery testified: "The Lord God has spoken it. . . . the Almighty God gave his Only Begotten Son. . . . He was crucified, died, and rose again the third day."[257]

- *Christ took upon Himself the sins and afflictions of all mortal beings.* The Savior assured Joseph Smith that He atoned for the sins of the world. Following are some of His many statements attesting to that fact: "The Lord your Redeemer suffered death in the flesh; wherefore he suffered the pain of all men, that all men might repent and come unto

---

252. Doctrine & Covenants 93:15.

253. Doctrine & Covenants 20:22.

254. Doctrine & Covenants 45:4.

255. Doctrine & Covenants 76:69.

256. Doctrine & Covenants 76:69, 39, 41–42; 93:38.

257. Doctrine & Covenants 20:16, 21, 23.

him."[258] "Jesus was crucified . . . for the sins of the world, yea, for the remission of sins unto the contrite heart."[259] "I am Jesus Christ, the Son of God, who was crucified for the sins of the world, even as many as will believe on my name."[260] "He came into the world, even Jesus, to be crucified for the world, and to bear the sins of the world."[261] "In all their afflictions he was afflicted. And . . . he redeemed them."[262] "My body . . . was laid down for you, and my blood . . . was shed for the remission of your sins."[263] "I, God, have suffered these things for all, that they might not suffer if they would repent."[264]

- *Christ initiated resurrection from death for all mankind.* The words of God the Father certify to the universal resurrection begun by Christ: "Righteousness . . . and truth . . . bear testimony of mine Only Begotten; his resurrection from the dead; yea, and also the resurrection of all men."[265] Joseph Smith revealed an unknown prophecy of John the Baptist that Christ "shall come . . . to bring to pass the resurrection from the dead."[266] Christ told the Prophet, "I say unto you, that through the redemption . . . is brought to pass the resurrection from the dead."[267]

---

258. Doctrine & Covenants 18:11.

259. Doctrine & Covenants 21:9.

260. Doctrine & Covenants 35:2.

261. Doctrine & Covenants 76:41.

262. Doctrine & Covenants 133:53.

263. Doctrine & Covenants 27:2.

264. Doctrine & Covenants 19:16.

265. Moses 7:62.

266. JST, Luke 3:5, 7.

267. Doctrine & Covenants 88:14.

The Savior authenticated His resurrection by appearing to Joseph Smith and Oliver Cowdery in the Kirtland Temple. As He stood before them, He announced, "I am he who liveth, I am he who was slain."[268] The Savior assured Joseph and Oliver of the reality of the resurrection in a revelation to them. He admonished them, "Doubt not, fear not. Behold the wounds which pierced my side, and also the prints of the nails in my hands and feet."[269]

- *Christ ascended into the heavens, where He reigns in power and glory.* The Savior told ten priesthood holders in the Whitney store in Kirtland that He "ascended up on high."[270] Joseph Smith and Oliver Cowdery said they "heard and bear witness to the words" of Christ, that He "ascended into heaven, to sit down on the right hand of the Father, to reign with almighty power."[271] The words of the Father also testify to the Savior's role: "He has taken his power on the right hand of his glory, and now reigneth in the heavens, and will reign till he descends on the earth to put all enemies under his feet."[272]

Christ Teaches of His Postmortal Life

The Savior finished His perfect atonement with His death and resurrection, but His mission was not yet complete. He assured His Latter-day Saints that He will return to earth. He declared, "I will come; and they shall see me in the clouds of heaven, clothed with power and great glory; with all

---

268. Doctrine & Covenants 110:4.

269. Doctrine & Covenants 6:36–37.

270. Doctrine & Covenants 88:6.

271. Doctrine & Covenants 20:16, 24.

272. Doctrine & Covenants 49:6.

the holy angels."[273] As to when He will return, He said, "The Son of Man ... cometh in an hour you think not."[274] He indicated, however, "The time is soon at hand."[275] Because of the uncertain time of His coming, He cautioned, "Be watchful and be sober ... for ... the Son of Man ... cometh in an hour you think not. Pray always ... that you may abide the day of his coming."[276] The words of the Father give emphasis and added certainty to Christ's promise: "I, the Lord God, have spoken it; but the hour and the day no man knoweth, neither the angels in heaven, nor shall they know until he comes."[277]

The Savior emphatically assured Joseph Smith, "Satan shall be bound."[278] He later promised Joseph, "I will come and reign."[279] Christ reinforced the prophecy that He will reign on earth when He said He will "come upon the earth ... and ... reign. ... For the great Millennium ... shall come."[280] He defined the Millennium with this statement: "I will ... dwell in righteousness with men on earth a thousand years, and the wicked shall not stand."[281]

The Savior affirmed His supremacy as He declared that He possessed "all power, even to the destroying of Satan and his works at the end of the world."[282] Christ taught, however, that Satan will not yield to him without a fight. He said there will be a "battle of the Great God; and the devil and his armies shall be cast away into their own place, that they shall not have power over the saints any more at all."[283]

---

273. Doctrine & Covenants 45:44.

274. Doctrine & Covenants 61:38.

275. Doctrine & Covenants 34:7.

276. Doctrine & Covenants 61:38–39.

277. Doctrine & Covenants 49:7.

278. Doctrine & Covenants 43:31.

279. Doctrine & Covenants 84:119.

280. Doctrine & Covenants 43:29–30.

281. Doctrine & Covenants 29:11.

282. Doctrine & Covenants 19:3.

283. Doctrine & Covenants 88:114.

Christ assured Joseph Smith that He will "deliver up the kingdom, and present it unto the Father, spotless, saying: I have overcome."[284] Joseph also learned that in "the fulness of time . . . the law and the testimony shall be sealed, and the keys of the kingdom shall be delivered up again unto the Father."[285]

The Savior told the Prophet, "I come quickly; and my reward is with me to recompense every man according as his work shall be."[286] He also said desires will play a part in the Judgment: "I, the Lord, will judge all men according to their works, according to the desire of their hearts."[287] Moses was told, "Jesus Christ [is] a righteous Judge."[288] The Lord cautioned Joseph, "Leave judgment alone with me, for it is mine."[289]

Joseph Smith learned that after delivering up His kingdom, Christ will "be crowned with the crown of his glory, to sit on the throne of his power to reign forever and ever."[290]

Thus, in and through all the glorious learning that came to the Prophet Joseph Smith and the Church during the Kirtland era, a sure and personal knowledge of the Savior was the ultimate experience. He schooled Joseph and others. They were tutored and given time to get to know Him. As a result, the infant Church took root.

284. Doctrine & Covenants 76:107.

285. JST, Luke 3:8.

286. Doctrine & Covenants 112:34.

287. Doctrine & Covenants 137:9.

288. Moses 6:57.

289. Doctrine & Covenants 82:23.

290. Doctrine & Covenants 76:108.

CHAPTER 6

WITNESSES OF THE SAVIOR

I know there is a God. . . . [He] has manifested himself to
men in our day, men whom we know, and I have heard bore this
testimony, that they have seen God, and that he lives.
—WANDLE MACE

The 1830s were a season of unparalleled revelations and visions to
Joseph Smith and the Saints of Kirtland, Ohio. The most significant visions were those of Deity. This was a time of long-awaited gospel restoration that required direct revelation and communication with the heavens.
Imagine living in Kirtland in the 1830s, when the revered Prophet often
communed with the Lord. He received revelation after revelation, thus
bolstering the Saints' faith as the Lord personally structured the newly
restored Church. In this revelatory period, Joseph was repeatedly in the
presence of the Lord—seeing Him, listening to Him, and attesting to His
specific guidance and instruction. Joseph used words and phrases such as
"Pentecost" and "time of rejoicing" to describe this season in Kirtland.

Picture the Saints' exhilaration and joy as they became aware that the
heavens were actually opening to them and their prophet. They heard the
Savior speak. They saw visions of Him. They received a divine witness of
Him through heavenly manifestations. They powerfully felt His presence

Kirtland Visions and Presence of Deity
Reported by Joseph Smith

Date	Where	Present	Journal Notation	Event
May 1831 Approximately	Smith Family Home	15* Smith and Lightner family members	"The Savior has been in your midst this night." Joseph Smith	First Church meeting with Smith family in Kirtland
June 3-6, 1831	Morley Farm	25* Church leaders including Joseph Smith Harvey Whitlock Lyman Wight	"I now see God and Jesus Christ at his right hand. . . . I should not feel death as I am now." Joseph Smith†	Ordination of first high priests
February 16, 1832	Johnson Farm	14* Brethren including Joseph Smith & Sidney Rigdon	"He lives for we saw him, even on the right hand of God." Joseph Smith & Sidney Rigdon	Vision of the eternal worlds (D&C 76)
March 18, 1833	Whitney Store	20* Priesthood leaders including Joseph Smith, John Murdock and Zebedee Coltrin	"Many of the brethren saw a heavenly vision of the savior." Joseph Smith‡	Ordination of First Presidency councilors
December 18, 1833	Johnson Inn	First Presidency of the Church & unnamed others	"I saw Adam... and [his children . . .]. The Lord appeared in their midst, & . . . bless them all." Joseph Smith	Bestowing of first patriarchal blessings
January 21, 1836	Kirtland Temple	16 Church leaders	"I beheld the . . . throne of God, whereon was seated the father and the son." Joseph Smith	First temple ordinances bestowed on key leaders
January 21, 1836	Kirtland Temple	16 Church leaders	"I saw the Twelve...and Jesus standing in their midst. . . . The Savior looked upon them and wept." Joseph Smith	First temple ordinances bestowed on key leaders
January 21, 1836	Kirtland Temple	16 Church leaders	"The Savior embraced . . . crowned and kissed each one [of the Twelve]." Joseph Smith	First temple ordinances bestowed on key leaders
January 21, 1836	Kirtland Temple	40 Church leaders	"The Visions of Heaven were opened to them. . . . Some of them saw the face of the Savior." Joseph Smith	First temple ordinances bestowed on key leaders
January 28, 1836	Kirtland Temple	100* high priests, seventies, and elders	"Zebedee Coltrin . . . saw the savior." Joseph Smith	First temple ordinances bestowed on key leaders
January 28, 1836	Kirtland Temple	100* high priests, seventies, and elders	"I see the Son of God sitting at the right hand of the Father." Joseph Smith	First temple ordinances bestowed on key leaders
March 30, 1836	Kirtland Temple	300* Leaders and Kirtland Stake members	"The Savior made his appearance to some while angels ministered to others." Joseph Smith	First temple ordinances bestowed on key leaders
April 3, 1836	Kirtland Temple	Joseph Smith & Oliver Cowdery	"We saw the Lord standing upon the breastwork of the pulpit." Joseph Smith and Oliver Cowdery	Christ accepting Kirtland Temple dedication

* Indicates the approximate number in attendance
† Lyman Wight and Harvey Whitlock also saw the Father and the Son on this occasion.
‡ John Murdock saw the Savior, and Zebedee Coltrin and Joseph Smith saw the Father also on this occasion.

Compiled by Karl Ricks Anderson

in meetings. They experienced the Savior's love, care, and concern for them and His latter-day Church. Such manifestations gave proof that He was resurrected and lives again. The Saints' faith was affirmed. The Savior literally was directing the Church in the last and final dispensation of His gospel.

Joseph Smith said that nothing is more fundamental than the "testimony of the apostles and prophets concerning Jesus Christ, that he died, was buried, and rose again the third day, and ascended up into heaven."[1] No evidence of His leadership made it more certain to these Latter-day Saints than to see Him, hear His voice, and converse with Him as did the apostles and prophets of earlier dispensations. Vital to the restoration of the gospel was that the Savior be at the helm—personally teaching and directing His prophet and His Church. This direct communication clearly defined from His own mouth that He lives and supervises His Father's work in this dispensation as He did anciently.

During the Kirtland years, surviving documentation attests that at least twenty-three Church leaders saw the Savior or heard Him speak—thus becoming latter-day witnesses of Him. Undoubtedly, even more witnesses than this saw Christ or heard His voice speaking to them, though many did not record their visions. Others did, but their records from the 1830s deteriorated or were lost. Records of their testimonies may yet surface. It is providential that so many records still survive.

Many who learn of these frequent visions may ask why the Savior and even God the Father manifested themselves so often in Kirtland. As noted in the accompanying chart (page 128), such visions seem to be connected with temple or other significant events.[2] When one examines these

---

1. Joseph Smith, *Elders' Journal* 1, no. 3 (July 1838): 44.

2. Some people try to draw a distinction between a vision and an appearance of Deity. This is difficult and perhaps unwise. It seems that Joseph Smith did not distinguish between the two. Generally he termed them all visions. Regarding his vision of Deity in the celestial kingdom (D&C 137), he said in verse 1, "whether in the body or out I cannot tell," apparently meaning that he didn't know if he was taken there to view the vision or if the vision came to him. When Christ stood "upon the

visitations of Deity, each seems to come during important *firsts* in the emerging dispensation. Some of these most sacred first steps were as follows:

- The ordination of high priests (June 1831).
- Christ showing and teaching the eternal plan of salvation (February 1832).
- The full organization of the First Presidency (March 1833).
- Administration of sacred endowment ordinances in a latter-day temple (January 1836).
- Restoration of priesthood keys of gathering, sealing, and redemption of the dead (April 1836).

The presence of Deity ratified and confirmed that each essential phase of the restoration in "the Ohio" was initiated and approved by the heavens. As in earlier gospel dispensations, each vision provides credence to the significance of the event. For example, at the baptism of Christ, God the Father and the Holy Ghost manifested Themselves. Their presence confirmed and ratified the critical importance of the baptismal ordinance. As Nephi of old stated, "If the Lamb of God . . . should have need to be baptized . . . how much more need have we . . . to be baptized."[3] Likewise, on the Mount of Transfiguration, the Father was manifest as the Savior bestowed the keys of Church presidency on Peter, James, and John.

Intense divine instruction was mandatory in Kirtland. It was a time of restoring Church organization—a time when divine priesthood keys and ordinances were being restored to the earth, a time when ordinances and initial endowments were again introduced and implemented, a time when

---

breastwork of the pulpit" in the Kirtland Temple (D&C 110:2), many might call that an appearance, but Joseph termed it a "vision" (v. 11.) Perhaps most illustrative, when God and Christ came to Joseph in the Sacred Grove, we would call that an appearance, yet it is officially referred to as the First Vision. Generally, I have used the term *vision*.

3. 2 Nephi 31:5.

the pure gospel of Jesus Christ was once again on the earth. Anticipated for eons, events that were now occurring ushered in the new and final dispensation of the gospel.

The Law of Witnesses

Participants in Kirtland's visions of Deity fulfill the Lord's "law of witnesses."[4] The Apostle Paul reiterated the ancient law of witnesses when he said, "In the mouth of two or three witnesses shall every word be established."[5] This is a law by which the Lord verifies truths. This law, which governs the Church today, was established by the Lord in the Old Testament and was further defined in the New Testament, the Book of Mormon, and the Doctrine and Covenants. Under this law, even Jesus' declaration of Himself as the Savior and Redeemer was not sufficient to substantiate the reality of His divinity. In addressing Jews who wanted to put Him to death, He said, "If I bear witness of myself, my witness is not true."[6]

He reminded His persecutors that there are three witnesses to His divinity. His first witness is John the Baptist, who "bare witness" that he "saw the Spirit descending from heaven like a dove" upon Christ.[7] The second witness is the Father who "hath borne witness of me."[8] The third witness is scripture. "Search the scriptures . . . they . . . testify of me."[9] Certainly, the law of witnesses was again formally engaged during the Kirtland period, when individuals and congregations witnessed the restoring process of the Savior's Church.

---

4. Robert L. Marrott, "Witnesses, Law of," in *Encyclopedia of Mormonism*, ed. Daniel H. Ludlow et al., 4 vols. (New York: Macmillan, 1992), 4:1569–70.

5. 2 Corinthians 13:1.

6. John 5:31. President Joseph Fielding Smith clarified what Christ meant: "If I stand alone and no one testifies for me, then you can reject my testimony because the witness would not be true" (*Doctrines of Salvation,* comp. Bruce R. McConkie, 3 vols. [Salt Lake City: Bookcraft, 1954–56], 1:206).

7. John 5:33; 1:32.

8. John 5:37. This witness came at Christ's baptism.

9. John 5:39.

The many witnesses of Christ in Kirtland paralleled His appearances to many witnesses and followers in past ages. When the Savior opened past gospel dispensations, He personally appeared, spoke, and associated with His followers one-on-one and in large groups. Thus we find in both the Old and New Testaments as well as in ancient America that noted witnesses emerged and new scriptures were born. After His resurrection, Christ appeared to women at His tomb and to His Apostles at various locations. He even appeared to more than "five hundred brethren at once."[10] The Old Testament records that in addition to appearing to prophets, the God of Israel appeared to "Aaron, Nadab, and Abihu, and seventy of the elders of Israel."[11] In ancient America, Christ appeared to His prophets as well as to His twelve Nephite disciples and great multitudes in the land of Bountiful. The Lord is consistent. He again invoked the law of witnesses in this last dispensation. Elder Bruce R. McConkie stressed how broadly Christ invoked the law of witnesses. He wrote: "We have no way of knowing how many mortal persons have seen the Lord. Individual saints and prophets have seen him in all dispensations, and sometimes he has appeared to large congregations. We know that 'many, exceedingly great many,' (Alma 13:12), as Alma expressed it, have enjoyed this privilege."[12]

Witnesses Build Faith in Christ

Through witnesses of divine manifestations, the faith of the Kirtland Saints intensified. Through creditable witnesses whom they knew and trusted, the faithful were reassured that Christ lives. They received confirmation that the resurrected Jesus Christ still guided His Church, as He always had throughout the ages. Their interaction and communication with

---

10. 1 Corinthians 15:6.

11. Exodus 24:9–10.

12. Bruce R. McConkie, *The Promised Messiah* (Salt Lake City: Deseret Book, 1978), 605.

Deity and angels provided strength, resolve, and power to sacrifice and make the Lord's work their first priority. Their interaction and communication also empowered them with faith to withstand the horrible onslaught of poverty, abuse, malicious plots, and persecutions that followed. The Prophet and other men and women witnessed and recorded their experiences of observing and perceiving divine presences in their midst.

Wandle Mace, converted in New York by missionaries from Kirtland, accepted the testimony of latter-day witnesses. Parley P. Pratt, one of those missionaries present during many visions, shared his mighty testimony and knowledge of spiritual experiences with Wandle, who believed and was baptized by Parley. Three years after Wandle's baptism, a well-known atheist openly challenged his testimony of the existence of God. Wandle responded:

> I know there is a God. . . . Our God is the god of the Bible . . . holy men testify of him[,] having seen and heard[,] as having talked with him face to face which facts are recorded in the Bible.
>
> This same God has manifested himself to men in our day, men whom we know, and I have heard bore this testimony, that they have seen God, and that he lives.[13]

In 1884, George Q. Cannon, first counselor in the First Presidency, firmly established that large numbers of early Saints saw the Savior. While still a youth, George met many of the Kirtland witnesses of Christ. Speaking of Joseph Smith and Oliver Cowdery beholding the Savior in the Kirtland Temple, he said, "These witnesses are also supplemented by hundreds of others who have beheld in vision and otherwise, glorious personages in these

---

13. Wandle Mace, Autobiography, typescript, 1809–1846, 78–79, L. Tom Perry Special Collections, Harold B. Lee Library, Brigham Young University, Provo, Utah; hereafter cited as BYU Special Collections.

last days."[14] He then described the increased faith that came to the Church through their testimonies: "There are men alive who have beheld the Son of God, who have heard His voice, and who have been ministered unto by Him in this our day and generation. In the face of these testimonies, which cannot be impeached successfully, is it any wonder that faith grows in the hearts of the people of God, the Latter-day Saints?"[15]

Twenty-three Witnesses Who Saw the
Savior or Heard His Voice

Of the hundreds of witnesses referred to by George Q. Cannon, only about twenty-three from Kirtland can be firmly identified, but that number is still impressive. Of these estimated twenty-three witnesses, eleven can be identified by name. The other fourteen cannot be identified by name but by groupings, largely specified by Joseph Smith. But like their unidentified ancient counterparts, they also saw and became witnesses of "glorious personages." Five identified witnesses also saw God the Father and the Savior together.

These twenty-three witnesses are listed below, either by name or in groups. The first list of eleven names is divided into two categories—those who saw the Savior and those who heard Him speak to them. This list provides a summary and at least one statement of testimony borne of their experiences. Detailed accounts for each vision are referenced in subsequent chapters.

Eight Witnesses Who Saw the Savior

Joseph Smith: While in Kirtland, Joseph witnessed at least ten visions of Christ, seven of which also included God the Father. Joseph testified of one of these visions of Christ, saying, "I saw ... Jesus."[16]

---

14. George Q. Cannon, in *Journal of Discourses,* 26 vols. (London: Latter-day Saints' Book Depot, 1854–86), 25:158.

15. Cannon, in *Journal of Discourses,* 25:158.

16. Joseph Smith, *History of The Church of Jesus Christ of Latter-day Saints,* ed. B. H. Roberts, 7 vols., 2d

Sidney Rigdon: Sidney, who stood next to Joseph Smith in the First Presidency, was usually present when visions of Deity descended upon Joseph and the other brethren. It seems probable that he received more than one vision. He also saw God the Father. Sidney joined Joseph in testifying in Hiram, "We saw [Christ] and . . . we conversed [with Christ]."[17]

Lyman Wight: Lyman was the first high priest ordained in the Church. Lyman eventually became a member of the Quorum of the Twelve Apostles. He probably attended three meetings in Kirtland where the Savior appeared. He saw a vision of the Father and the Son. Lyman "saw the face of the Savior."[18]

Harvey Whitlock: Harvey was born in Massachusetts in 1809. He attended the fourth conference of the Church on the Morley farm in June 1831 and was ordained a high priest there. Harvey was twenty-two years old when he beheld a vision of the Father and the Son. "[Harvey] testified . . . he saw . . . Jesus."[19]

John Murdock: John was converted by four missionaries sent to the Lamanites. Joseph and Emma Smith adopted John's twins, who survived their mother's death in childbirth. John gave a detailed account of one of the Savior's appearances in the School of the Prophets. John said, "I . . . beheld the face of the Lord."[20]

Zebedee Coltrin: Zebedee was one of the first seven presidents of the Seventy. He was blessed by the First Presidency to have "heavenly visions

ed. rev. (Salt Lake City: The Church of Jesus Christ of Latter-day Saints, 1932–51), 2:381; Dean C. Jessee, Mark R. Ashurst-McGee, and Richard L. Jensen, eds, *Journals, 1832–1839*, vol. 1 of the Journals series of *The Joseph Smith Papers,* edited by Dean C. Jessee, Ronald K. Esplin, and Richard Lyman Bushman (Salt Lake City: Church Historian's Press, 2008), 1:168.

17. Doctrine & Covenants 76:14.

18. George A. Smith, in *Journal of Discourses,* 11:4.

19. Address of Zebedee Coltrin at a meeting of high priests in Spanish Fork, Utah. February 5, 1878, in *They Knew the Prophet,* ed. Hyrum L. Andrus and Helen Mae Andrus, (Salt Lake City: Deseret Book, 1999), 30.

20. *John Murdock,* "John Murdock Journal, 1792–1871," typescript, BYU Special Collections, 164.

and the ministry of Angels."[21] He recorded several visions—at least one of which included both the Father and the Son. In one of Zebedee's accounts he testified of Christ, "I saw Him!"[22]

Oliver Cowdery: Oliver, the second elder and one of the Three Witnesses of the Book of Mormon, stood at Joseph's side when they received priesthood keys from John the Baptist, Peter, James, John, Moses, Elias, and Elijah. He saw the Savior and heard His voice in New York. He saw the Savior and heard Him speak in the Kirtland Temple. He was present in six meetings when the Savior was seen. He testified with Joseph Smith, "We saw the Lord . . . [and heard] the voice of Jehovah."[23]

Martin Harris: Martin was one of the Three Witnesses of the Book of Mormon. He moved from New York in 1831 and remained principally in Kirtland until 1870—longer than any of the other witnesses. Martin attended nearly every meeting where the Savior appeared in Kirtland. In Joseph Smith's 1832 Kirtland account of his history, he recorded that "the Lord appeared unto him [Martin]"[24] in New York as he helped Joseph financially.

Three Witnesses Who Heard the Savior's Voice

Martin Harris: In Kirtland, Martin reaffirmed his witness of the Book of Mormon as he testified, "I heard the voice of God."[25]

David Whitmer: David was one of the Three Witnesses of the Book of

---

21. Kirtland Council Minute Book, typescript by Lyndon W. Cook, 1978, Church History Library, The Church of Jesus Christ of Latter-day Saints, Salt Lake City, Utah, 178.

22. Zebedee Coltrin, in *Salt Lake School of the Prophets Minute Book, 1883* (Salt Lake City: Pioneer Press, 1992), 54.

23. Doctrine & Covenants 110:2–3.

24. Karen Lynn Davidson, David J. Whittaker, Mark Ashurst-McGee, and Richard L. Jensen, eds., *Histories, 1832–1844*, vol. 1 of the Histories series of *The Joseph Smith Papers*, edited by Dean C. Jessee, Ronald K. Esplin, and Richard Lyman Bushman (Salt Lake City: Church Historian's Press, 2012), 1:15.

25. William Harrison Homer, "The Passing of Martin Harris," *Improvement Era* 29 (March 1926): 470.

Mormon. He witnessed significant miracles in New York. Because he was presiding in Missouri, David was one of the nine men sitting at the prestigious Melchizedek Priesthood pulpits at the dedication of the Kirtland Temple. He attended four meetings where Christ appeared and may have been one of whom Joseph said "saw glorious visions also."[26] In Ohio, David bore his witness of the Book of Mormon, saying, "The voice of God declared it."[27]

Newel K. Whitney: Newel was the second bishop to serve in Kirtland. His store became the first bishops' storehouse for the Church. Newel attended most of the meetings where the Savior appeared in vision in Kirtland. Bishop Whitney "heard [the Lord's] voice from heaven."[28]

Warren S. Snow: Warren was called to missions in Delaware and Vermont. He was a captain of the Nauvoo Legion. The Lord gave Warren a divine manifestation in the Kirtland Temple. Warren testified, "I heard the voice of God."[29]

Twelve Unidentified Witnesses Who Saw the Savior

The following groupings describe at least twelve witnesses who Joseph Smith or John Murdock said saw the Savior.[30]

Three Witnesses Reported by John Murdock

As Saints gathered in Kirtland at the first baptisms in November and December 1830, great heavenly manifestations were given to the faithful. John Murdock was baptized in November and recorded, "Others said they

---

26. *History of the Church,* 2:381; Jessee, Ashurst-McGee, and Jensen, *Journals,* 1:170.

27. In Ezra Booth to Ira Eddy, October 24, 1831, "Mormonism—No. III," *[Ravenna] Ohio Star* 2 (October 27, 1831): 3. Booth indicated that all Three Witnesses bore this testimony.

28. Orson F. Whitney, in Conference Report, June 1, 1919, 47.

29. Warren Snow, in *Millennial Star* 26 (January 23, 1864): 51.

30. The estimated number of unidentified witnesses may appear to be low, but the count has purposely been adjusted down to be conservative and to avoid double counting of the definite witnesses attending the meetings described.

23 Estimated Witnesses Who Saw the Savior or Heard His Voice

Date	Location	Name or Group	Relevant Statement	Event
Various dates	Various locations	Joseph Smith Jr.*	"I saw … Jesus"	Various significant events
February 16, 1832	Johnson Farm	Sidney Rigdon†	"We saw and … conversed [with Christ]"	Vision of the eternal worlds (D&C 76)
June 3-6, 1831	Morley Farm	Lyman Wight†	"Saw the face of the Savior"	Ordination of first high priests
June 3-6, 1831	Morley Farm	Harvey Whitlock†	"Testified … he saw … Jesus"	Ordination of first high priests
March 18, 1833	Whitney Store	John Murdock	"I … beheld the face of the Lord"	Ordination of First Presidency counselors
March 18, 1833 and January 28, 1836	Whitney Store and Kirtland Temple	Zebedee Coltrin†	"I saw Him!"	Ordinations and temple ordinances
April 3, 1836	Kirtland Temple	Oliver Cowdery	"We saw the Lord. … [and heard] the voice of Jehovah"	Christ accepting Kirtland Temple dedication
Various dates	Various locations	David Whitmer‡	"the voice of God declared it"	Testimony in Kirtland as a Book of Mormon Witness
Various dates	Various locations	Martin Harris‡	"The Lord appeared unto him [Martin]"	Testimony in Kirtland as a New York eyewitness of Christ
About December 1831	Whitney Home	Newel K. Whitney	"Heard [the Lord's] voice from heaven"	Related to his call as Bishop
1836	Kirtland Temple	Warren Snow	"I heard the voice of God"	Kirtland Temple endowment meeting
November and December 1830	Baptismal site	3 Witnesses (at least) reported by John Murdock in 1830	"Others said they saw the Lord"	First Kirtland baptisms
March 18, 1833	Whitney Store	3 Witnesses (at least) reported by Joseph Smith in 1833	"Many of the brethren saw a heavenly vision of the Savior"	Ordination of First Presidency counselors
January 21, 1836	Kirtland Temple	3 Witnesses (at least) reported by Joseph Smith in January 1836	"Some of them saw the face of the Savior"	First temple ordinance bestowed on key leaders
March 30, 1836	Kirtland Temple	3 Witnesses (at least) reported by Joseph Smith in March 1836	"The Savior made His appearance to some"	Solemn assembly and final Kirtland Temple ordinance

Other members of the First Presidency (such as Frederick G. Williams, Hyrum Smith, and Joseph Smith Sr.) as well as all members of the Quorum of the Twelve and ten members of the Kirtland high council and Missouri presidents and high council are not listed above but may have been part of the fourteen estimated unidentified witnesses. Virtually all of these were present during visions of Deity in Kirtland (see chapter 6).

* Joseph Smith saw Christ at least ten times in Kirtland. At least seven of these included the Father. In addition, he saw Christ or heard His voice at least four times in New York, the testimony of which was borne in Kirtland. The vision in the Sacred Grove also included the Father.

† These men also saw God, the Father in their vision.

‡ Although David Whitmer and Martin Harris saw or heard Christ speak in New York, they frequently bore testimony of those experiences in Kirtland (see chapter 8).

Compiled by Karl Ricks Anderson

saw the Lord."[31] It seems likely that the term "others" would imply at least three.

At Least Three Witnesses Reported by Joseph Smith in 1833

About twenty members of the School of the Prophets gathered in the schoolroom of the Whitney store on March 18, 1833. They participated in events surrounding the ordination of Joseph Smith's counselors in the First Presidency. In fulfillment of a promise given by Joseph Smith, the Savior appeared to the pure in heart. Joseph concluded, "Many of the brethren saw a heavenly vision of the Savior."[32] It is probable that "many" would number at least five. Two of those brethren are known to have been John Murdock and Zebedee Coltrin; therefore, perhaps three remain unidentified.

At Least Three Witnesses Reported by Joseph Smith in January 1836

In the final temple meeting of the day on January 21, 1836, when the ordinance of anointing with oil was introduced, at least three brethren in addition to Joseph Smith saw the Savior. Forty brethren were present, including the First Presidency of the Church, Joseph's scribe, the stake presidency and the bishopric in Zion (Missouri), and the high councilors of Kirtland and Zion. Joseph Smith records, "The visions of heaven were opened. . . . Some of them saw the face of the Savior, and others were ministered unto by holy angels."[33] Although the exact number who saw Christ is not known, it

---

31. John Murdock, "A Brief Synopsis of the Life of John Murdock: Taken from an Abridged Record of His Journal," 11, BYU Special Collections.

32. *History of the Church,* 1:335. Known members of the School of the Prophets included Joseph Smith, Zebedee Coltrin, John Murdock, Sidney Rigdon, Frederick G. Williams, Joseph Smith Sr., Hyrum Smith, Samuel H. Smith, William Smith, Ezra Thayre, Newel K. Whitney, Martin Harris, Lyman Johnson, Orson Hyde, Solomon Humphrey, Sylvester Smith, Orson Pratt, and Levi Hancock.

33. *History of the Church,* 2:382; Jessee, Ashurst-McGee, and Jensen, *Journals,* 1:170.

is probable that "some" of those forty in attendance would number at least three.

At Least Three Witnesses Reported by Joseph Smith in March 1836

About three hundred brethren met in the long-awaited solemn assembly in the Kirtland Temple on March 30, 1836. Participants included the First Presidency, the Twelve, the seventies, the high councils, the bishoprics, the elders, and all the official members of the Kirtland Stake. As part of this meeting and in fulfillment of another promise made by Joseph Smith, the Savior was present. Joseph recorded, "The Savior made His appearance to some."[34] It is probable that "some" would number at least three.

As a result of these visions, witnesses of Christ walked again among people on earth. At least twenty-three latter-day witnesses (see chart, p. 138) testified of Him throughout this newly settled region in Ohio. Hundreds of other witnesses to Christ's glory joined with these twenty-three (see chapter 7). They bore testimony of events not seen or heard on earth since the time of Christ's resurrection, when He appeared to so many of His disciples.

Possible Additional Witnesses

The conservative estimate of twenty-three witnesses forms a base number, but the actual number of those who saw the Savior or heard His voice in Kirtland is not known. It is probable that there were more witnesses than these. George Q. Cannon's statement that Joseph Smith and Oliver Cowdery's Kirtland Temple vision is "supplemented by hundreds of others who have beheld . . . glorious personages" could lead to a conclusion that many of those hundreds of others also had their experiences in Kirtland. This seems to be a reasonable conclusion because Kirtland was the

---

34. *History of the Church*, 2:432; Jessee, Ashurst-McGee, and Jensen, *Journals*, 1:215–16.

latter-day location of most visions of Deity during the Church's early days. The Church was in Kirtland longer than any other location. Joseph Smith also declared Kirtland to be "a Pentecost . . . long to be remembered."[35]

A further example that these numerical estimates of witnesses are conservative is found in the instruction the Prophet gave to the Twelve Apostles in November 1835. As he prepared them for sacred ordinances in the Kirtland Temple, he said, "All who are prepared, and are sufficiently pure to abide the presence of the Savior, will see Him in the Solemn Assembly."[36] The word "all" probably means more than just a few. There is no way of knowing the exact number who were prepared and sufficiently pure as they entered the solemn assembly on March 30, 1836. Of the three hundred attendees, 115 were leaders who had been instructed in various meetings and admonished by scripture to prepare themselves. Three is a conservative estimate for the solemn assembly, and some might conclude that the number who saw the Savior was much greater.

Historical accounts certify that Joseph consistently tried to prepare Church leaders to see the Savior. In 1833, Joseph wrote a letter to Missouri officials encouraging them to prepare for this great experience in the Kirtland Temple. He encouraged their preparation by sharing a promise made by the Lord Himself:

> The brethren in Kirtland pray for you unceasingly. . . . The Lord commanded us, in Kirtland, to build a house of God, . . . this is the word of the Lord to us, and we must, yea, the Lord helping us, we will obey: as on conditions of our obedience He has promised us great things; yea, even a visit from the heavens to honor us with His own presence. We greatly fear before the Lord lest we should fail of this

---

35. *History of the Church,* 2:432–33; Jessee, Ashurst-McGee, and Jensen, *Journals,* 1:216.

36. *History of the Church,* 2:310; Davidson, Whittaker, Ashurst-McGee, and Jensen, *Histories,* 1:123.

great honor, which our Master proposes to confer on us; we are seeking for humility and great faith lest we be ashamed in His presence.[37]

Yet another example of possibly more unidentified witnesses of the Savior is found in the original Quorum of the Twelve Apostles. Not one in the list of individual witnesses was a member of that quorum. Yet Joseph Smith worked diligently to prepare them to see the Savior. While it is probable that some of the estimated three witnesses in the solemn assembly were Apostles, it seems uncharacteristic that not more of them would have seen the Savior. A statement by Elder David Patten may bear out this assertion. Within a few weeks after the Kirtland Temple dedication, David told Abraham Smoot, possibly referring to the Twelve Apostles, that "Jesus Christ was seen of them."[38] Another indicator that more Church leaders might have seen or heard the Savior speak to them comes from Orson Pratt, also of the original Twelve. He testified, "God was there . . . the visions of the Almighty were opened to the minds of the servants of the living God; . . . they saw the heavens opened; they beheld the angels of God; they heard the voice of the Lord; and they were filled from the crown of their heads to the soles of their feet with the power and inspiration of the Holy Ghost."[39]

---

37. *History of the Church*, 1:316–17.

38. David Patten, in Wilford Woodruff, *Wilford Woodruff's Journal, 1833–1898*, ed. Scott G. Kenney, typescript, 9 vols. (Midvale, Utah: Signature Books, 1983–85), 1:67. David does not specify the date of the vision; however, the account correlates closer with the January 28 meeting than with any other. There are three clues to the date of the meeting: (1) Wilford Woodruff said it was "an account of the endowment." In Joseph Smith's account of the January 28 meeting, he said the "Holy Anointing" was given in the meeting. This anointing was one of the ordinances of the Kirtland endowment. (2) The Father and the Son appeared in vision. Except for January 21, no account exists for another meeting during this time where both the Father and the Son appear in vision. This account is the second account of the Father and the Son appearing in this January 28 meeting. (3) David Patten was present. David was not present on January 21, when both the Father and the Son were seen, but he and other members of the Twelve were present on January 28.

39. Orson Pratt, in *Journal of Discourses*, 18:132.

Still, not all early leaders recorded their visions of the Savior. Some felt they were too sacred to record. One such person was Oliver Cowdery, who participated in most meetings where the Savior was seen. Conservative Oliver did not even record his vision documented in Doctrine and Covenants 110. Of the visions in which he participated on January 21, 1836, Oliver wrote, "I only say, that the heavens were opened to many, and great and marvelous things were shown."[40] Others may also have written of such an experience in a general way without recording the specifics of seeing Deity.[41] For example, Joseph Smith, who apparently saw the Father and the Son in the January 28, 1836, Kirtland Temple meeting, merely recorded, "[I saw] a glorious vision."[42] The First Presidency and the Twelve probably didn't record their visions because Joseph Smith asked them not to. In an instruction meeting of these brethren, Joseph said, "If God gives you a manifestation, keep it to yourselves."[43]

Many more than just a few, then, stand as witnesses that the Lord again appeared in vision and spoke to men personally in Kirtland as He did anciently. The named and the unnamed, the faithful and those who faltered have all agreed that indeed Deity was there, and the restored work was divinely ratified.

---

40. Leonard J. Arrington, "Oliver Cowdery's Kirtland, Ohio, 'Sketch Book,'" *BYU Studies* 12, no. 4 (Summer 1972): 419.

41. Some feel that Lorenzo Snow was also a witness of the Savior at the time of his baptism in Kirtland. After his baptism, Lorenzo knelt in supplication for personal knowledge of the Savior. The Lord answered his prayer. Lorenzo described a manifestation that came while he knelt to pray: "I had no sooner opened my lips in an effort to pray, than I heard a sound, just above my head, like the rustling of silken robes, and immediately the Spirit of God descended upon me, completely enveloping my whole person, filling me, from the crown of my head to the soles of my feet. . . . I then received a perfect knowledge that God lives, that Jesus Christ is the Son of God" (Eliza R. Snow Smith, *Biography and Family Record of Lorenzo Snow* [Salt Lake City: Deseret News, 1884], 7–8). Later, as the fifth president of the Church, President Snow, said, "No man ever did or ever could receive a more perfect knowledge in regard to the existence of God and of the truth of this work than God gave to me by revelation and the opening of the heavens" (in Conference Report, April 7, 1894).

42. *History of the Church*, 2:387; Jessee, Ashurst-McGee, and Jensen, *Journals*, 1:175. See Chapter 12, pp. 225–47 herein, for more on sources of details of the vision.

43. *History of the Church*, 2:309; Davidson, Whittaker, Ashurst-McGee, and Jensen, *Histories*, 1:122.

CHAPTER 7

Secondary Witnesses
of the Savior

I saw the glory and felt the power, but did not see the vision.
—Philo Dibble

In addition to the many direct witnesses of the Savior, visions of Deity created an abundance of secondary witnesses who were present when the Savior appeared but did not see the vision itself. Nevertheless, these men and women witnessed outward manifestations of divine power and glory. Records indicate that more than two hundred men and women became secondary witnesses. These secondary witnesses had parallel experiences to witnesses in past dispensations. For example, when the Lord appeared to Paul as he journeyed to Damascus, others who accompanied him became secondary witnesses to his vision. Paul's companions didn't see the Savior directly, but they saw the accompanying great light. Because they observed this outward manifestation of the vision, they knew that Paul saw the Savior.

Paul states:

> Suddenly there shone from heaven a great light round about me. And I fell unto the ground, and heard a voice saying unto me, Saul, Saul, why persecutest thou me? And I

answered, Who art thou, Lord? And he said unto me, I am Jesus of Nazareth, whom thou persecutest. And they that were with me saw indeed the light . . . but they heard not the voice of him that spake to me.[1]

Moses is an example of an Old Testament parallel. During the time he was in the presence of the Lord on the mount, the children of Israel became secondary witnesses as they saw an intensive bright light. They compared that light or "glory of the lord" that surrounded Moses and the mount to a "devouring fire."[2] When Moses descended the mount from the presence of the Lord, the distinguishing outward manifestation of his experience shone in his face. What the children of Israel particularly noticed was "that the skin of Moses' face shone."[3] Because his face bore this divine radiance, they knew that Moses was in God's power.

The same phenomenon is true of those present during visions of Deity in Kirtland. Outward manifestations they mentioned the most were feeling a sense of divine power and seeing light or glory around or upon recipients of the visions. They often noted the light or glow that was reflected from the Prophet's face.

Few accounts of these secondary witnesses have survived. Specific remembrances in surviving accounts are also few. Many who were present may even have been witnesses of the Savior, but accounts are not specific enough to fully establish the fact. For example, Hyrum Smith and Roger

---

1. Acts 22:6–9. There is confusion in the book of Acts about whether the men heard Christ's voice. Robert Matthews, a scholar of the Joseph Smith Translation, resolves the confusion between two accounts in Acts (chapters 9 and 22). Brother Matthews explained, "It is recorded in Acts 9:7: 'And the men which journeyed with him stood speechless, hearing a voice, but seeing no man.' However, in Acts 22:9, as Paul was making a defense at Jerusalem, he recounts the event thus: 'And they that were with me saw indeed the light, and were afraid; but they heard not the voice of him that spake to me.' Evidently here is a misstatement of fact. As corrected by the Prophet, the passage in Acts 9:7 is altered to agree with that in chapter 22. This would seem to be the reasonable conclusion, for surely the voice and message of the Lord was for Paul alone, although his companions in travel might be permitted to see the light and thereby be assured of the unusual event that was taking place" ("A Walk through the Bible with the Prophet Joseph Smith," Thirty-first Annual Joseph Smith Memorial Sermon, Utah State University South Stake Center, Logan, Utah, December 9, 1973, 10).

2. Exodus 24:17.

3. Exodus 34:35.

Orton attended the January 28, 1836, meeting when Joseph Smith and Zebedee Coltrin witnessed their divine visions.[4] Harrison Burgess said that the power of God was manifest to all of them. Harrison also recorded that Joseph, Hyrum, and Roger were all "enveloped in the light."[5] Because Hyrum and Roger were enveloped in the same light as Joseph, it seems probable that they also saw Deity and became witnesses. Because the account does not specify that Hyrum and Roger saw a vision of Deity, however, they are thus categorized as secondary witnesses.

More Than Two Hundred Secondary Witnesses

Historical accounts certify that more than two hundred individuals, like Paul's companions on the road to Damascus, witnessed outward manifestations of visions of Deity in Kirtland. The actual number is in all probability greater, but existing records cannot document a higher number with certainty.[6]

---

4. Joseph Smith, *History of The Church of Jesus Christ of Latter-day Saints*, ed. B. H. Roberts, 7 vols., 2d ed. rev. (Salt Lake City: The Church of Jesus Christ of Latter-day Saints, 1932–51), 2:387.

5. Harrison Burgess, Autobiography, in *Windows: A Mormon Family*, comp. and ed. Kenneth Glyn Hales (Tucson, Ariz.: Skyline Printing, 1985), 102–3.

6. As an example, no doubt many more secondary witnesses arose from the dedication day in the Kirtland Temple. Accounts indicate that on March 27, 1836, the Savior may have been present although unseen (see chapter 12, pp. 225–47 herein). Meetings on March 27 may have been like the one Mary Elizabeth Lightner reported on the Morley farm in 1831 (see chapter 9, pp. 171–85 herein). Joseph Smith announced that the Savior was present, but the eyes of those there were veiled so that they could not see Him. Yet those present detected His certain presence because all felt an unmistakable power and saw a glorious light reflected through Joseph. Statements made by Saints in meetings of March 27 signify that there were secondary witnesses. Outward manifestations are identified by attendees on that day: "I saw the glory of God" (Leonard J. Arrington, "Oliver Cowdery's Kirtland, Ohio, 'Sketch Book,'" *BYU Studies* 12, no. 4 [1972]: 426). "A sense of divine presence was realized by all present, and each heart was filled with 'joy inexpressible and full of glory'" (Eliza R. Snow, in Edward W. Tullidge, *The Women of Mormondom* [New York: Tullidge & Crandall, 1877; repr., Salt Lake City: n.p., 1975], 95). "The glory of God came down on the Elders" (Benjamin Brown, in Steven C. Harper, "Kirtland Temple Experience," in *Opening the Heavens: Accounts of Divine Manifestations, 1820–1844*, ed. John W. Welch and Erick B. Carlson [Provo, Utah: Brigham Young University Press, 2005], 337). "All the congregation [was] moved upon by an invisible power. . . . The people of the neighborhood came running together [hearing an unusual sound within, and seeing a bright light . . . resting upon the Temple]" (Joseph Smith, *History of The Church of Jesus Christ of Latter-day Saints*, ed. B. H. Roberts, 7 vols., 2d ed. rev. [Salt Lake City: The Church of Jesus Christ of Latter-day Saints, 1932–51], 2:428).

Following are descriptions of meetings where the Savior was present and that produced secondary witnesses, those who were in the meeting and witnessed manifestations of divine glory but did not see the vision itself. Some secondary witnesses are identified by name with their specific explanations. For each meeting, estimates are given of the number of secondary witnesses who saw or felt the outward manifestations of visions of Deity.

Thirty Secondary Witnesses at Baptisms and Confirmations, November 1830

John Murdock was baptized on November 5, 1830, and confirmed two days later. He recorded, "On Sunday evening they confirmed about thirty; I was one of the number. . . . the Spirit rested on me as it never did before and others said they saw the Lord, and had visions."[7] Philo Dibble remembered the outward manifestations that were seen at baptisms during this period:

> There were many signs and wonders seen in the heavens . . . both by Saints and strangers. A pillar of light was seen every evening for more than a month hovering over the place where we did our baptizing. One evening . . . the moon was not to be seen that night. Although it was cloudy, it was as light as noonday, and we could seemingly see . . . farther that night than we could in the day time.[8]

Fifteen Secondary Witnesses at May 1831 Meeting

Mary Elizabeth Lightner records that it was made known to Joseph Smith and Martin Harris that the Savior was present in an 1831 meeting in Kirtland. Attending were "the Smith family . . . from the old gentleman and his wife to all the sons and daughters."[9] Mary said of that visitation:

---

7. John Murdock, "A Brief Synopsis of the Life of John Murdock: Taken from an Abridged Record of His Journal," 11, L. Tom Perry Special Collections, Harold B. Lee Library, Brigham Young University, Provo, Utah; hereafter cited as BYU Special Collections,

8. "Philo Dibble's Narrative," in *Four Faith Promoting Classics* (Salt Lake City: Bookcraft, 1968), 78.

9. Mary Elizabeth Lightner, typescript, April 14, 1905, 1, BYU Special Collections. The estimate of

Those who looked at him [Joseph] that day said *there was a search light within him, over every part of his body.* I never saw anything like it on the earth. . . .

. . . [The] power rested down upon the congregation. Every soul felt it. The spirit rested upon us in every fiber of our bodies."

Mary spoke of the dramatic change in Joseph Smith's body. She said,

"All at once his countenance changed and he stood mute . . . ; he got so white that anyone who saw him would have thought he was transparent. . . . I shall remember it and see in my mind's eye as long as I remain upon the earth.[10]

Through this experience, Mary became an effective secondary witness of the Savior. Throughout her life she bore a strong witness of His presence.

Twenty-two Secondary Witnesses at Ordination of First High Priests

Lyman Wight, Harvey Whitlock, and Joseph Smith saw both the Father and the Son as the first high priests were ordained at the fourth conference of the Church. During the meeting at least twenty-two high priests and other ordained members witnessed outward manifestations of glory and power emanating from the vision.[11] John Whitmer became a secondary witness, of which

---

fifteen secondary witnesses includes Joseph Smith Sr., Lucy Mack Smith, their eight children (minus Joseph) and spouses of those who were married, and Mary Lightner and her mother.

10. Lightner, typescript, 1.

11. Those ordained were Lyman Wight , John Murdock, Reynolds Cahoon, Harvey Whitlock, Hyrum Smith, Parley P. Pratt, Thomas B. Marsh, Isaac Morley, Edward Partridge, Joseph Wakefield, Martin Harris, Ezra Thayre, Ezra Booth, John Corrill, Samuel H. Smith, Solomon Hancock, Simeon Carter, Wheeler Baldwin, Jacob Scott, Joseph Smith Sr., John Whitmer, Joseph Smith Jr., and Sidney Rigdon. Others known to be present were Zebedee Coltrin and Levi Hancock. See *Far West Record: Minutes of The Church of Jesus Christ of Latter-day Saints, 1830–1844*, ed. Donald Q. Cannon and Lyndon W. Cook (Salt Lake City: Deseret Book, 1983), 6.

he wrote matter-of-factly in his history: "The glory of the Lord shone around."[12] It was said of Lyman Wight that "his countenance was a brilliant, transparent white."[13] Levi Hancock stated that "Lyman [Wight] was white."[14] Lyman Wight wrote, "I . . . saw the visible manifestations of the power of God."[15]

Twelve Secondary Witnesses at Hiram, Ohio, February 16, 1832

Joseph Smith and Sidney Rigdon beheld the Father and the Son as they sat enwrapped in the vision of the eternities as described in Doctrine and Covenants 76. Philo Dibble wrote, "There were other men in the room, perhaps twelve." He attested to the outward manifestations of the vision, which made him a secondary witness: "I saw the glory and felt the power, but did not see the vision." He also said, "Joseph sat . . . all the time in the midst of a magnificent glory."[16] Philo especially noted Joseph's countenance: "His face shone as if it were transparent."[17]

Fourteen Secondary Witnesses in the School of the Prophets, March 18, 1833

About twenty high priests met in the School of the Prophets on March 18, 1833.[18] It was to become a day of visions. Joseph Smith said, "Many of

---

12. *From Historian to Dissident: The Book of John Whitmer,* ed. Bruce N. Westergren (Salt Lake City: Signature Books, 1995), 70.

13. Zebedee Coltrin, in Hyrum Andrus, "Little Known Friends of the Prophet Joseph Smith," 1963 seminar on the Prophet Joseph Smith, Brigham Young University, 47–48, in Calvin R. Stephens, "The Life and Contributions of Zebedee Coltrin" (master's thesis, Brigham Young University, 1974), 14.

14. Levi Hancock, Autobiography, copied by Clara E. H. Lloyd, typescript, 33, BYU Special Collections.

15. "Lyman Wight," Saints without Halos, accessed March 1, 2012, http://www.saintswithouthalos.com/m/310603-06_x4.phtml#endzc.

16. Philo Dibble, "Recollections of the Prophet Joseph Smith," *Juvenile Instructor* 27 (May 15, 1892): 303–4. It is not known who the other eleven were.

17. "Philo Dibble's Narrative," 81.

18. Known members of the School of the Prophets were Joseph Smith, Sidney Rigdon, Frederick G. Williams, Joseph Smith Sr., Hyrum Smith, Samuel H. Smith, William Smith, Ezra Thayre,

the brethren saw a heavenly vision of the Savior, and concourses of angels, and many other things."[19]

Approximately six high priests, including Joseph Smith, Zebedee Coltrin, and John Murdock, saw visions of Deity. Those who didn't see Deity apparently felt an unmistakable presence and became secondary witnesses through observing outward manifestations. Zebedee described the feeling that accompanied the visions as "a sensation . . . of consuming fire."[20] He described the accompanying light as brilliant.[21] Zebedee summed up the overwhelming intensity of these manifestations this way: "[The] glory and brightness . . . and . . . power was so great that had it continued much longer I believe it would have consumed us."[22]

Thirty-six Secondary Witnesses in the Kirtland Temple, January 21, 1836

Approximately three brethren in addition to Joseph Smith saw the Savior in the Kirtland Temple when the ordinance of anointing with oil was introduced. The other thirty-six who were present became secondary witnesses as they participated in outward manifestations of the visions.[23] In describing outward manifestations of power and glory in meetings that day, Joseph said "the power of the Highest rested upon us, [and] the house was filled with the glory of God."[24] He added, "We all communed with the

Newel K. Whitney, Martin Harris, Lyman Johnson, Orson Hyde, Solomon Humphrey, Sylvester Smith, Orson Pratt, Levi Hancock, Zebedee Coltrin, and John Murdock.

19. *History of the Church,* 1:335.

20. Zebedee Coltrin, in *Salt Lake School of the Prophets Minute Book, 1883* (Salt Lake City: Pioneer Press, 1992), 54.

21. Coltrin, in *Minute Book,* 54.

22. Zebedee Coltrin, address at a meeting of high priests in Spanish Fork, Utah, February 5, 1878, Church History Library, The Church of Jesus Christ of Latter-day Saints, Salt Lake City, Utah, hereafter cited as Church History Library, in *The Prophet Joseph: Essays on the Life and Mission of Joseph Smith,* ed. Larry C. Porter and Susan Easton Black (Salt Lake City: Deseret Book, 1988), 111.

23. Others present included the First Presidency, Joseph's scribe, the stake presidency and bishopric in Zion (Missouri), and the high councilors of Kirtland and Zion.

24. *History of the Church,* 2:381; Dean C. Jessee, Mark Ashurst-McGee, and Richard L. Jensen, eds., *Journals,*

heavenly host."[25] Warren Parrish was one who certainly became a secondary witness and may have seen the Savior directly. Joseph wrote that Warren "saw, in a vision, the armies of heaven . . . and many things which I saw."[26]

One Hundred Secondary Witnesses in the Kirtland Temple, January 28, 1836

"About a hundred of the high priests, seventies and elders" met in the upper part of the Kirtland Temple on January 28, 1836.[27] They saw visions of Deity and other great spiritual manifestations. In describing the outward manifestations accompanying the visions of Deity that day, Harrison Burgess said "all at once there was a Heavenly and Divine Atmosphere surrounded them."[28] He also said, "All who were in the room felt the power of God . . . and the power of God was made manifest [to all these in the assembly], the remembrance of which I shall never forget while I live upon the earth."[29] Harrison confirmed that he was a secondary witness as he also testified, "I beheld the room lighted up with a peculiar light such as I had never seen before."[30] Joseph Smith cited another manifestation: "President Sylvester Smith saw a pillar of fire rest down and abide upon the heads of the quorum, as we stood in the midst of the Twelve."[31] Harrison also identified Roger Orton, another person in attendance, as a secondary witness when he wrote, "Roger Orton [was] enveloped in the light."[32]

1832–1839, vol. 1 of the Journals series of *The Joseph Smith Papers,* edited by Dean C. Jessee, Ronald K. Esplin, and Richard Lyman Bushman (Salt Lake City: Church Historian's Press, 2008), 1:170.

25. *History of the Church,* 2:382; Jessee, Ashurst-McGee, and Jensen, *Journals,* 1:170.

26. *History of the Church,* 2:381; Jessee, Ashurst-McGee, and Jensen, *Journals,* 1:170.

27. Burgess, Autobiography, 102–3.

28. *Diary of Charles Lowell Walker,* ed. Karl Larson and Katherine Miles Larson, 2 vols. (Logan: Utah State University Press, 1980), 2:483.

29. Burgess, Autobiography, 102–3.

30. Burgess, Autobiography, 102–3.

31. *History of the Church,* 2:386; Jessee, Ashurst-McGee, and Jensen, *Journals,* 1:174.

32. Burgess, Autobiography, 102–3.

William Smith, Hyrum's younger brother, was probably also in this same category given that Joseph wrote, "William Smith . . . saw the heavens opened."[33] Hyrum was at least a secondary witness and probably saw the Savior in the Kirtland Temple. Harrison wrote, "Hyrum Smith [was] enveloped in the light. . . . Hyrum exclaimed, 'I behold the angels of heaven.'"[34]

Witnesses to Christ's Revelations

Seldom did Joseph Smith ever receive revelations from the Lord in private with no others present. His scribe at least was usually present. Joseph's normal mode was to invite others to join him. For example, in Hiram, Ohio, when the vision recorded in Doctrine and Covenants 76 was given, "perhaps twelve" others were present in addition to Joseph and Sidney Rigdon.[35] In the Whitney store, where section 84 was received, six elders who gathered at first were joined later by at least five others. Ten brethren were gathered when the Lord dictated Doctrine and Covenants 88. At times those who joined with Joseph had requested the revelation and knelt with the Prophet to petition the Lord in prayer.

As the brethren and sisters observed the process of Christ revealing His word to Joseph Smith, they became witnesses to Christ's revelations. They could perceive that the Savior was near and bestowed inspiration, knowledge, and revelation upon Joseph. They noticed a change in him. It seems that whether Joseph was receiving revelation from Christ or seeing a vision of Him, the outward manifestations others noticed were the same. Many mention that they detected a light or a heavenly glow surrounding Joseph, especially in his face.

This phenomenon has parallels in past dispensations. As Abinadi was receiving and speaking the word of the Lord under inspiration to King Noah and his priests, the record indicates, "his face shone with exceeding luster, even as Moses' did while in the mount of Sinai."[36]

---

33. *History of the Church*, 2:387; Jessee, Ashurst-McGee, and Jensen, *Journals*, 1:174.

34. Burgess, Autobiography, 102–3.

35. Dibble, "Recollections," 303.

36. Mosiah 13:5.

In our own dispensation, Orson Pratt, present when Doctrine and Covenants 51 was revealed, observed that "Joseph's face was exceedingly white, and seemed to shine."[37] Heber C. Kimball said, "When the Spirit of God was in him . . . his countenance was as white as the whitest thing you ever saw."[38] Brigham Young, another witness, explained the source of this change in countenance:

> Those who were acquainted with him knew when the Spirit of revelation was upon him, for his countenance wore an expression peculiar to himself while under that influence. He preached by the Spirit of revelation, and taught in his council by it, and those who were acquainted with him could discover it at once, for at such times there was a peculiar clearness and transparency in his face.[39]

Zebedee Coltrin also testified to the effect of receiving revelation manifest on the Prophet's face. Zebedee said to John Taylor that "he had seen Joseph giving revelation when he could not look on his face, so full was he [Joseph] of the glory of God, and the house was full of the same glory."[40] Zebedee testified that "when Joseph came out of the translating room after having received the revelation on the word of wisdom . . . his face shone with brilliance."[41]

Philo Dibble added his account to those of others who noticed changes in the Prophet's face. Recalling his observation of Joseph in the translating room at the Johnson home, Philo used the same terminology as Orson Pratt and Zebedee Coltrin that his face, like that of Moses and Abinadi,

---

37. Orson Pratt, in *Millennial Star* 36 (August 11, 1874): 498.

38. Heber C. Kimball, in *Journal of Discourses*, 26 vols. (London: Latter-day Saints' Book Depot, 1854–86), 6:35.

39. Brigham Young, in *Journal of Discourses*, 9:89.

40. Coltrin, in *Minute Book*, 63.

41. Minutes of a meeting of high priests in Spanish Fork, Utah, February 5, 1878, in Church History Library, in Stephens, "Contributions of Zebedee Coltrin," 44.

shone. He said it shone "as if it were transparent." Apparently, the brilliance noted by so many also characterized Joseph's clothing. Philo noted that in the Johnson translating room, "Joseph wore black clothes, but at this time seemed to be dressed in an element of glorious white."[42]

Some witnesses simply bore their testimony without mentioning what spiritual manifestation they received. Joel Johnson was one. He said, "I was often present when the word of the Lord came from His mouth, and was written down by his scribe. I knew, and now know, that it was the word of the Lord to all men."[43]

Joseph also manifested a change in facial expression when he was speaking under the Lord's influence. Edward Stevenson, fourteen, heard the Prophet speak and wrote, "He began relateing his vision . . . his countanance seemed to me to assume a heavenly whiteness."[44]

Lorenzo Snow noted the same outward manifestation when Joseph preached. He related: "I heard the Prophet discourse upon the grandest of subjects. At times he was filled with the Holy Ghost, speaking as with the voice of an archangel and filled with the power of God, his whole person shone and his face was lightened until it appeared as the whiteness of the driven snow."[45]

God's revelations to the Prophet Joseph Smith created a large pool of latter-day witnesses. These witnesses received an unquestionable testimony that the Lord lived and directed His Saints. These witnesses built faith and strength in others as they shared their testimony of Christ's leadership. Knowledge of this leadership through His presence and through revelations given to Joseph Smith validated the Saints' sacrifice.

---

42. "Philo Dibble's Narrative," 81.

43. Joel Hills Johnson, "Autobiography," in *Voice from the Mountains: Being a Testimony of the Truth of the Gospel of Jesus Christ, as revealed by the Lord to Joseph Smith, Jr.* (Salt Lake City: Juvenile Instructor Office, 1881), 13.

44. *Autobiography of Edward Stevenson 1820–1897*, ed. Joseph Grant Stevenson (Provo, Utah: Stevenson's Genealogical Center, 1986), 7.

45. LeRoi C. Snow, "How Lorenzo Snow Found God," *Improvement Era* 40 (February 1937): 84.

CHAPTER 8

JOSEPH AND THE THREE WITNESSES
TESTIFY IN KIRTLAND

The Lord opened the heavens upon me and I saw the Lord and he spake unto
me saying . . . behold I am the Lord of glory I was crucified for the world.
—JOSEPH SMITH

The Savior either appeared to or spoke with four men while they lived in New York: Joseph Smith, Oliver Cowdery, Martin Harris, and David Whitmer. He appeared to Joseph Smith, Oliver Cowdery, and Martin Harris[1]; He spoke to them and to David Whitmer. Two men, Joseph Smith and Oliver Cowdery, heard His voice at the time John the Baptist appeared. The Three Witnesses—Oliver Cowdery, Martin Harris, and David Whitmer—heard the Savior's voice at the time the angel Moroni showed them the ancient records from which the Book of Mormon was translated. The Three Witnesses certified that when viewing the plates, "the voice of the Lord" instructed them in their duties, which clearly indicates that Christ was the speaker.[2] After they had all moved to Kirtland in 1831, these four witnesses bore forceful testimony of these events.

---

1. Joseph Smith–History 1:17; *Personal Writings of Joseph Smith*, comp. and ed. Dean C. Jessee, rev. ed. (Salt Lake City: Deseret Book, 2002), 13–14.

2. See "The Testimony of the Three Witnesses" in the introduction to the Book of Mormon. Based

Although these experiences with Deity occurred in New York, these men became witnesses of Christ in Kirtland because of what they had seen and heard. During the Kirtland years these men often affirmed the reality of their divine experiences. In Kirtland they testified of seeing or hearing God the Father and His Son, Jesus Christ. Because of these witnesses, listeners and readers in Ohio received assurance that Christ lived and directed the Church. Skeptics and believers alike, in this newly settled area, listened with interest when these men related latter-day encounters with Deity. Even skeptics visually responded with respect to the sincerity of these witnesses. Lorenzo Snow, who waited five years to embrace the restored gospel after hearing it, remembered his first impressions of Joseph Smith in Hiram: "He was only twenty-five years of age and was not, at that time, what would be called a fluent speaker. His remarks were confined principally to his own experiences. . . . He simply bore his testimony to what the Lord had manifested to him. . . . He . . . seemed to affect the whole audience with the feeling that he was honest and sincere."[3]

---

upon the written testimony and later statements of the Three Witnesses, it is not clear whether the voice was that of God the Father or Jesus Christ. Each of the witnesses identified the divine voice as being that of either "God" or "the Lord." The two names are used interchangeably by all Three Witnesses without being more specific. "God" is a title; "the Lord" is also a title. The two titles in general usage can mean either God the Father or Jesus Christ. Analyzing the usage of these two titles at the time of the Three Witnesses reveals that in most cases they pertain to Jesus Christ. To determine how the Three Witnesses might have interpreted the titles, we can look at revelations given to them by the Savior around the time they saw the Book of Mormon plates in June 1829. In an April 1829 revelation to Oliver Cowdery, the Savior said, "Behold, I am God. . . . Behold the wounds which pierced my side, and also the prints of the nails in my hands and feet" (D&C 6:2, 37). In a May 1829 revelation to David Whitmer, the Savior said, "Behold, I am God. . . . I am Jesus Christ, the Son of the living God, who created the heavens and the earth, a light which cannot be hid in darkness" (D&C 14:2, 9). Also in May 1829, immediately following the Three Witnesses' view of the plates, the Savior said to Oliver Cowdery and David Whitmer, "For, behold, the Lord your Redeemer suffered death in the flesh. . . . Behold, I, Jesus Christ, your Lord and your God, and your Redeemer . . . have spoken it. Amen" (D&C 18:11–47). In these revelations, the Savior used the titles "God" and "the Lord" to mean Himself. It seems, therefore, reasonable to assume that the Three Witnesses probably meant to convey that it was the Savior's voice they heard.

3. LeRoi C. Snow, "How Lorenzo Snow Found God," *Improvement Era* 40 (February 1937): 83.

Although the visions in New York occurred individually and at different times, they were all recorded in Kirtland. It was in Kirtland that Joseph Smith first recorded that he saw Christ in 1820, writing plainly, "I saw the Lord."[4] It was in Kirtland that Joseph disclosed that Martin Harris had seen Christ eight years before. Joseph explained that because of Martin Harris's faith and support of the Prophet, "the Lord appeared unto him in a vision and shewed unto him his marvilous work which he was about to do."[5] It was also in Kirtland that Joseph disclosed that in 1829 Oliver Cowdery had seen the Savior as well. Joseph recorded that the "Lord appeared unto a young man by the name of Oliver Cowd[e]ry and shewed unto him the plates in a vision and also the truth of the work and what the Lord was about to do through me."[6]

Joseph Smith's Accounts of the First Vision

Joseph Smith talked many times about his First Vision, which took place in Palmyra, New York. Probably more information about this vision surfaced in Kirtland than in New York. These accounts certify that Joseph the Prophet did bear his witness to members and nonmembers alike. He testified that Christ the Son and God the Father addressed him, called him by name, and instructed him in the grove in the spring of 1820. Details about young Joseph's life-changing experience come from his personal recounting of his First Vision. Various documents and histories preserved from the Kirtland era attest that in Kirtland, Joseph wrote his first formal account of the vision and also frequently told others about it.

Lorenzo Snow learned of Joseph's powerful conviction when he heard

---

4. Karen Lynn Davidson, David J. Whittaker, Mark Ashurst-McGee, and Richard L. Jensen, eds., *Histories, 1832–1844,* vol. 1 of the Histories series of *The Joseph Smith Papers,* edited by Dean C. Jessee, Ronald K. Esplin, and Richard Lyman Bushman (Salt Lake City: Church Historian's Press, 2012), 1:12–13.

5. Davidson, Whittaker, Ashurst-McGee, and Jensen, *Histories,* 1:15.

6. Davidson, Whittaker, Ashurst-McGee, and Jensen, *Histories,* 1:16.

the Prophet speak about his vision shortly after Joseph arrived in Kirtland in 1831:

> As I looked upon him and listened, I thought to myself that a man bearing such a wonderful testimony as he did, and having such a countenance as he possessed, could hardly be a false prophet. He certainly could not have been deceived, it seemed to me, . . . he testified that he had had a conversation with Jesus, the Son of God, and had talked with Him personally, as Moses talked with God upon Mount Sinai, and that he had also heard the voice of the Father.[7]

Joseph, who in 1832 wrote a short history of his life, focused on his First Vision. Interestingly, he began his history by giving credit to the Savior. He testified that he had done "the mighty acts" of his divine calling "in the name of Jesus Ch[r]ist the son of the living God."[8] He then formally testified that Christ brought forth His Church and restored it by His own hand. The Prophet described his vision:

> I cried unto the Lord for mercy for there was none else to whom I could go and to obtain mercy and the Lord heard my cry in the wilderness and while in <the> attitude of calling upon the Lord . . . a piller of . . . light above the brightness of the sun at noon day come down from above and rested upon me and I was filled with the spirit of god and the <Lord> opened the heavens upon me and I saw the Lord and he spake unto me saying Joseph <my son> thy sins are forgiven thee. go thy <way> walk in my statutes and

7. Snow, "Lorenzo Snow," 83.

8. Davidson, Whittaker, Ashurst-McGee, and Jensen, *Histories,* 1:10.

keep my commandments behold I am the Lord of glory I was crucifyed for the world.[9]

In an 1832 meeting near Cleveland, Ohio, Joseph boldly bore public witness of Christ's appearance to him. The Reverend Richmond Taggart heard and recorded Joseph's testimony in a letter written on March 2, 1833. He wrote: "The following Curious occurrence occurred last week in Newburg [Ohio] about 6 miles from this Place [Cleaveland]. Joe Smith the great Mormonosity was there and held forth, and among other things he told them he had seen Jesus Christ and the Apostles and conversed with them."[10]

In 1834, Joseph traveled to Michigan on a proselytizing mission. There, Edward Stevenson, fourteen years old, saw and heard the Prophet speak. He vividly remembered that in multiple meetings Joseph described the Savior's appearance to him when he was Edward's age:

> In the midst of many large congregations, the Prophet testified with great power concerning the visit of the Father and the Son, and the conversation he had with them. Never before did I feel such power as was manifested on these occasions. . . .
>
> Although a mere humble widow's son, I felt proud and blessed of God, when he honored us by coming under our roof and partaking of our hospitality. . . . We were proud,

---

9. Davidson, Whittaker, Ashurst-McGee, and Jensen, *Histories,* 1:12–13.

10. Reverend Richmond Taggart to the Reverend Jonathon Goings, March 2, 1833, 2, American Baptist Historical Society, Rochester, New York, in Gregory A. Prince, *Power from on High: The Development of Mormon Priesthood* (Salt Lake City: Signature Books, 1995), 8, in *Early Mormon Documents,* comp. and ed. Dan Vogel, 5 vols. (Salt Lake City: Signature Books, 1995–2003), 1:205.

indeed, to entertain one who had conversed with the Father and the Son.[11]

On another occasion Edward wrote of the Prophet speaking:

> Let me as a living witness speak. . . . With uplifted hand he [Joseph Smith] said: "I am a witness that there is a God, for I saw Him in open day, while praying in a silent grove, in the spring of 1820." He further testified that God, the Eternal Father, pointing to a separate personage, in the likeness of Himself, said: "This is my Beloved Son hear ye Him." O how these words thrilled my entire system, and filled me with joy unspeakable to behold one who, like Paul the apostle of olden time, could with boldness testify that he had been in the presence of Jesus Christ![12]

In still another recollection, Edward related more of the details of Joseph's vision: "The Prophet related [that] a bright light began to shine around him (like unto Paul's vision) the brightness of which at first alarmed him, but his fear was soon dispelled by the voice of the Father introducing His Only Begotten Son to him, who spoke to the young man, and instructed him."[13]

Joseph Curtis, also from Michigan, attended some of the same meetings that Edward Stevenson attended. Curtis, who later joined the Church, recalled of Joseph's testimony, "He [Joseph Smith] went [into the Grove] with a determinatio[n] . . . to enquire of the lord himself after some strugle

---

11. Edward Stevenson, *Reminiscences of Joseph, the Prophet, and the Coming Forth of the Book of Mormon* (Salt Lake City: Edward Stevenson, 1893), 4–5.

12. Edward Stevenson, "In Early Days: The Home of My Boyhood," *Juvenile Instructor* 29, no. 14 (July 15, 1894): 443–44.

13. Edward Stevenson, "The Three Witnesses to the Book of Mormon," in *Millennial Star* 48, no. 22 (May 31, 1886): 341.

the Lord manifested to him that the different sects were [w]rong also that the Lord had a great work for him to do."[14]

A highly celebrated event occurred when Joseph related the First Vision to Matthias (or Joshua), a Jewish minister who visited Joseph in Kirtland in 1835. Joseph's scribe wrote the account and stated that the Prophet's words were "nearly as follows":

> I retired to the silent grove and there bowed down before the Lord. . . . I called on the Lord in mighty prayer. A pillar of fire appeared above my head; which presently rested down upon me, and filled me with unspeakable joy. A personage appeared in the midst of this pillar of flame, which was spread all around and yet nothing consumed. Another personage soon appeared like unto the first: he said unto me thy sins are forgiven thee. He testified also unto me that Jesus Christ is the Son of God. I saw many angels in this vision.[15]

Joseph related his vision to other visitors to Kirtland. One visitor, Erastus Holmes, had been a member of the Methodist Church and was excommunicated for receiving Mormon elders into his house. Joseph recorded Holmes's visit: "This afternoon, Erastus Holmes, of Newbury, Ohio, called on me. . . .

"I . . . gave him a brief relation of my experience . . . up to the time I received my first vision, which was when I was about fourteen years old."[16]

---

14. Joseph Curtis, "History of Joseph Curtis son of Nahum & Millicent Curtis Which was born Dec. 24, 1818 in the town of [-] Erie Co. Penn.," circa 1881, 5–6, Church History Library, The Church of Jesus Christ of Latter-day Saints, Salt Lake City, Utah, hereafter cited as Church History Library, in Vogel, *Early Mormon Documents*, 1:36.

15. Dean C. Jessee, "The Early Accounts of Joseph Smith's First Vision," *BYU Studies* 9, no. 3 (Spring 1969): 284.

16. Joseph Smith, *History of The Church of Jesus Christ of Latter-day Saints*, ed. B. H. Roberts, 7 vols., 2d ed. rev. (Salt Lake City: The Church of Jesus Christ of Latter-day Saints, 1932–51), 2:312; Dean C. Jessee, Mark Ashurst-McGee, and Richard L. Jensen, eds., *Journals, 1832–1839*, vol. 1 of the

Parley P. Pratt wrote to members of the Church in Canada in November 1836. He noted that Joseph Smith, at the pulpit in the Kirtland Temple, told the congregation details of his vision. He recorded, "Br. S[mith] gave the history of these things relating many particulars of the manner of his first vissions &c."[17]

John Alger, a young boy, provides another Kirtland recollection of Joseph speaking of his vision. John lived in Kirtland and related the following in a talk he gave in 1893. A listener was impressed and recorded John's message: "Br. John Alger said . . . he heard the Prophet Joseph relate his vision of seeing The Father and the Son, That God . . . said 'Joseph this is my beloved Son hear him.' . . . He immediately saw the Savior."[18]

During the Kirtland years many of Joseph's associates heard him relate details of his First Vision. Orson Pratt, who boarded with Joseph in Kirtland, said of the First Vision, "I have often heard him relate it."[19]

John Taylor, who became the third president of the Church, met Joseph in Kirtland in 1837. He later said, "I can tell you what he told me about it. . . . He went to the Lord. . . . and asked him, and the Lord revealed himself to him together with his Son Jesus, and, pointing to the latter, said: 'This is my beloved Son, hear him.'"[20]

These accounts attest to the fact that while in Kirtland, Joseph wanted the world to know that the Father and the Son personally opened a new

Journals series of *The Joseph Smith Papers,* edited by Dean C. Jessee, Ronald K. Esplin, and Richard Lyman Bushman (Salt Lake City: Church Historian's Press, 2008), 1:100.

17. Parley P. Pratt to the Elders and Brethren of The Church of Latter Day Saints in Canada, November 27, 1836, John Taylor Papers, Manuscript, Church History Library, in Vogel, *Early Mormon Documents,* 1:207.

18. *Diary of Charles Lowell Walker,* ed. A. Karl Larson and Katherine Miles Larson, 2 vols. (Logan: Utah State University Press, 1980), 2:755–56, in Vogel, *Early Mormon Documents,* 1:208.

19. Orson Pratt, in *Journal of Discourses,* 26 vols. (London: Latter-day Saints' Book Depot, 1854–86), 7:220.

20. John Taylor, in *Journal of Discourses,* 21:161.

gospel dispensation. The young boy's vision in this day and age would change the Christian world's concept of Deity.

Oliver Cowdery's Visions of the Almighty

Oliver Cowdery arrived in Ohio in November 1830. While in New York, Oliver saw the Savior in vision as he was being prepared to assist Joseph Smith in the process of translating the Book of Mormon. Joseph described Oliver's vision, saying,

> [The] Lord appeared unto a young man by the name of Oliver Cowd[e]ry and shewed unto him the plates in a vision and also the truth of the work and what the Lord was about to do through me his unworthy Servant therefore he was desirous to come and write for me. . . . I cried unto the Lord that he would provide for me to accomplish the work whereunto he had commanded me. [21]

In December 1830 an Ohio newspaper reported that Oliver publicly testified that he experienced a vision of Christ. "Mr. Oliver Cowdry [Cowdery] has his commission directly from the God of Heaven. . . . He has personally conversed [with Jesus Christ]." [22]

Oliver also heard Christ's voice in the spring of 1829 when John the Baptist ordained him and Joseph to the Aaronic Priesthood. In 1834, Oliver wrote an article for the Church newspaper in Kirtland, in which he publicly bore colorful testimony of what he termed "the vision of the Almighty." He shared interesting details for the world to see: "The Lord . . . condescended to manifest to us his will. On a sudden, as from the midst of eternity, the

---

21. Davidson, Whittaker, Ashurst-McGee, and Jensen, *Histories*, 1:16.

22. "The Book of Mormon," *Painesville [Ohio] Telegraph*, December 7, 1830, 3. The newspaper reporter could have confused Oliver's accounts of the vision of Christ with accounts of when Oliver just heard His voice. The reference to "conversed" could pertain to Oliver's hearing the Lord's voice on two prior occasions.

voice of the Redeemer spake peace to us. . . . Our eyes beheld—our ears heard. . . . We were rapt in the vision of the Almighty! Where was room for doubt? No where: uncertainty had fled, doubt had sunk, no more to rise."[23]

On another occasion while in Kirtland, Oliver reflected:

> One word from the mouth of the Savior, from the bosom of eternity, strikes [everything] into insignificance, and blots it forever from the mind! . . . The certainty that we heard the voice of Jesus, and the truth unsullied as it flowed from a pure personage, dictated by the will of God, is to me, past description, and I shall ever look upon this expression of the Savior's goodness with wonder and thanksgiving while I am permitted to tarry, and in those mansions where perfection dwells and sin never comes, I hope to adore in that DAY which shall never cease![24]

In 1835, Oliver testified simply of this same event, "We . . . called upon the name of the Lord, and he answered us out of the heavens."[25] Edward Stevenson, who met Oliver in 1834, said, "I have often heard him bear a faithful testimony."[26]

The Three Witnesses Testify of the Lord's Voice

During the Ohio period the Three Witnesses of the Book of Mormon— Oliver Cowdery, David Whitmer, and Martin Harris—frequently

---

23. Oliver Cowdery, letter in *Messenger and Advocate* 1, no. 2 (November 1834): 15.

24. Cowdery, letter in *Messenger and Advocate* 1, no. 2 (November 1834): 16.

25. This statement by Oliver Cowdery was recorded October 2, 1835, in the Patriarchal Blessing book of Joseph Smith Sen., in Joseph F. Smith Jr. [Joseph Fielding Smith], "Restoration of the Melchizedek Priesthood," *Improvement Era* 7 (October 1904): 942.

26. Life sketch in *[Salt Lake City, Utah] Deseret News*, January 28, 1897, repr., "Elder Edward Stevenson," in *Millennial Star* 59 (February 18, 1897): 108.

reaffirmed their printed testimonies as recorded in every Book of Mormon.[27] In their formal statement the witnesses attest with their signatures that they heard the voice of God declare to them that the plates "have been translated by the gift and power of God." They also testified that "the voice of the Lord commanded us that we should bear record of it."[28]

Certainly the most impressive and formal confirmation of their testimony occurred during a conference in Orange, Ohio, in October 1831, near Kirtland. The Three Witnesses stood in front of possibly one hundred people and reaffirmed their written testimony. Luke Johnson, who attended this conference, recalled the impressive sight when the Three Witnesses along with the Eight Witnesses, "with uplifted hands, bore their solemn testimony to the truth of that book, as did also the Prophet Joseph."[29]

In Ohio, Oliver, David, and Martin frequently testified to large groups of hearing the Lord's voice when they were permitted to see the gold plates in New York. Ezra Booth, a former Methodist minister, wrote of their testimony: "You have probably read the testimony of the three witnesses. . . . These witnesses testify, that . . . the voice of God declared it to be a Divine Record. To this they frequently testify, in the presence of large congregations."[30]

Rebecca Swain Williams, wife of Frederick G. Williams, frequently associated with Oliver Cowdery, David Whitmer, and Martin Harris in Kirtland and knew them well. She wrote to her non-Mormon father, Isaac Swain, in June 1834, imploring him to accept the testimony of the Three Witnesses relative to the Book of Mormon. In her letter, she stated, "I have heard the same story . . . from the three witnesses themselves. I heard them

---

27. See "Testimony of the Three Witnesses" in the introduction of the Book of Mormon.

28. See 157n2.

29. "History of Luke Johnson: By Himself," *Millennial Star* 26 (December 31, 1864): 835.

30. Ezra Booth to Ira Eddy, October 24, 1831, "Mormonism—No. III," *[Ravenna] Ohio Star* 2 (October 27, 1831): 3.

declare [their testimonies] in public. . . . They were men of good character and their word is believed."[31]

Other accounts affirm the fact that the Three Witnesses bore testimonies separately. For example, Luman Shurtliff, an Ohio convert, writes in his journal that he walked some distance to spend an afternoon with David Whitmer:

> Mr. Daton [Dayton] kindly offered to go with me to Brother David Whitmer and give me an introduction to him. As all of the higher officers were absent, I thought this would be my best way of learning what I wanted to know, and as Mr. Whitmer was one of the witnesses of the Book of Mormon, I thought I could learn something.
>
> We walked to Mr. Whitmer's. I got the necessary introduction and took dinner and spent the afternoon in hearing him relate things about the angel showing him the plates from which the Book of Mormon was translated. I also asked him all the questions I had a wish to ask.[32]

Martin Harris was the last witness to certify his testimony in Kirtland. In 1869, William Homer, a missionary related to Martin through marriage, visited Kirtland and recorded Martin's still-impressive testimony. As Martin and Homer stood together in the Kirtland Temple, the following exchange occurred:

> "Do you still believe . . . that Joseph Smith was a prophet?" . . . A changed old man stood before me. . . . It was a man with a message, a man with a noble conviction

---

31. Rebecca Swain Williams to Isaac Swain, June 4, 1834, in Nancy Clement Williams, *After One Hundred Years!* (Independence, Mo.: Zion's Printing & Publishing Company, 1951), 200.

32. Luman Andros Shurtliff, Autobiography, typescript, 24, L. Tom Perry Special Collections, Harold B. Lee Library, Brigham Young University, Provo, Utah.

in his heart, a man inspired of God and endowed with divine knowledge. Through the broken window of the Temple shone the winter sun, clear and radiant.

"Young man," answered Martin Harris with impressiveness, "Do I believe it! Do you see the sun shining! Just as surely as the sun is shining on us and gives us light, and the [moon] and stars give us light by night, just as surely as the breath of life sustains us, so surely do I know that Joseph Smith was a true prophet of God, chosen of God to open the last dispensation of the fulness of times; so surely do I know that the Book of Mormon was divinely translated. I saw the plates; I saw the Angel; I heard the voice of God. . . . I might as well doubt my own existence as to doubt . . . the divine calling of Joseph Smith." . . . A halo seemed to encircle him. A divine fire glowed in his eyes. His voice throbbed with the sincerity and the conviction of his message.[33]

The witnesses were not always valiant in Church activity, but their testimonies of the Savior and the Book of Mormon—what they had heard and seen—never wavered. They were witnesses of the sacred, and they remained true to that testimony.

---

33. William Harrison Homer, "The Passing of Martin Harris," *Improvement Era* 29 (March 1926): 469–70.

CHAPTER 9

VISIONS OF DEITY ASSOCIATED
WITH CHURCH STRUCTURE

Brothers and Sisters, the Saviour has been in your midst.
I want you to remember it.
—JOSEPH SMITH

From 1830 to 1833 at least five visions or visitations of the Savior were received during critical events or meetings held as Church organization was being put in place. Three of these visitations included God the Father. The Lord bestowed these visions not only to Joseph Smith but also to many others. Seven witnesses are identified by name; in addition, others are cited in various accounts. As will be noted, those who became witnesses to the resurrected Christ during this period could number as many as fifteen. In addition, these visions resulted in about sixty secondary witnesses who would have observed the outward manifestations associated with them.

Visions Begin with Baptisms and Meetings

The Chagrin River was the site of the earliest baptisms in Kirtland. Philo Dibble, one of Ohio's first converts, reported heavenly manifestations. He wrote: "There were many signs and wonders seen in the heavens above and in the earth beneath in the region of Kirtland, both by Saints and strangers. A pillar of light was seen every evening for more than a month hovering over the place where we did our baptizing."[1]

John Murdock remembered that people saw visions and even the Savior. He recorded similar events while he was being confirmed a member of the Church: "The Spirit rested on me as it never did before and others said they saw the Lord, and had visions."[2] This heavenly presence reassured these newly baptized Saints that Christ lives and leads them in His Church.

Christ was present in a meeting held after the Prophet's family arrived in Kirtland in 1831. His presence was made known to Joseph Smith and Martin Harris.[3] Mary Elizabeth Lightner, thirteen years old at the time, attended and made a record of the meeting.[4] She implied that Joseph might have seen the Savior, dramatically recalling, "Joseph began talking. Suddenly he stopped and seemed almost transfixed. He was looking ahead into space and his face outshone the candle that was on the shelf back of him. . . . He looked as though a searchlight was inside his face shining through every pore."[5] Mary later said that this experience was so vivid she could never forget it. Seventy-four years later, in 1905, she electrified an audience of prospective missionaries in Provo, Utah, when she told them:

1. "Philo Dibble's Narrative," in *Four Faith Promoting Classics* (Salt Lake City: Bookcraft, 1968), 78.

2. John Murdock, "A Brief Synopsis of the Life of John Murdock: Taken from an Abridged Record of His Journal," 11, L. Tom Perry Special Collections, Harold B. Lee Library, Brigham Young University, Provo, Utah; hereafter cited as BYU Special Collections.

3. Martin Harris lived longer in Kirtland than did the other Book of Mormon witnesses. He moved from New York in 1831, and except for brief visits to Missouri and his former home in Palmyra, New York, he remained in Kirtland until 1870, when he moved to Utah.

4. Mary Elizabeth Rollins Lightner identified this meeting as the first meeting the Prophet held in Kirtland. Joseph arrived about February 1, 1831, but the meeting could not have occurred before May because, she said, the whole Smith family attended. Lucy Mack Smith, William Smith, and others arrived in May from New York.

5. "Life Story of Mary Elizabeth Rollins Lightner," in *Our Pioneer Heritage,* comp. Kate B. Carter, 20 vols. (Salt Lake City: Daughters of Utah Pioneers, 1958–77), 5:306.

I am the only living witness who was at the first meeting that the Prophet [Joseph Smith] held in Kirtland. . . .

. . . Joseph and Martin Harris came in. Joseph looked around very solemnly. It was the first time some of them had ever seen him.

Said he, "There are enough here to hold a little meeting." They got a board and put it across two chairs to make seats. Martin Harris sat on a little box at Joseph's feet. They sang and prayed. Joseph got up and began to speak to us. As he began to speak very solemnly and very earnestly, all at once his countenance changed and he stood mute.[6]

He looked over the congregation as if to pierce every heart. He said, "Do you know who has been in your midst this night?" One of the Smith family said, "An angel of the Lord." . . . Martin Harris . . . said, "I know, it was our Lord and Saviour, Jesus Christ." Joseph put his hand on Martin's head and answered, "Martin, God revealed that to you. Yes, Brothers and Sisters, the Saviour has been in your midst. I want you to remember it. He cast a veil over your eyes for you could not endure to look upon Him."[7]

Christ's visit must have comforted Joseph and the other Saints from New York. They were reassured that their new church was truly the restored Church of Jesus Christ. After they obeyed the Lord by leaving their homes, possessions, and some family members, and making severe sacrifices to come to Ohio, the Lord visibly manifested that they were about His work. He had not forgotten them.

---

6. Mary Elizabeth Lightner, typescript, April 14, 1905, 1, BYU Special Collections.

7. Carter, "Mary Elizabeth Rollins Lightner," 5:306.

Visions As First High Priests Are Ordained

During the first Kirtland Church conference in June 1831, the Father and the Son first manifested themselves together in Kirtland to Joseph Smith, Lyman Wight, and Harvey Whitlock. This vision came as the priesthood gathered in the log schoolhouse on the Isaac Morley farm to ordain the high priests. According to Levi Hancock, as the meeting began, Joseph "looked at Lyman [Wight] and said to him, 'You shall see the Lord' . . . and laid his hands upon him and blessed him with the visions of heaven."[8]

Philo Dibble, who was present, recorded, "Joseph Smith . . . said that before the conference closed there were those present who should see the heavens open and bear record of the coming of the Son of Man, and that the man of sin should be revealed."[9]

The man of sin (the adversary) attempted to stop the proceedings as the ordinations began. He seized several men, including Harvey Whitlock. Exercising the power of his priesthood, Joseph cast Satan out of the meeting. After he departed, a glorious vision of the Father and the Son—reminiscent of the Prophet's Sacred Grove experience—burst upon them. Levi Hancock recalled, "Joseph Smith then stepped out on the floor and said, 'I now see God, and Jesus Christ at his right hand, let them [enemies] kill me, I should not feel death as I am now.'"[10]

Lyman Wight, who later became a member of the Quorum of the Twelve, saw the same vision. He was the first high priest ordained in the restored Church. John Whitmer, the recently called Church historian, recorded, "The Spirit . . . fell upon Lyman, and he . . . saw the he[a]vens opened, and the Son of man sitting on the right hand of the Father. Making intercession for his brethren. the Saints."[11]

---

8. Levi Hancock, Autobiography, copied by Clara E. H. Lloyd, typescript, 33, BYU Special Collections.

9. Philo Dibble, "Recollections of the Prophet Joseph Smith," *Juvenile Instructor* 27 (May 15, 1892): 303.

10. Hancock, Autobiography, 33.

11. *From Historian to Dissident: The Book of John Whitmer,* ed. Bruce N. Westergren (Salt Lake City:

Philo wrote, "Lyman Wight stepped into the middle of the room and bore record of the coming of the Son of Man."[12] Relying on accounts of others, George A. Smith, longtime Church historian and Apostle, stated, "Lyman Wight bore testimony that he saw the face of the Savior."[13]

Harvey Whitlock was the third person to witness this remarkable vision. Zebedee Coltrin remembered that "Joseph rebuked the power that had seized him [Harvey Whitlock], and it left him, and he testified, as Lyman had done, that he saw the heavens open, and Jesus . . . on the right hand of the Father."[14]

Philo recorded even more details:

> Harvey Whitlock stepped into the middle of the room with his arms crossed, bound by the power of Satan. . . .
>
> Joseph then approached Harvey and asked him if he believed in God. Then we saw a change in Harvey. He also bore record of the opening of the heavens and of the coming of the Son of Man, precisely as Lyman Wight had done.[15]

In addition to these three men, others may have seen this vision. Without specifying names, George A. Smith simply stated that "others had visions."[16] The visions of the Father and the Son certified heaven's approbation at the bestowal of priesthood authority on this occasion.

Signature Books, 1995), 69.

12. Dibble, "Recollections," 303.

13. George A. Smith, in *Journal of Discourses,* 26 vols. (London: Latter-day Saints' Book Depot, 1854–86), 11:4.

14. Zebedee Coltrin, address at a meeting of high priests in Spanish Fork, Utah, February 5, 1878, in *They Knew the Prophet,* ed. Hyrum L. Andrus and Helen Mae Andrus (Salt Lake City: Deseret Book, 1999), 30.

15. Dibble, "Recollections," 303.

16. Smith, in *Journal of Discourses,* 11:4.

Christ Calls Newel K. Whitney as Bishop

On December 4, 1831, the Lord said, "And now, verily I say unto you, my servant Newel K. Whitney is the man who shall be appointed and ordained unto this power [as bishop]. This is the will of the Lord your God, your Redeemer. Even so. Amen."[17] When Joseph Smith extended the call, Newel was hesitant. Orson F. Whitney, Newel's son, relates that the Lord confirmed the call with His own voice to Newel:

> Though in natural gifts few men were better quali-
> fied for such a position, he . . . distrusted his ability. . . . In
> his perplexity he appealed to the prophet: "I cannot see
> a Bishop in myself, Brother Joseph; but if you say it's the
> Lord's will, I'll try." "You need not take my word alone,"
> answered the Prophet, kindly, "Go and ask Father for your-
> self." Newel felt the force of this mild rebuke, but deter-
> mined to do as he was advised. His humble, heartfelt prayer
> was answered. In the silence of night and the solitude of his
> chamber he heard a voice from heaven: "Thy strength is in
> me." The words were few and simple, but they had a world
> of meaning. His doubts were dispelled like the dew before
> the dawn. He straightway sought the Prophet, told him he
> was satisfied, and was willing to accept the office to which
> he had been called.[18]

Newel and his wife, Elizabeth Ann, had a prior experience with a heavenly vision and a celestial voice. Before Joseph came to Kirtland, they were praying. Elizabeth described the vision and voice that came to them:

---

17. Doctrine & Covenants 72:8.

18. Andrew Jenson, *Latter-day Saint Biographical Encyclopedia,* 4 vols. (Salt Lake City: Andrew Jenson History Company, 1901–36; repr., Salt Lake City: Western Epics, 1971), 1:224.

It was midnight—my husband and I were in our house at Kirtland, praying to the Father to be shown the way when the Spirit rested upon us and a cloud overshadowed the house. It was as though we were out of doors. The house passed away from our vision. We were not conscious of anything but the presence of the spirit and the cloud that was over us. We were wrapped in the cloud. A solemn awe pervaded us. We saw the cloud and felt the Spirit of the Lord. Then we heard a voice out of the cloud saying, "Prepare to receive the word of the Lord, for it is coming." At this we marveled greatly, but from that moment we knew that the word of the Lord was coming to Kirtland.[19]

On another occasion during a meeting at the Whitney home, Philo Dibble tells of another great vision. He said, "The heavens were opened and the Spirit of God filled the house and rested upon all the congregation to overflowing, little children not excepted. Prophesying and singing the songs of Zion were indulged in until morning."[20]

Visions at the Organization of the First Presidency

Unprecedented visions came on March 18, 1833—the day Joseph ordained Sidney Rigdon and Fredrick G. Williams as his counselors in the First Presidency of the Church. The visions occurred during a meeting of the School of the Prophets in the Whitney store. Specific accounts identify that in addition to Joseph Smith, John Murdock and Zebedee Coltrin also saw the Savior that day.[21] Beyond the vision of the Savior, Zebedee saw God

---

19. Jenson, *Latter-day Saint Biographical Encyclopedia,* 1:223.

20. Dibble, "Narrative," 77–78.

21. The detailed account of the First Presidency organizational meeting is found in Joseph Smith, *History of The Church of Jesus Christ of Latter-day Saints,* ed. B. H. Roberts, 7 vols., 2d ed. rev. (Salt Lake City: The Church of Jesus Christ of Latter-day Saints, 1932–51), 1:334–35. John Murdock's

the Father. Written accounts verify that he spoke of this vision on at least seven occasions.[22] Joseph Smith said that many of the probable twenty or so persons who attended the school also saw the Savior and many other things. Therefore, it is possible to conjecture that at least three others also saw these visions. Joseph formally recorded the events of this meeting in which the visions took place:

> Great joy and satisfaction continually beamed in the countenances of the School of the Prophets, and the Saints, on account of the things revealed, and our progress in the knowledge of God. The High Priests assembled in the school room of the Prophets, and were organized according to revelation; prayer by Sidney Rigdon. . . .
>
> . . . I laid my hands on Brothers Sidney and Frederick, and ordained them to take part with me in holding the keys of this last kingdom, and to assist in the Presidency of the High Priesthood, as my Counselors; after which I . . . gave much instruction . . . with a promise that the pure in heart should see a heavenly vision; and after remaining a short

---

and Zebedee Coltrin's accounts evidently both came from this meeting. Several facts that place these accounts at this meeting are as follows: (1) The meeting was apparently a meeting of the School of the Prophets. Joseph Smith indicated it was for high priests (terminology used for the 1833 School of the Prophets). John Murdock and Zebedee Coltrin were both high priests and members of the school, which was "organized according to revelation," apparently a reference to Doctrine & Covenants 88, which organized the school (*History of the Church,* 1:334). (2) This meeting essentially fits the time frame given by John and Zebedee. (3) Their accounts fit Joseph Smith's description of the meeting. (4) No other meeting during this time indicates visions of Deity. (5) Joseph's account as well as John's and Zebedee's all confirm Joseph's promise that they would see a vision. (6) A short time was spent in prayer prior to the vision; John called it a "prayer meeting."

22. Zebedee Coltrin gave his testimony five times in meetings of high priests from September 1880 to June 1887 and twice at the School of Prophets in Salt Lake City in October 1883 at John Taylor's invitation. One week following this testimony, on October 12, 1883, Zebedee was admitted to the school by vote. Four brethren who knew him and had confidence in him in Kirtland were present— John Taylor, Wilford Woodruff, Lorenzo Snow, and Erastus Snow. On October 11, 1883, Wilford Woodruff recorded in his journal the Coltrin account of seeing both the Father and the Son.

time in secret prayer, the promise was verified; for many present had the eyes of their understanding opened by the Spirit of God, so as to behold many things. . . . Many of the brethren saw a heavenly vision of the Savior, and concourses of angels, and many other things, of which each one has a record of what he saw.[23]

That Joseph Smith saw the Savior on this stunning day of visions is demonstrated by his descriptive conversations. First, Joseph promised a vision of the Lord to those who could "humble" themselves and "exercise strong faith."[24] Second, after Christ appeared, Joseph asked if they saw Him.[25] Third, Joseph then identified Him, saying, "That is Jesus."[26]

John Murdock as a Witness

John Murdock was one of the witnesses whose record is preserved. John recorded one of the most complete descriptions of Christ:

> We had a number of prayer meetings, in the Prophet's Chamber, in which we obtained great blessings. In one of those Meetings [School of the Prophets] the Prophet told us, if we could humble ourselves before God, and exercise strong faith, we should see the face of the Lord. And about midday, the visions of my mind were opened, and the eyes of my understanding were enlightened, and I saw the form of a man, most lovely! The visage of his face was sound and fair as the sun. His hair, a bright silver grey, curled in most

---

23. *History of the Church*, 1:334–35.

24. John Murdock, "John Murdock Journal, 1792–1871," typescript, BYU Special Collections, 14.

25. Zebedee Coltrin, in *Salt Lake School of the Prophets Minute Book, 1883* (Salt Lake City: Pioneer Press, 1992), 54.

26. Coltrin, in *Minute Book*, 54.

majestic form, His eyes, a keen penetrating blue, and the skin of his neck a most beautiful white, and He was covered from the neck to the feet with a loose garment, pure white, whiter than any garment I have ever before seen. His countenance was most penetrating, and yet most lovely! And while I was endeavoring to comprehend the whole personage, from head to feet, it slipped from me, and the Vision was closed up. But it left on my mind the impression of love, for months, that I never before felt, to that degree![27]

Later in life, John abridged his journal and further identified that the personage he saw in his vision was Christ. He elaborated, "I . . . was with Bro. Joseph a part of the winter receiving instruction . . . and beheld the face of the Lord according to the promise and prayer of the Prophet."[28]

Similarities to the Mount of Transfiguration

The vision of the Father and the Son, as the First Presidency was being fully organized, is consistent with the presence of the Father and the Son during the past dispensation of Christ and the Apostles. Just as Peter, James, and John ascended the Mount of Transfiguration to receive Christ's instructions and the keys of their ministry, so did Sidney Rigdon and Fredrick G. Williams ascend to the upper schoolroom of the Whitney store, where Joseph instructed and ordained them "to take part with him in holding the keys of this last kingdom."[29] Just as on the Mount of Transfiguration, where God the Father and Jesus Christ manifested themselves in celestial glory, so did They manifest themselves in the upper schoolroom of the Whitney

---

27. Murdock, "Brief Synopsis," 13–14.

28. Murdock, "John Murdock Journal," 163–64.

29. *History of the Church*, 3:387; 1:334.

store. The Apostles on the mount said of Christ, "His face did shine as the sun, and his raiment was white as the light."[30]

In the New Testament, Mark describes Christ's appearance on the mount: "And his raiment became shining, exceeding white, as snow; so white as no fuller on earth could whiten them."[31] In the Whitney store schoolroom vision, John Murdock noted the Savior's face and clothing just as Mark described: "His face was . . . fair as the sun," and His garment was "pure white, whiter than any garment I have ever before seen."[32] John Murdock indicated that he noticed that the Savior's eyes were blue. In one of Joseph Smith's accounts of the First Vision, he told Alexander Neibaur that the Savior had blue eyes.[33]

By adding this vision to the vision of Moses, Elias, and Elijah in the Kirtland Temple, Kirtland becomes a latter-day counterpart of the ancient Mount of Transfiguration.

Zebedee Coltrin as a Witness

Another preserved record is that of Zebedee Coltrin. Zebedee was one of the initial seven presidents of the Seventy. He was blessed by the First Presidency to have "heavenly visions and the ministry of Angels."[34] Leaders of the Church have always held Zebedee in high regard. For example, President George Albert Smith paid tribute to Zebedee in the October 1934 general conference. He named him from the pulpit as one of forty-eight leaders in the first one hundred years who were "some of the greatest men that have ever lived upon the earth . . . who from this pulpit have instructed

---

30. Matthew 17:2.

31. JST, Mark 9:2.

32. Murdock, "Brief Synopsis," 14.

33. Alexander Neibaur, Autobiography, May 24, 1844, Church History Library, The Church of Jesus Christ of Latter-day Saints, Salt Lake City, Utah, 15; hereafter cited as Church History Library.

34. Kirtland Council Minute Book, typescript by Lyndon W. Cook, 1978, Church History Library, 178.

the Latter-day Saints in the years gone by . . . men that we love and venerate. . . . They were super-men that God called to lead . . . who have devoted themselves to the Church until the Lord summoned them home."[35]

On March 18, 1833, Zebedee saw the Savior in the School of the Prophets in the Whitney store and testified:

> At one of these meetings after the organization of the school . . . when we were all together, Joseph having given instructions, and while engaged in silent prayer, kneeling, . . . each one praying in silence, no one whispered above his breath, [I saw] a personage . . . Joseph asked if we saw him. I saw him and supposed the others did, and Joseph answered that is Jesus, the Son of God, our elder brother.[36]

Then, speaking of seeing a vision of God the Father, Zebedee continued:

> Afterward Joseph told us to resume our former position in prayer, which we did. Another person came . . . He was surrounded as with a flame of fire. I experienced a sensation that it might destroy the tabernacle as it was of consuming fire of great brightness. The Prophet Joseph said this was the Father of our Lord Jesus Christ.[37]

President John Taylor, who knew Zebedee in Kirtland, invited him in 1883 to share his experiences with the School of the Prophets in Salt Lake City. Concluding his testimony to the General Authorities gathered in the school, Zebedee testified, "I saw Him." The brethren asked Zebedee about the clothing the Father wore. Brother Coltrin said:

---

35. George Albert Smith, in Conference Report, October 1934, 52.

36. Coltrin, in *Minute Book,* 54.

37. Coltrin, in *Minute Book,* 54.

I did not discover His clothing for He was surrounded as with a flame of fire, which was so brilliant that I could not discover anything else but His person. I saw His hands, His legs, His feet, His eyes, nose, mouth, head and body in the shape and form of a perfect man. . . . This appearance was so grand and overwhelming that it seemed I should melt down in His presence, and the sensation was so powerful that it thrilled through my whole system and I felt it in the marrow of my bones.[38]

Then, in October 1883 in Salt Lake City, Zebedee concluded his testimony by repeating the initial charge that Joseph Smith gave in 1833 to those at the Kirtland School of the Prophets, most of whom were later ordained as General Authorities. Joseph told them, "Brethren, now you are prepared to be the apostles[39] of Jesus Christ, for you have seen both the Father and the Son and know that They exist and that They are two separate personages."[40]

That Joseph Smith also saw God the Father at this time is verified by Zebedee's account of Joseph's conversations. First, after the Savior appeared, Joseph told them to "resume our former position in prayer." Next, after the Father appeared, Joseph identified whom they had seen. "Joseph said this was the Father of our Lord Jesus Christ," Zebedee said.[41] Finally, Joseph confirmed the vision of both members of the Godhead, "Brethren, . . . you have seen both the Father and the Son."[42]

---

38. Coltrin, in *Minute Book,* 54.

39. The word *apostles* here is used in a general priesthood sense of representing the Lord instead of in the administrative sense of being a member of the Quorum of the Twelve Apostles. The Lord used the word in this general sense in Doctrine & Covenants 84:63 when He told high priests, "You are mine apostles, even God's high priests." This vision took place almost two years before the Quorum of the Twelve Apostles was formed.

40. Coltrin, in *Minute Book,* 54–55.

41. Coltrin, in *Minute Book,* 54.

42. Coltrin, in *Minute Book,* 54–55.

Christ Seen in Vision When First Patriarchal
Blessings Are Given

Joseph Smith saw Christ in vision on December 18, 1833, at the John Johnson Inn in Kirtland. Joseph received the vision as he gave a patriarchal blessing to his father, Joseph Smith Sr.[43] Oliver Cowdery, who recorded the blessing, emphasized that Joseph saw the vision as he was blessing his father. In fact, Oliver repeated it twice. He wrote, "Thus spake the Seer, and these are the words which fell from his lips, while the visions of the Almighty were open to his view,"[44] and "These blessings were given by vision and the spirit of prophecy."[45]

In the vision, Joseph saw Adam and his posterity at Adam-ondi-Ahman. While viewing the vision, he described the scene as part of the blessing to his father:

> Three years previous to the death of Adam, he called Seth, Enos, Cainan, Mahalaleel, Jared, Enoch and Methuselah who were high priests with the residue of his posterity who were righteous, into the valley of Adam-ondi-Ahman, and there bestowed upon them his last blessing. . . . and they rose up and blessed Adam, and called him Michael, the Prince, the Archangel.[46]

Continuing his description of the vision, Joseph said he also saw Christ in their midst: "And the Lord appeared unto them, . . . and the Lord

---

43. Oliver Cowdery recorded in the Church's first patriarchal blessing book that the first patriarchal blessings "were pronounced by Joseph Smith, Jr., the first elder and first patriarch of the Church . . . by vision and the spirit of prophecy" (Joseph Fielding Smith, *Church History and Modern Revelation*, 2 vols. [Salt Lake City: Deseret Book, 1953], 1:473).

44. Smith, *Church History and Modern Revelation*, 1:473.

45. Smith, *Church History and Modern Revelation*, 1:473.

46. Smith, *Church History and Modern Revelation*, 1:473.

administered comfort unto Adam, and said unto him: I have set thee to be at the head, a multitude of nations shall come of thee, and thou art a prince over them forever."[47]

So important was this vision to Joseph that he repeated it twice more. One year later he included it in the Doctrine and Covenants as section 107, verses 53–55. Six years later he related it to Church leaders as follows: "I saw Adam in the valley of Ah-dam-ondi-Ahman—he called together his children & blessed them with a Patriarchal blessing. The Lord appeared in their midst, & he (Adam) blessed them all, & foretold what should befall them to the latest generation."[48]

It is apparent that during this critical organizational period of the infant Church, many received a witness that Deity directed the important work in which they were involved. They also became acquainted with the nature of Deity—the God whom they worshipped. The Savior was truly no stranger in Kirtland.

---

47. Smith, *Church History and Modern Revelation*, 1:473–74.

48. *The Words of Joseph Smith*, comp. and ed. Andrew F. Ehat and Lyndon W. Cook (Provo, Utah: Brigham Young University Religious Studies Center, 1980), 9.

CHAPTER 10

CHRIST CONVERSES WITH
JOSEPH AND SIDNEY IN A VISION
OF THE ETERNITIES

I, Joseph, the prophet, in spirit beheld, Eternity sketch'd in a vision
from God, Of what was, and now is, and yet is to be.
—JOSEPH SMITH

Christ's personal guidance of Joseph and the Church reached an apex in an upper room of a rural Ohio farmhouse on February 16, 1832. A vision recorded as Doctrine and Covenants 76 is so significant and superlative that the Lord, Joseph Smith, and others referred to it as "the vision."[1] Given to Joseph Smith and Sidney Rigdon in Hiram, Ohio, the vision is possibly the most comprehensive of all Joseph's visions. The Savior's broad and lengthy firsthand tutelage assured Joseph and Sidney that the Father and His Son, Jesus Christ, created and controlled the universe. This instruction spelled out the origin and destiny of all mankind. During this vision, Christ revealed to them the most fundamental doctrine of the Church—the plan of salvation. The presence of the Father and the Son at the beginning of the vision signified to Joseph and the Saints that this

---

1. Doctrine & Covenants 76:28, 49, 113; Joseph Smith, *History of The Church of Jesus Christ of Latter-day Saints,* ed. B. H. Roberts, 7 vols., 2d ed. rev. (Salt Lake City: The Church of Jesus Christ of Latter-day Saints, 1932–51), 2:492, 505; 5:402; 6:477.

was true doctrine. It was a major departure from religious doctrines of the day, and for those who accepted it, it changed their concept of heaven.

Two presidents of the Church to whom Joseph directly taught the vision ranked its importance and effect on them. Brigham Young explained, "The vision given to Joseph Smith and Sidney Rigdon is the greatest vision I ever knew given to the children of men, incorporating more in a few pages than any other revelation I have any knowledge of."[2] Wilford Woodruff responded to this vision by saying:

> When I first read that vision it swept away a vail that had been around me all my life; it opened my understanding and shook off my shackles. There was something in it so different from the old sectarian notion—something that swept away the idea of one heaven, one hell, and that those who do not go to one place must go to the other, and that all in heaven have an equal glory, and all in hell an equal misery. There always appeared something very inconsistent connected with the doctrine of future rewards and punishments as taught by modern divines; but when I got hold of the vision, I saw more light, more consistency, and Godlike mercy and justice than I had ever seen in my life. . . .
>
> . . . The vail was taken from my eyes, and . . . I was made to comprehend that every man is rewarded according to the deeds done in the body.[3]

Joseph Smith highlighted the importance of man's eternal destiny and his need to study it. He explained:

---

2. Brigham Young, in *Journal of Discourses*, 26 vols. (London: Latter-day Saints' Book Depot, 1854–86), 8:36.

3. Wilford Woodruff, in *Journal of Discourses*, 8:265–66.

All men know that they must die. And it is important that we should understand the reasons and causes of our exposure to the vicissitudes of life and of death, and the designs and purposes of God in our coming into the world, our sufferings here, and our departure hence. What is the object of our coming into existence, then dying and falling away, to be here no more? It is but reasonable to suppose that God would reveal something in reference to the matter, and it is a subject we ought to study more than any other. We ought to study it day and night, for the world is ignorant in reference to their true condition and relation. If we have any claim on our Heavenly Father for anything, it is for knowledge on this important subject.[4]

The Vision as a Tour of the Eternities

The vision could well be viewed as a comprehensive tour of the eternities. Joseph Smith said this vision included three things: "what was, and now is, and yet is to be."[5] The vision is often referred to as a vision of the three degrees of glory, but it encompasses much more than that. Joseph said God "sketch'd" eternity for him and Sidney.[6] The vision began with key events in the premortal existence such as the premortal council, the Creation, and Satan's rebellion and expulsion. It concluded with the Savior unveiling the three degrees of glory to them.

---

4. *History of the Church*, 6:50.

5. *Times and Seasons* 4 (February 1, 1843): 82 [v. 11]. Joseph Smith rendered the vision in poetic form in 1843. These words come from verses in that poem. In his journal, he wrote, "In reply to W. W. Phelps's *Vade Mecum*, or 'Go with me' . . . I dictated an answer: [It consisted of the 'Revelation known as the Vision of the Three Glories,' Doctrine & Covenants, section lxxvi, made into verse.]" (*History of the Church*, 5:288). No matter the origin of the verses, Joseph took responsibility for them by signing his response to Phelps. For further reference, see the poem in *Times and Seasons* 4 (February 1, 1843): 82–85.

6. *Times and Seasons* 4 (February 1, 1843): 82 [v. 11].

Who Guided Joseph and Sidney on Their Celestial Tour?

None other than the Savior guided Joseph and Sidney on their celestial tour. They testified of "Jesus Christ . . . whom we saw and with whom we conversed in the heavenly vision."[7] To converse means to have a two-way conversation. Fifteen verses make reference to Joseph and Sidney hearing the Savior speak to them during the vision:

- "We conversed [with Jesus Christ] in the heavenly vision."
- "We heard the voice bearing record that he is the Only Begotten of the Father."
- "The Lord commanded us that we should write the vision."
- "Thus came the voice of the Lord unto us."
- "Thus saith the Lord concerning all those who . . . suffered themselves through the power of the devil to be overcome."
- "I say that it had been better for them never to have been born."
- "Concerning [the sons of perdition] I have said there is no forgiveness in this world nor in the world to come."
- "The voice out of the heavens bore record unto us."
- "I, the Lord, show it by vision unto many."
- "We heard the voice, saying: Write the vision."
- "We bear record—for we . . . heard."
- "The Lord commanded us to write [the vision . . . of the terrestrial]."
- "[We] heard the voice of the Lord saying: These all shall bow the knee."
- "We were commanded to write [the end of the vision]."
- "He commanded us we should not write [the mysteries of his kingdom]."[8]

---

7. Doctrine & Covenants 76:14.

8. Doctrine & Covenants 76:14–115.

How Did the Savior Teach Joseph and Sidney?

During the vision the Savior used a show-and-tell teaching technique. He instructed Joseph and Sidney by first showing them scenes from the eternal worlds and then conversing about those worlds. The two men confirmed this interpretation as they wrote, "Great and marvelous are the works of the Lord, and the mysteries of his kingdom which he showed unto us, which surpass all understanding in glory, and in might, and in dominion."[9]

Philo Dibble, one of the first Ohio converts, was present in the room. He provides an observer's viewpoint of the vision:

> Joseph would, at intervals, say: "What do I see?" as one might say while looking out the window and beholding what all in the room could not see. Then he would relate what he had seen or what he was looking at. Then Sidney replied, "I see the same." Presently Sidney would say "what do I see?" and would repeat what he had seen or was seeing, and Joseph would reply, "I see the same."
>
> This manner of conversation was repeated at short intervals to the end of the vision.[10]

While showing eternity to them, the Savior continued to interpret what they were seeing. For example, the following verses demonstrate how Christ did indeed both tell and show:

- "We beheld . . . the Son, on the right hand of the Father. . . . And we heard the voice bearing record that he is the Only Begotten of the Father."
- "We saw . . . an angel of God . . . who rebelled against the

---

9. Doctrine & Covenants 76:114.

10. Philo Dibble, "Recollections of the Prophet Joseph Smith," *Juvenile Instructor* 27 (May 15, 1892): 303–4.

Only Begotten Son. . . . And [he] was called Perdition . . . he was Lucifer, a son of the morning."

- "We saw a vision of the sufferings of those with whom [Lucifer] made war and overcame . . . thus came the voice of the Lord unto us: . . . all those who know my power, and have been made partakers thereof, and . . . deny the truth and defy my power—They are . . . sons of perdition . . . doomed to suffer the wrath of God, with the devil and his angels in eternity; . . . Yea, verily, the only ones who shall not be redeemed in the due time of the Lord."

- "We saw and heard . . . concerning them who shall come forth in the resurrection of the just. . . . These shall dwell in the presence of God and his Christ forever and ever."

- "We saw the terrestrial world. . . . These are they who died without law . . . the spirits of men kept in prison . . . Who received not the testimony of Jesus in the flesh, but afterwards received it. . . . Honorable men of the earth, who were blinded by the craftiness of men."

- "We saw the glory of the telestial. . . . These are they who received not the gospel of Christ, neither the testimony of Jesus. . . . who deny not the Holy Spirit. . . . who shall not be redeemed from the devil until the last resurrection."

- "We saw the glory and the inhabitants of the telestial world . . . and heard the voice of the Lord saying: These all shall bow the knee, and every tongue shall confess to him who sits upon the throne forever and ever. . . . They shall be servants of the Most High; but where God and Christ dwell they cannot come, worlds without end."

- "He showed unto us [the mysteries of his kingdom] . . .
  [and] commanded us we should not write [them]."[11]

Apparently telling and showing Joseph and Sidney was not sufficient for them to fully understand what the Lord wanted to convey to them. He, therefore, introduced a gift that only God could give. He opened the eyes of their understanding. Joseph and Sidney made special note of this gift: "Our understandings were enlightened, so as to see and understand the things of God."[12] This additional sense of understanding was familiar to Joseph. He already knew and relied on it. He identified this sense another way in the Kirtland Temple when Christ appeared to him in 1836. He said, "The veil was taken from our minds, and the eyes of our understanding were opened."[13]

What Did Joseph and Sidney See in the Vision?

It appears that in addition to being taught, Joseph and Sidney may have witnessed a comprehensive view of earths and planets, perhaps in some small degree that which we experience as we view stunning images from the Hubble telescope. Joseph said, "The glories of the kingdoms [were] manifested to me in the vision."[14] Seven months later the Lord revealed, "The earth and all the planets . . . are kingdoms."[15] In summarizing their vision, Joseph and Sidney wrote, "Great and marvelous are the works of the Lord, and the mysteries of his kingdom which he showed unto us, which surpass all understanding in glory, and in might, and in dominion."[16] It seems that the normally eloquent Sidney struggled for words to describe the

---

11. Doctrine & Covenants 76:20, 23, 25–26, 30–33, 38, 50, 62, 71–75, 81–85, 109–12, 114–15.

12. Doctrine & Covenants 76:12.

13. Doctrine & Covenants 110:1.

14. *History of the Church*, 5:402.

15. Doctrine & Covenants 88:43, 47.

16. Doctrine & Covenants 76:114.

magnificence of the heavenly realms as he declared to a large congregation, "It is beauty, it is heaven, it is felicity to look on."[17]

The Lord undoubtedly prepared Joseph and Sidney for these "visions of the universe" two years earlier by expanding their minds and helping them understand the vastness of space.[18] While translating the book of Moses, Joseph dictated this to Sidney, his scribe, saying, "Were it possible that man could number the particles of the earth, yea, millions of earths like this, it would not be a beginning to the number of [God's] creations."[19] Joseph had also been somewhat prepared by these words of the Lord:

> Many worlds ... have passed away. ... and innumerable are they unto man. ... The heavens, they are many, and they cannot be numbered unto man; but they are numbered unto me, for they are mine. And as one earth shall pass away, and the heavens thereof even so shall another come; and there is no end to my works, neither to my words.[20]

Joseph Smith expressed some words that give further clues as to what they saw:

- "[God's] throne is the heavens."
- "I ... beheld ... Eternity sketch'd."
- "I beheld the ... starry world."
- "As the stars are all diff'rent ... so differs the glory of these."

---

17. *Times and Seasons* 5 (May 1, 1844): 524. Elder Neal A. Maxwell characterized the splendor Joseph and Sidney may have observed in these words: "As we look at the universe, we do not see unexplained chaos or cosmic churn. ... It is like viewing a divinely choreographed, cosmic ballet—spectacular, subduing, and reassuring!" ("Our Creator's Cosmos," in *By Study and by Faith: Selections from the Religious Educator*, ed. Richard Neitzel Holzapfel and Kent P. Jackson [Provo, Utah: Brigham Young University Religious Studies Center, 2009], 48).

18. A phrase coined by Elder Neal A. Maxwell in his charge to the author, July 9, 1994.

19. Moses 7:30.

20. Moses 1:35, 37–38.

- "I beheld the terrestrial . . . which excels . . . in glory . . . light . . . [and] splendor."
- "I beheld the celestial, in glory sublime; which is the most excellent kingdom that is."
- "The stars are all different in lustre and size."[21]

The vastness of space and innumerable worlds must have been astonishing to Joseph and Sidney because astrophysicists of that day had such a limited understanding of space. Perhaps the leading early 1800s astronomer was Frederick William Herschel (1738–1822). He examined every star in the standard star charts of his day, and by 1802 he had counted only something more than 90,000 stars in the Milky Way galaxy through his 40-foot telescope, which looked like a giant cannon.[22] Joseph's understanding certainly put him at odds with experts of his day.

How Long Was the Vision?

This may have been Joseph's longest vision. Sidney Rigdon said he and Joseph sat there "for hours" enwrapped in vision.[23] One can hardly imagine how glorious this must have been to have the Savior show glorious scenes, answer questions, and instruct in the mysteries of the eternities for what could have been many hours.[24]

---

21. *Times and Seasons* 4 (February 1, 1843): 82–85 [vv. 4, 11, 58, 59, 65, 66, 69]. All statements come from Joseph Smith's poem (189n5).

22. J. C. Evans, "Frederick William Herschel (1738–1822)," Physics and Astronomy Department, George Mason University, 1995, accessed March 2012, http://physics.gmu.edu/~jevans/astr103 /CourseNotes/ECText/Bios/herschel.htm.

23. Wilford Woodruff, *Wilford Woodruff's Journal, 1833–1898,* ed. Scott G. Kenney, typescript, 9 vols. (Midvale, Utah: Signature Books, 1983–85), 2:376.

24. Another estimate of the length of the vision comes from Philo Dibble, who estimated it was about ninety minutes. Philo is not the best witness, however, because he was not in the room for the whole vision. He said he was "in the room . . . during a part of the time—probably two-thirds of the time . . . which I think was over an hour" (Dibble, "Recollections," 303–4). Sidney would be a better witness of the length because he was there the whole time.

What Was the Scope of Their Celestial Tour?

The vision contained many visions, not just one. These visions began with seeing God the Father and His Son Jesus Christ and possibly the Creation and the premortal council in Kolob.[25] The understanding of Joseph and Sidney widened far beyond the realms of this world as they "beheld round the throne, holy angels and hosts, and sanctified beings from worlds that have been."[26] Christ explained that He created and is the Savior of this and all other worlds.[27] The vision continued with a vision of the war in heaven and Lucifer being cast out of heaven, a vision of the sons of perdition, a vision of the celestial kingdom, a vision of the terrestrial kingdom, and finally, a vision of the telestial kingdom.[28] Verses 91–112 of Doctrine and Covenants 76 represent a summary and comparison of the three kingdoms of glory.

How Much of the Vision Could Joseph Teach the Church?

As Joseph and Sidney concluded recording the vision, they wrote, "He commanded us we should not write [the works of the Lord, and the mysteries of his kingdom] while we were yet in the Spirit."[29] From this, it appears that the vision, similar to the Book of Mormon, contained a sealed portion not to be revealed at that time. Joseph recorded:

Paul ascended into the third heavens, and he could

---

25. Doctrine & Covenants 76:20–27. In his poem, Joseph Smith said the righteous will be shown God's plans "from the council in Kolob, to time on the earth" (*Times and Seasons* 4 [February 1, 1843]: 82 [vv. 5–7]). Because the vision elaborates on the exalted status of Satan before the world was (D&C 76:25–27), it shows that the Lord revealed much concerning the premortal plan of God to Sidney and Joseph.

26. *Times and Seasons* 4 (February 1, 1843): 82 [v. 17].

27. Joseph wrote of this part of the vision: "By him [Christ], of him [Christ], and through him [Christ], the worlds were all made, Even all that career in the heavens so broad, Whose inhabitants, too, from the first to the last, Are sav'd by the very same Saviour of ours" (*Times and Seasons* 4 [February 1, 1843]: 83 [vv. 19–20]).

28. Doctrine & Covenants 76:25–29, 30–49, 50–70, 71–80, 81–90.

29. Doctrine & Covenants 76:114–15.

understand . . . the telestial, the terrestrial, and the celestial glories or kingdoms. . . . I could explain a hundred fold more than I ever have of the glories of the kingdoms manifested to me in the vision, were I permitted, and were the people prepared to receive them.

The Lord . . . [communicates] light and intelligence and the knowledge of his ways as they can bear it.[30]

As we study subsequent revelations and teachings of Joseph Smith, we see his statement borne out. The Lord communicates light, intelligence, and knowledge of His ways gradually as the Saints are prepared to receive them.[31] He described this progressive acquisition of knowledge as "line upon line, precept upon precept; and I will try you and prove you herewith."[32] Apparently, the Lord restricted Joseph Smith from teaching all the doctrines he received.[33] The vision could be compared to a deep well of pure water (even "living water"[34]) containing knowledge and truths from which Joseph would have gladly given the Saints to drink had he been allowed.[35] As the Saints prepared themselves to receive additional knowledge and truths, Joseph was able to draw living water from the deep well and teach them.

The Lord continued building on the base of the vision in subsequent revelations. For example, the following December the Lord revealed more details about the resurrection of the dead and the celestial, terrestrial, and

---

30. *History of the Church,* 5:402.

31. When the Lord revealed higher ordinances and principles implemented in Nauvoo, Joseph observed, "There was nothing made known to these men but what will be made known to all the Saints of the last days, so soon as they are prepared to receive, and a proper place is prepared to communicate them, even to the weakest of the Saints; therefore let the Saints be diligent . . . and wait their time with patience in all meekness, faith, perseverance unto the end" (*History of the Church,* 5:2).

32. Doctrine & Covenants 98:12.

33. Doctrine & Covenants 76:114–15.

34. Doctrine & Covenants 63:23.

35. Doctrine & Covenants 76:7, 14.

telestial kingdoms of glory.[36] He added further insight and understanding by unfolding knowledge that "the earth and all the planets. . . . are kingdoms, and any man who has seen any or the least of these hath seen God moving in his majesty and power."[37]

In July 1835, Joseph purchased the Egyptian papyrus scrolls. Through these scrolls, Christ taught Joseph even more details about the premortal life—principles of astronomy, the Creation, and the Council in Heaven. Speaking to the Saints in Nauvoo in 1843, Joseph related even more details about the resurrection, which he said he had previously "seen in vision."[38] "I actually saw men, before they had ascended from the tomb, as though they were getting up slowly. They took each other by the hand."[39] Following this comment, he said, "All your losses will be made up to you in the resurrection, provided you continue faithful. By the vision of the Almighty I have seen it."[40] It is not known what visions he was referring to, but it is possible that they were part of the visions recorded as Doctrine and Covenants 76.

In the King Follett Discourse given in 1844, some two months before his martyrdom, Joseph revealed even more specific information concerning the resurrection, heavenly kingdoms, and the second death. Probably realizing his own impending death, Joseph likely felt a sense of urgency to teach so much in so little time.

How Prepared Were the Saints to Receive the Vision?

The vision was a significant trial for members of the Church. It required a complete restructuring of their prior Christian beliefs in life after death, including the doctrine of one heaven and one hell. The Lord, knowing that

---

36. Doctrine & Covenants 88:14–32.

37. Doctrine & Covenants 88:43, 47.

38. *History of the Church,* 5:361.

39. *History of the Church,* 5:362.

40. *History of the Church,* 5:362.

this new doctrine would be a trial for the Church, commanded Joseph almost three months before that he was to "call upon the inhabitants of the earth, and bear record, and prepare the way for the commandments and revelations which are to come."[41] The Lord also warned Church members, "For he will give unto the faithful line upon line, precept upon precept; and I will try you and prove you herewith."[42]

Many members were not prepared for the trials this new doctrine and revelation would impose. Joseph Holbrook, a faithful Kirtland Saint, was called on a mission to the eastern United States. He recorded an incident in which Saints in Genesee, New York, refused to accept the vision. He said,

> On April 29 [1833], I took leave of my family for a mission to the world with brother Truman O. Angel to the east. [We] traveled 14 miles to Warsaw. On the 30th [we] traveled 26 miles. We met with the brethren of the church of Genesee, held a prayer meeting and found there was a wrong spirit with some of the brethren, the presiding elder even forbidding us to believe in the vision of Joseph Smith and Sidney Rigdon.[43]

Even strong Church leaders struggled to fully accept the new doctrine. Brigham Young was one such leader. Brigham was perhaps Joseph's most supportive follower and friend throughout the Prophet's life. Despite Brigham's loyalty to Joseph, his reaction was underwhelming at best. He publicly stated, "When the Vision came first to me . . . I did not reject it!" He then explained, "After all, my traditions were such, that . . . it was directly contrary and opposed to my former education. I said, Wait a little. . . . I could not understand it."[44]

---

41. Doctrine & Covenants 71:4.

42. Doctrine & Covenants 98:12.

43. Joseph Holbrook, Autobiography, typescript, 27, L. Tom Perry Special Collections, Harold B. Lee Library, Brigham Young University, Provo, Utah.

44. Young, in *Journal of Discourses*, 6:280–81.

On another occasion Brigham Young stated:

> When God revealed to Joseph Smith and Sidney Rigdon
> that there was a place prepared for all, according to the light they
> had received and their rejection of evil and practice of good, it
> was a great trial to many, and some apostatized because God was
> not going to send to everlasting punishment heathens and in-
> fants, but had a place of salvation, in due time, for all, and would
> bless the honest and virtuous and truthful, whether they ever
> belonged to any church or not. It was a new doctrine to this gen-
> eration, and many stumbled at it.[45]

Joseph Smith advised missionaries going to England to "remain
silent concerning the . . . vision . . . until such time as the work [is] fully
established."[46] Zealous missionaries eager to spread the newly revealed truths
of the gospel sometimes disregarded Joseph's advice, however. One case involved John Goodson, a recent Canadian convert, who sailed to England
with the first group of missionaries in 1837. Heber C. Kimball relates Elder
Goodson's violation of instructions:

> A minister by the name of Timothy R. Matthews, a
> brother-in-law to Joseph Fielding, received them very kindly,
> and invited them to preach in his church, which was accepted,
> and in it they preached several times, when a number, amongst
> whom were Mr. Matthews and his lady, believed their testi-
> mony, and the truths which they proclaimed. Mr. Matthews
> had likewise borne testimony to his congregation of the truth
> of these things, and that they were the same principles that were
> taught by the Apostles anciently; and besought his congrega-
> tion to receive the same. Forty of his members went forward

---

45. *Discourses of Brigham Young*, ed. John A. Widtsoe (Salt Lake City: Bookcraft, 1998), 390–91.
46. *History of the Church*, 2:492.

and were baptized, and the time was appointed when he was to be baptized. In the interval, however, Brother Goodson, contrary to my counsel and positive instructions, and without advising with any one, read to Mr. Matthews the vision seen by President Joseph Smith and Sidney Rigdon, which caused him to stumble, and darkness pervaded his mind; so much so, that at the time specified he did not make his appearance, but went and baptized himself in the river Ouse; and from that time he began to preach baptism for the remission of sins. He wrote to Rev. James Fielding saying that his best members had left him.[47]

The dramatic way the vision unfolded and the firm testimony not only of Joseph and Sidney but also of observing secondary witnesses in the room became important to members and nonmembers alike. The vision opened with Christ sitting on the right hand of the Father on His throne. The presence of the Father and the Son and the knowledge that Christ Himself revealed this new doctrine was a comfort and strength and built faith in members who felt challenged. No other doctrine or revelation was taught with such clarity, power, and length. Possibly, no other doctrine is more fundamental to the foundation of the Church and is, to a large extent, what differentiates the Church doctrinally from other churches of the world. This may be why the Savior used three human senses to teach these leaders. They saw with their physical eyes—He showed them the overall elements of the plan of salvation; they heard with their ears—He taught them with His voice; they felt His Spirit within them—He enlightened their understandings in a clear and comprehensive way.

Reports of the Vision Produce Ridicule and Contempt

According to Sidney Rigdon, when word of the vision spread to the community, hostility raised its ugly head. As part of the adversary's continuing

---

47. Heber C. Kimball, in Orson F. Whitney, *Life of Heber C. Kimball* (Salt Lake City: Bookcraft, 1945), 148.

effort to defeat Joseph and prevent the establishment of the Lord's kingdom, he exacted a price from Joseph and Sidney. Within five weeks, while under cover of darkness that matched the deed, a vicious mob broke into the homes where Joseph and Sidney were living. The mob dragged them from their beds and inflicted intense personal injury on both. Their injuries remained with them throughout their lives. Tragically, others suffered as well. When Joseph was dragged out of his house into the cold night, Joseph and Emma's adopted son, Joseph, was exposed to the frigid air. Joseph explained the consequences: "During the mobbing one of the twins contracted a severe cold, continued to grow worse until Friday, and then died."[48] It appears that there was a relationship between the great spiritual experiences granted to Joseph and Sidney and the subsequent onslaught inflicted by the adversary. In an 1844 Church conference talk in Nauvoo, Sidney remembered the ridicule and repercussion that resulted from the vision:

> The world being entirely ignorant of the testimony of the prophets and without knowledge of what God was about to do; treated all we said with pretended contempt, and much ridicule . . . They not only ridiculed us for what we did say in public, but threatened and inflicted much personal abuse. . . . We were obliged to retire to our secret chambers, and commune ourselves with God. . . . If we had told the people what our eyes behold this day, we should not be believed; but the rascals would have shed our blood. . . . If a mob came upon us, we had to run and hide ourselves to save our lives. . . . These were the beginning of good days; shut up in a room, eating nothing but dry johnny cake and buttermilk; every man who had a little farm, or clothes, sold them and distributed what he had among the rest, and did the best they could. I had nothing to eat, nothing to wear, and yet it was the beginning of good days. Some say I want

---

48. *History of the Church,* 1:265.

plenty to eat, plenty to drink, plenty to wear and a good house to live in, and say they, then I will believe; but God will not give it, until you have proved yourselves to him. . . . Get the visions of heaven, and seek not what you shall eat or what you shall drink, but seek the will of God; get into the presence of God, and then you will have johnny cake and milk and water no more.[49]

Testimony of Joseph and Sidney

The testimony that Joseph and Sidney bore of Christ is powerfully simple yet magnificent. It certainly ranks among the strongest of any testimonies ever been borne of Him in any age. They testified:

And now, after the many testimonies which have been given of him, this is the testimony, last of all, which we give of him: That he lives! For we saw him, even on the right hand of God; and we heard the voice bearing record that he is the Only Begotten of the Father—That by him, and through him, and of him, the worlds are and were created, and the inhabitants thereof are begotten sons and daughters unto God.[50]

Joseph Smith certified the source of this vision:

Nothing could be more pleasing to the Saints . . . than the light which burst upon the world through the . . . vision. Every law, every commandment, every promise, every truth, and every point touching the destiny of man, from Genesis to Revelation . . . witnesses the fact that that document [D&C 76]

49. *Times and Seasons* 5 (May 1, 1844): 523.

50. Doctrine & Covenants 76:22–24.

is a transcript from the records of the eternal world. . . . Every honest man is constrained to exclaim: *"It came from God."*[51]

Late in his life, Joseph added, "I . . . truly did see Eternity . . . in a vision from God. . . . It came unto me by the spirit direct."[52] No testimony of Christ could be any more clear and concise as the one Joseph and Sidney bore: "He lives!"[53] How did they know this of a surety? Because they "saw him . . . and . . . heard the voice bearing record that he is the Only Begotten of the Father."[54] In 1843, one year before his death, Joseph reflected on this vision and confirmed his simple yet impressive testimony of Christ, declaring, "He lives; yea he lives!"[55]

Sidney Rigdon's Testimonies of the Vision

Sidney Rigdon was an eloquent witness of Christ through the vision, and he frequently bore testimony of it. One public example of his witness of this vision occurred four years later in Medina, Ohio, a town about forty-five miles southwest of Kirtland. Charles Olcott, a reporter for the *Ohio Free Press,* wrote that Sidney presented six days of lectures. He was impressed that Sidney had personally conversed with the Savior in vision. He wrote of his lasting impression:

> Elder Sidney Rigdon, a preacher, of the new sect styling themselves "Latter Day Saints," . . . delivered an interesting series of Lectures. . . . The audiences were very full, and profoundly attentive. . . .
>
> [He said] that . . . direct communications with the Almighty, which have been long lost . . . have been again

---

51. *History of the Church,* 1:252–53.

52. *Times and Seasons* 4 (February 1, 1843): 82 [vv. 11–15].

53. Doctrine & Covenants 76:22.

54. Doctrine & Covenants 76:23.

55. *Times and Seasons* 4 (February 1, 1843): 82 [v. 18].

resumed by a New Dispensation. . . . The Latter Day Saints have now, frequent intercourse . . . with the Creator, by means of visions, revelations, &c., which [Sidney Rigdon] confirmed by some striking narratives from his own personal experience. . . .

These tremendous doctrines, promulgated by the Elder with a closeness of reasoning and eloquence of declamation seldom surpassed, were calculated to make as they have made, a powerful and no doubt a lasting impression on most of his hearers.[56]

Sidney Rigdon bore a powerful testimony of this vision in April 1844 at the last Church conference before Joseph's martyrdom. The Prophet heard once again, perhaps for the last time, Sidney's powerful testimony of the vision they had experienced together as they communed with Deity:

God had great things to say for the salvation of the world. . . . We were obliged to retire to our secret chambers, and commune ourselves with God. . . . There we sat in secret and beheld the glorious visions, and powers of the kingdom of heaven, pass and repass. . . . This was the period when God laid the foundation of the church, and he laid it firm'y, truly, and upon eternal truth. If any man says it is not the work of God, I know they lie. . . . I have the testimony of Jesus which is the spirit of prophecy; I have slept with it, I have walked with it; the idea has never been out of my heart for a moment, and I will reap the glory of it when I leave this world. . . . I know God, I have gazed upon the glory of God, the throne, visions and glories of God, and the visions of eternity in days gone by . . . when Jehovah looked on.[57]

---

56. Oliver Cowdery, "Ohio Free Press," *Messenger and Advocate* 2, no. 8 (May 1836): 315–16.

57. *Times and Seasons* 5 (May 1, 1844): 523–24. See 193n17.

Wilford Woodruff recorded Sidney's words that day as follows:

> There we talked wept, & prayed & the Angels Adminis-
> tered unto us & the spirit of God was with us & the heavens
> opened unto us. . . .
>
> . . . Have I not seen Gods glory by the visions of Heaven?
> Yea I have. . . .
>
> . . . We rejoiced in the things God was revealing unto us. . . .
>
> . . . It was at this time we sat for hours in the *Visions* of
> *heaven* around the throne of God & gazed upon the [scenes]
> of Eternity.[58]

Observations of Others Who Were Present

As with many visions received in Kirtland, other attendees attested
to the obvious outward manifestations of the vision. In addition to seeing
the glory and feeling the power, those present must have sat in awe as they
observed Joseph and Sidney explore eternity with the Savior. Philo Dibble
described the scene of the vision from the perspective of those watching.
He said, "During the whole time not a word was spoken by any other person. Not a sound nor motion made by anyone but Joseph and Sidney, and it
seemed to me that they never moved a joint or limb during the time I was
there, which I think was over an hour, and to the end of the vision."[59]

Regarding the impact the vision had upon Sidney Rigdon, Philo said,
"Sidney sat limp and pale, apparently as limber as a rag, observing which,
Joseph remarked, smilingly, 'Sidney is not used to it as I am.'"[60] In relating
this on another occasion, Philo described it this way: "I did not see the same
glory attending Sidney [Rigdon]. Joseph appeared as strong as a lion, but

---

58. Woodruff, *Journal*, 2:374–77.

59. Dibble, "Recollections," 304.

60. Dibble, "Recollections," 304.

Sidney seemed as weak as water, and Joseph, noticing his condition smiled and said, 'Brother Sidney is not as used to it as I am.'"[61]

The vision indeed proved to be a wellspring of eternal truth from which Joseph Smith taught for the rest of his life. It is significant that another witness was required to testify with Joseph of this magnificent experience. Neither Joseph nor Sidney ever denied the events of that day and what they had learned.

---

61. "Philo Dibble's Narrative," in *Four Faith Promoting Classics* (Salt Lake City: Bookcraft, 1968), 81.

CHAPTER 11

A House of the Lord
on Earth Again

Joseph [Smith] . . . received a pattern also, as did Moses
for the tabernacle, and Solomon for his temple.
—Brigham Young

"Organize yourselves . . . and establish a house, even a house . . . of glory, a house of order, a house of God."[1] With these words pronounced in 1832, Christ commanded His poverty-stricken Saints to build the Kirtland Temple, a latter-day house of the Lord. The temple was a priority because in it ancient priesthood ordinances would once again be performed.

Thousands of years had elapsed since the Lord first commanded His ancient people to build sanctuaries and temples. In 1841 the Savior made it clear that building temples and instituting sacred ordinances had always been important to Him. He said, "I commanded Moses that he should build a tabernacle . . . and to build a house in the land of promise, that those ordinances might be revealed which had been hid from before the world was."[2]

Anciently as the Lord commanded the children of Israel to build their

---

1. Doctrine & Covenants 88:119.

2. Doctrine & Covenants 124:38.

holy tabernacles and sanctuaries, He directed Moses in specific architectural details for these edifices. For example, on Mt. Sinai the Lord showed Moses the pattern, content, and dimensions for the tabernacle.[3] He then cautioned Moses, "Look that thou make them after their pattern, which was shewed thee in the mount."[4] In His command to erect a sanctuary, the Lord directed that it should be made "according to all that I shew thee, after the pattern of the tabernacle."[5]

By revelation the Lord gave David, Solomon's father, the pattern for building Solomon's temple. The model was so clearly presented that David said, "The Lord made me understand in writing by his hand upon me, even all the works of this pattern."[6] Because most of his early life and reign was a time of war, David had "shed much blood," and the Lord gave his son Solomon the responsibility to build the majestic structure.[7] The Lord promised Solomon that he would be given the capability to build the temple "if thou wilt walk in my statutes, and execute my judgments, and keep all my commandments to walk in them; then will I perform my word with thee, which I spake unto David thy father."[8]

The Lord caused the Kirtland Temple, though different in design, to be erected in the same manner as He caused the tabernacle and Solomon's temple to be built. He commanded the Saints, through His latter-day prophet, to build it.[9] By vision He showed the completed temple to Joseph Smith and his counselors almost three years before it was built. In a revelation, the Lord directed that three brethren be selected to build it

---

3. Exodus 25–27.

4. Exodus 25:40.

5. Exodus 25:9.

6. 1 Chronicles 28:19.

7. 1 Chronicles 22:7–9.

8. 1 Kings 6:12.

9. Doctrine & Covenants 88:119.

according to the manner He would show them.[10] Truman O. Angell recorded Frederick G. Williams's narrative about how the entire First Presidency saw the temple:

> Joseph received the word of the Lord for him to take his two counselors, Williams and Rigdon, and come before the Lord and He would show them the plan or model of the House to be built. We went upon our knees, called on the Lord, and the Building appeared within viewing distance. I being the first to discover it. Then all of us viewed it together. After we had taken a good look at the exterior, the Building seemed to come right over us, and the Makeup of this Hall seemed to coincide with what I there saw to a minutia.[11]

The Lord did more than just give Joseph the pattern and dimensions of the temple.[12] As He did with Moses on Mount Sinai, He cautioned the

---

10. Doctrine & Covenants 95:14.

11. "Truman Angell Autobiography," in *Our Pioneer Heritage*, comp. Kate B. Carter, 20 vols. (Salt Lake City: Daughters of Utah Pioneers, 1958–77), 10:198; Truman O. Angell, Journal, 4, L. Tom Perry Special Collections, Harold B. Lee Library, Brigham Young University, Provo, Utah; hereafter cited as BYU Special Collections. The First Presidency saw the plan or model of the Kirtland Temple before it was built, but it is not certain what level of detail the Lord revealed. Many features in the temple were common to carpenters' manuals and pattern books of that day, but the temple also has many unique features not usually found in buildings at the time. Features that stand out include the following: (1) Four tiers of pulpits on each end of the upper and lower halls. (2) Two large assembly rooms, one above the other, which are basically mirror images. (3) Canvas curtains, or veils, attached to the ceiling that allowed for privacy in the priesthood pulpits behind each set of veils. (4) Four large canvas curtains, or veils, attached to the ceiling that could be dropped between pew boxes to divide the main assembly halls into four equal sections to accommodate separate simultaneous meetings. (5) Windows in every interior and exterior wall, allowing rooms to be lit by natural light. In the third floor attic story, especially, interior windows in the five smaller rooms transmitted light. (6) A light well in the front hallway foyer placed between the two main floors of the temple. The light well was placed just behind the large exterior window in the front wall of the temple. This well allowed light to reflect up or down and pass through the large interior windows at the east end of the two large assembly halls on the first and second floors.

12. Doctrine & Covenants 95:15.

Prophet, "It must be done according to the pattern which I have given unto you."[13] Using much the same language He used with Solomon, the Lord promised Joseph that He would enable him to build the Kirtland Temple. He said, "If you keep my commandments you shall have power to build it."[14]

In each of these three houses of the Lord—the tabernacle, Solomon's temple, and the Kirtland Temple—the Lord demonstrated intense personal interest and involvement. With each one, He

- Gave the initial commandment.
- Revealed the pattern.
- Specified the dimensions.
- Outlined cautions.
- Gave power for its completion.

Brigham Young illustrates that Joseph Smith's need for instruction was similar to that of Moses, David, and Solomon. Brigham said:

> The Church, through our beloved Prophet Joseph, was commanded to build a temple to the Most High, in Kirtland, Ohio. Joseph received not only revelation and commandment to build a temple but a pattern also, as did Moses for the tabernacle and Solomon for his temple; without a pattern, Joseph could not know what was wanted, having never seen a temple and having not experienced its use.[15]

---

13. Doctrine & Covenants 94:2.

14. Doctrine & Covenants 95:11.

15. *Discourses of Brigham Young,* ed. John A. Widtsoe (Salt Lake City: Bookcraft, 1998), 415.

The Lord Enabled the Saints to Build the Temple

We pay tribute to the Kirtland Saints for constructing the temple, but the Lord Himself made it possible for His house to be built. For the early members of the Church, it was an unthinkable task. Consider the existing obstacles:

- Most members were poverty stricken.
- The Church had no financial reserves. (Cost of the temple would be about forty thousand dollars.)
- Few members had construction experience.
- Few members were available to contribute time and resources. (Only 175 Church members lived in the Kirtland area in 1833.)[16]
- The Church did not own the land upon which the temple was to be built.
- Few members possessed construction tools.
- Church enemies swore to stop temple construction.

The following Kirtland Saints painted a dismal picture of their circumstances:

Eliza R. Snow: "The Saints were few in number, and most of them very poor; and, had it not been for the assurance that God had spoken, and had commanded that a house should be built to his name, . . . an attempt towards building that Temple, under the then existing circumstances, would have been, by all concerned, pronounced preposterous."[17]

Benjamin F. Johnson: "There were but few saints in Kirtland, and those all of the poorer class. . . .

---

16. *A Profile of Latter-day Saints of Kirtland, Ohio, and Members of Zion's Camp, 1830–1839,* comp. Milton V. Backman Jr. (Provo, Utah: BYU Department of Church History and Doctrine, 1982), 83.

17. *Eliza R. Snow, an Immortal: Selected Writings of Eliza R. Snow,* ed. Nicholas G. Morgan Sr. (Salt Lake City: Nicholas G. Morgan Sr. Foundation, 1957), 54.

" . . . there was not a scraper and hardly a plow that could be obtained among the Saints."[18]

Brigham Young: "They did not have molasses to eat with their johnny cake. Sometimes they had shoes, and sometimes not; sometimes they would have tolerable pants, and, sometimes, very ragged ones."[19]

Heber C. Kimball: "The church was in a state of poverty and distress . . . it appeared almost impossible that the commandment could be fulfilled, at the same time our enemies were raging and threatening destruction upon us."[20]

Joseph Smith: "Our means are already exhausted, and we are deeply in debt, and know of no means whereby we shall be able to extricate ourselves."[21]

Joel Hills Johnson: "We had but very few friends . . . while we had thousands of enemies who were holding their secret meetings to devise a plan to thwart and overthrow all our arrangements. We were obliged to keep night watchers to prevent being mobbed and our workers being overthrown."[22]

Heber C. Kimball: "We were persecuted . . . there were mobs gathering all around us to destroy us, and prevent us from building the Temple. . . . we took our firelocks, to reinstate our brethren, and in the night we layed upon the floor . . . so as to be ready to keep our enemies at bay."[23]

Brigham Young: "The [Saints] were too few in numbers, too weak in

---

18. Benjamin F. Johnson, *My Life's Review* (Independence, Mo.: Zion's Printing and Publishing Co., 1947), 15–16.

19. In Andrew Karl Larson, *Erastus Snow: The Life of a Missionary and Pioneer for the Early Mormon Church* (Salt Lake City: University of Utah Press, 1971), 466.

20. *Times and Seasons* 6 (January 15, 1845): 771.

21. Joseph Smith, *History of The Church of Jesus Christ of Latter-day Saints*, ed. B. H. Roberts, 7 vols., 2d ed. rev. (Salt Lake City: The Church of Jesus Christ of Latter-day Saints, 1932–51), 1:450.

22. Joel Hills Johnson, Excerpts from Autobiography (1802–1868), typescript, 5, BYU Special Collections; Church History Library, The Church of Jesus Christ of Latter-day Saints, Salt Lake City, Utah.

23. *Times and Seasons* 6 (July 15, 1845): 972.

faith, and too poor in purse. . . . a mere handful of men, living on air, and a little hominy and milk . . . holding the sword in one hand to protect themselves from the mob, while they placed the stone and moved the trowel with the other."[24]

In light of these staggering realities, the only solution was to petition the Lord. Heber C. Kimball told of Sidney Rigdon's intense petitions: "He frequently used to go upon the walls of the building both by night and day and frequently wetting the walls with his tears, crying aloud to the Almighty to send means whereby we might accomplish the building."[25]

The Lord reassured the Saints by promising them, "It is my will that you should build a house. . . . you shall have power to build it."[26] The Lord, true to His promise, provided help to the Saints so that the Temple could be built. For example, He answered prayers for financial assistance by providing members who contributed much-needed funds at critical times.

The most dramatic example of the Lord's intervention occurred when He inspired John Tanner to come to Kirtland. John came as a direct result of Joseph Smith praying for two thousand dollars to pay off a mortgage on the temple property. John's timely financial assistance prevented a foreclosure as described in the following account:

> About the middle of December he received an impression by dream or vision of the night, that he was needed and must go immediately to [Kirtland]. . . . His neighbors . . . tried their utmost to dissuade him; but he knew the will of God in the present crisis and nothing could deter him from doing it.
>
> On Christmas day he commenced his journey with all

---

24. Brigham Young, in *Journal of Discourses,* 26 vols. (London: Latter-day Saints' Book Depot, 1854–86), 2:31.

25. *Times and Seasons* 6 (April 15, 1845): 867.

26. Doctrine & Covenants 95:11.

his earthly effects, and in the dead of Winter traveled the distance of five hundred miles, to Kirtland. . . .

On his arrival in Kirtland, he learned that at the time he received the impression . . . the Prophet Joseph and some of the brethren had met in prayer-meeting and asked the Lord to send them a brother or some brethren with means to assist them. . . .

. . . He loaned the prophet two thousand dollars.[27]

The Lord also caused members who had lesser means, such as Vienna Jaques, to contribute. She assisted when the Church was buying land for the temple. Vienna's conversion to the Church began through a vision the Lord gave her of the Book of Mormon. She left Massachusetts with her life savings, fourteen thousand dollars of which the Lord prompted her to donate. The Lord confirmed His support to Joseph Smith in a "whispering" that told him, "Joseph, thou art indebted to thy God for the offering of thy Sister Vienna, which proved a savor of life as pertaining to thy pecuniary concerns. . . . The Lord hath done this."[28]

The Lord also provided manpower. He moved upon experienced craftsmen to accept the gospel and move to Kirtland. Men of great faith like Brigham Young, Joseph Young, Lorenzo Young, Artemus Millett, and Truman O. Angel assumed major roles in constructing the temple. Few workers initially resided near Kirtland, but the Lord eventually sent sufficient manpower to complete the work. While the temple was being built, Joseph Smith bestowed formal blessings on 119 men who had helped build it.[29]

Finally, the Lord answered prayers for protection from menacing mobs.

27. "Sketch of an Elder's Life," in *Scraps of Biography* in *Classic Experiences and Adventures* (Salt Lake City: Bookcraft, 1969), 12.

28. *History of the Church,* 1:408.

29. *History of the Church,* 2:205–6.

Joel Johnson said, "The Lord had promised . . . to keep a stronghold in Kirtland for the space of five years; therefore we were warned of all the devices of our enemies in time to elude them until the temple was completed, the saints endowed [with power,] and the five years expired."[30]

Oliver Huntington, the Prophet's bodyguard, tells how one of the many prayers for protection was answered:

> Joseph Smith was guarded day and night by his brethren from mob violence. . . .
>
> [One night] Joseph was listening to the prayer of a little boy in the room adjoining. The boy prayed for the Prophet, that he might be secure and safe from his enemies, the mob, that night. . . .
>
> . . . Joseph turned to his brethren and told them all to go to bed and all sleep and rest themselves that night, for God had heard and would answer that boy's prayer. They all went to bed and slept safely until morning undisturbed.[31]

Unseen forces also protected the Saints. In January 1836, just before the completion of the temple, Joseph Smith reported, "Eld. Roger Orton saw a . . . <mighty> Angel riding upon a horse of fire with a flaming sword in his hand followed by five others—encircle the house & protect the saints."[32]

Most observers of 1830s history would conclude that without divine intervention, the task of temple construction would have been impossible

---

30. Johnson, Excerpts from Autobiography, 5; Doctrine & Covenants 64:21.

31. Max H. Parkin, *Conflict at Kirtland* (Salt Lake City: Department of Seminaries and Institutes of Religion, 1967), 206.

32. *History of the Church*, 2:386–87; Dean C. Jessee, Mark R. Ashurst-McGee, and Richard L. Jensen, eds., *Journals, 1832–1839*, vol. 1 of the Journals series of *The Joseph Smith Papers*, edited by Dean C. Jessee, Ronald K. Esplin, and Richard Lyman Bushman (Salt Lake City: Church Historian's Press, 2008), 1:174.

for this small band of people. One non-Mormon historian and specialist in early architecture and building construction observed: "The Kirtland Temple stands as a monument to Joseph Smith and to those faithful souls. . . . It appears a miracle the temple was constructed." She concluded, "They were inspired by almost superhuman exertion of body and brilliance of mind, by their devotion . . . to the visions and revelations."[33]

Because of their implicit faith that the Lord had spoken and promised them power to build the temple, early members were resolute. Their determination is memorialized by Joseph Smith's statement to one of the faithful, William W. Phelps. He declared: "The Lord commanded us in Kirtland to build an house of God . . . this is the word of the Lord to us, & we must—yea the Lord helping us we will obey." Joseph was also given another promise from the Lord. He said, "On conditions of our obedience, he has promised <us> great things, yea <even> a visit from the heavens to honor us with his own presence."[34]

Days of Rejoicing Follow Temple Dedication

After a nearly three-year seemingly impossible feat to build the Kirtland Temple, it was ready to dedicate to the Lord. The long-awaited day of dedication—Sunday, March 27, 1836—burst upon a city bulging with visitors. Not even a seven-hour dedication service would deter Saints who had labored and sacrificed all they possessed for this Christ-inspired temple.

Personal comforts were discarded as brotherly love dictated occupying every possible space. One thousand Saints squeezed together into a space that accommodates barely four hundred today.

Joseph Smith estimated that by 7:00 A.M. that day, more than one thousand persons waited near the temple doors. Between 7:00 and 8:00 A.M. a

---

33. Mrs. Peter S. Hitchcock, "Joseph Smith and the Kirtland Temple," in *Lake County Historical Society Quarterly* 7, no. 4 (November 1965): 5, 2.

34. *Personal Writings of Joseph Smith*, comp. and ed. Dean C. Jessee, rev. ed. (Salt Lake City: Deseret Book, 2002), 293.

number of Church leaders and ushers entered the building. At 8:00 A.M. the temple doors opened, and about one thousand people entered the main hall. The doors were finally closed when all available seats were occupied. Hundreds could not enter the building; therefore, a second dedicatory service was scheduled to be held the following Thursday, March 31.

Joseph read the inspired dedicatory prayer. This prayer, recorded in the Doctrine and Covenants, contains a petition that the Kirtland Temple may be "a house of prayer, a house of fasting, a house of faith, a house of learning, a house of glory, a house of order, a house of God."[35]

The joy and gratitude of the Kirtland Saints were unrestrained. The Lord had kept His promises and given them ability and power sufficient to complete the temple. He had also kept His promise to visit and honor them with His presence. He rewarded their sacrifices and efforts by endowing them with long-promised sacred ordinances. He showered them with unparalleled spiritual manifestations. The Saints sang glorious hymns of praise and thanks to the Lord. Their voices ascended to heaven in refrains from joyful songs such as "Now Let Us Rejoice." Their voices were joined by heavenly choirs that also celebrated this long-awaited day. In fact, choirs of angels were frequently heard singing in the Kirtland Temple during this period. At the conclusion of the dedicatory prayer, the choir sang:

> *We'll sing and we'll shout with the armies of heaven—*
> *Hosanna, hosanna to God and the Lamb!*
> *Let glory to them in the highest be given,*
> *Henceforth and forever: amen and amen!*[36]

W. W. Phelps wrote this stirring anthem, "The Spirit of God," for the dedication of the temple. The words of this hymn were so significant that

---

35. Doctrine & Covenants 109:8.

36. *History of the Church*, 2:427; "The Spirit of God," *Hymns of The Church of Jesus Christ of Latter-day Saints* (Salt Lake City: The Church of Jesus Christ of Latter-day Saints, 1985), no. 2.

they were printed on white satin for the dedication ceremonies.[37] Following this hymn, the Savior's ultimate sacrifice was commemorated as the Saints partook of the sacrament of the Lord's Supper. Then, after concluding remarks, they "sealed the proceedings of the day by . . . shouting hosanna, hosanna, hosanna to God and the Lamb, three times, sealing it each time with amen, amen, and amen."[38]

Hosanna Shout

These sacred words of unrestrained praise have become known as the Hosanna Shout, currently used at all temple dedications. President Gordon B. Hinckley termed the Hosanna Shout "beautiful words of worship"[39] and a "sacred salute to the Father and the Son."[40] The Hosanna Shout is far more significant than might be generally understood. It is a formal heaven-sent shout of acclaim to Deity that God gave to Joseph Smith. Joseph said, "God had shown to me [the order] which is as follows: . . . all the quorums were to shout with one accord a solemn Hosanna to God and the Lamb, with an Amen, Amen and Amen."[41]

The shout expressed the Saints' gratitude toward and praise of Deity. When the Hosanna Shout was introduced in the Kirtland Temple, meeting minutes indicated that the shout allowed participants who felt a great intensity of the Spirit to give vent to the Spirit by shouting aloud. Joseph Smith wrote, "Many arose and spoke, testifying that they were filled with the Holy Ghost, which was like fire in their bones, so that they could not hold their peace, but were constrained to cry hosanna to God and the Lamb, and glory

---

37. Susa Young Gates, "Our Hymn Book," *Relief Society Magazine* 9, no. 7 (July 1922): 352.

38. *History of the Church*, 2:427–28; Jessee, Ashurst-McGee, and Jensen, *Journals*, 1:210.

39. Gordon B. Hinckley, "'An Humble and a Contrite Heart,'" *Ensign*, November 2000, 89.

40. Gordon B. Hinckley, "This Great Millennial Year," *Ensign*, November 2000, 69.

41. *History of the Church*, 2:391; Jessee, Ashurst-McGee, and Jensen, *Journals*, 1:181.

in the highest."[42] It is as if God desired to give the Saints a way to formally express their innermost worship and gratitude.

At the conclusion of the dedicatory prayer, Joseph Smith petitioned in prayer, "Help us by the power of thy Spirit, that we may mingle our voices with those bright, shining seraphs around thy throne, with acclamations of praise, singing Hosanna to God and the Lamb!"[43]

The Hosanna Shout is possibly ongoing at the throne of God, as may be inferred from the dedicatory prayer. Church presidents John Taylor and Lorenzo Snow, who were both in Kirtland with the Prophet Joseph Smith, suggested that the precedence for the Hosanna Shout was established in the premortal existence. John said, "Indeed the shout was . . . older than the everlasting hills . . . aye, older than the earth. . . . For was not this the shout which shook the heavens before the foundations of the earth were laid, when 'the morning stars sang together and all the sons of God shouted for joy?'"[44]

Lorenzo Snow suggested at the dedication of the Salt Lake Temple that the first Hosanna Shout had occurred "when . . . all the sons of God shouted for joy"[45] in premortality. Remembering Kirtland, he also said:

> The words of the shout . . . were introduced by President Joseph Smith at the Kirtland Temple. . . . This is no ordinary order . . . [it is] a sacred shout, and employed only on extraordinary occasions. . . . we want the brethren and sisters not only to express the words, but that their hearts shall be full of thanksgiving to the God of heaven, who has

---

42. *History of the Church*, 2:392; Jessee, Ashurst-McGee, and Jensen, *Journals*, 1:181–82.

43. Doctrine & Covenants 109:79.

44. B. H. Roberts, *The Life of John Taylor* (Salt Lake City: Bookcraft, 1963), 366, 365.

45. Lael J. Woodbury, "Hosanna Shout," in *Encyclopedia of Mormonism*, ed. Daniel H. Ludlow et al., 4 vols. (New York: Macmillan, 1992), 2:659; Job 38:7.

accomplished, through our agency, this mighty and extra-ordinary labor.[46]

Lorenzo also taught that the Hosanna Shout would "herald the Messiah when he comes in the glory of the Father."[47]

Erastus Snow recalled the celestial spirit and angelic messengers that accompanied the Hosanna Shout. He said, "Angels came and worshipped with us and some saw them, yea even twelve legions of them, the chariots of Israel and the horsemen thereof."[48]

Benjamin Brown chronicled the miracle of a baby participating in the Hosanna Shout. He wrote:

> One woman ... brought her child about 2 months old ... the woman & child entered and the child did not cry a word from 8 till 4 in the after noon. But when the saints all shouted Hosana the child was nursing But let go & shouted also when the saints paused it paused when they shouted it shouted for three times when they shouted amen it shouted also for three times then it resumed its nursing without any alarm.[49]

Wilford Woodruff indicated that even one year after the dedication, angels shouted along with Saints in the Kirtland Temple who were rendering thanks and adoration to Deity. After describing the order of giving the shout, he concluded, "If ever a shout entered the Cabinet of heaven[,] that

46. Lorenzo Snow, *Millennial Star* 29 (July 4, 1892): 418.

47. "Hosanna Shout," in *Encyclopedia of Mormonism*, 2:659.

48. Erastus Snow, "A Journal or Sketch of the Life of Erastus Snow," typescript, 6, BYU Special Collections.

49. Benjamin Brown, Steven C. Harper, "A Pentecost and Endowment Indeed": Six Eyewitness Accounts of the Kirtland Temple Experience," in *Opening the Heavens: Accounts of Divine Manifestations, 1820–1844,* ed. John W. Welch and Erick B. Carlson (Provo, Utah: Brigham Young University Press, 2005, and Salt Lake City: Deseret Book, 2005), 336.

did & was repeated by angels on high & caused the power of God to rest upon us."[50]

The Lord has directed the building of His temples from the beginning. The patterns have always been His, as have the proceedings and ordinances performed within these sacred structures. How comforting to note that whatever confusion rages in the world, the Lord is always the same, and His Houses will always be sanctuaries to bless His children.

---

50. Wilford Woodruff, *Wilford Woodruff's Journal, 1833–1898,* ed. Scott G. Kenney, typescript, 9 vols. (Midvale, Utah: Signature Books, 1983–85), 1:132–33.

CHAPTER 12

VISIONS OF DEITY IN THE
KIRTLAND TEMPLE

I am he who liveth, I am he who was slain.

—DOCTRINE & COVENANTS 110:4

In the Kirtland Temple, visions of Deity and unparalleled spiritual manifestations flowed down upon the Saints. Most visions came during meetings as Joseph Smith conducted recently revealed sacred temple ordinances. When the Saints erected the first house of the Lord in this last dispensation, with humble faith and under direction of their prophet, they fully expected to see or feel the presence of the Savior and experience heavenly manifestations. Joseph taught the new Twelve Apostles, "All who are prepared and are sufficiently pure to abide the presence of the Saviour will see him in the solem assembly."[1]

Letters from Church leaders indicated that ordinary Church members had been prepared to expect visions and heavenly manifestations. In one letter they wrote: "Within that house God will pour out his spirit in great

---

1. Dean C. Jessee, Mark Ashurst-McGee, and Richard L. Jensen, eds., *Journals, 1832–1839,* vol. 1 of the Journals series of *The Joseph Smith Papers,* edited by Dean C. Jessee, Ronald K. Esplin, and Richard Lyman Bushman (Salt Lake City: Church Historian's Press, 2008), 99.

majesty and glory and encircle his people with fire more gloriously and marvelously than at Pentecost because the work to be performed in the last days is greater than was in that day."[2]

Modern-Day Pentecost

Because people of that period knew the Bible, they were familiar with the pentecostal period in the New Testament that surrounded the ascension of Christ and the descent of the Holy Ghost in Jerusalem. Large numbers of Jews witnessed speaking in tongues and seeing "cloven tongues like as of fire."[3] After the outpourings of the Holy Ghost, the Saints of the primitive Church had visions, participated in healings, and beheld wonders and signs. So it was in Kirtland. These modern disciples likewise experienced such spiritual manifestations.

The magnitude, depth, and variety of these manifestations in the Kirtland Temple compelled the Prophet Joseph Smith to record the following:

> It was a Pentecost and an endowment indeed, long to be remembered, for the sound shall go forth from this place into all the world, and the occurrences of this day shall be handed down upon the pages of sacred history, to all generations; as the day of Pentecost, so shall this day be numbered and celebrated as a year of jubilee, and time of rejoicing to the Saints of the Most High God.[4]

The Lord's inspired prophets of old foresaw and taught of future pentecostal periods such as Kirtland's. Joel prophesied anciently: "I will pour out my spirit upon all flesh; and your sons and your daughters shall prophesy, your

---

2. Sidney Rigdon, Newel K. Whitney, and Oliver Cowdery, May 6, 1834, in Stanley R. Gunn, *Oliver Cowdery: Second Elder and Scribe* (Salt Lake City: Bookcraft, 1962), 101.

3. Acts 2:3.

4. Joseph Smith, *History of The Church of Jesus Christ of Latter-day Saints,* ed. B. H. Roberts, 7 vols., 2d ed. rev. (Salt Lake City: The Church of Jesus Christ of Latter-day Saints, 1932–51), 2:432–33; Jessee, Ashurst-McGee, and Jensen, *Journals,* 1:216.

old men shall dream dreams, your young men shall see visions: And also upon the servants and upon the handmaids in those days will I pour out my spirit."[5]

During Pentecost, Peter recognized that Joel's prophecy had descended upon the Saints in Jerusalem. He informed the Jews: "These are not drunken, as ye suppose. . . . But this is that which was spoken by the prophet Joel."[6] The manifestations spoken of by Peter were not the complete fulfillment of Joel's prophecy, however. As Moroni instructed young Joseph in 1823, he "quoted the second chapter of Joel, from the twenty-eighth verse to the last. He also said that this was not yet fulfilled, but was soon to be."[7]

Lorenzo Snow declared that the fulfillment of Joel's prophecy began for the Latter-day dispensation in the Kirtland Temple. He said:

> [The] magnificent [Kirtland] Temple was completed and dedicated to the Lord in the presence of thousands. The day of blessings, and of rejoicings in the history of the Saints, had now arrived. . . . The youth, the middle aged, both men and women, clothed with the spirit of inspiration, would speak, as with the tongue of angels. . . . One would exercise the gift of tongues, another that of interpretation, and some would have the gift of prophecy. One would speak of the blessings of faith, another would testify of knowledge, and some would have the spirit of exhortation. Thus were their gifts exercised, and all edified together, proving they lived in the time of the fulfilment of Joel's prophecy.[8]

This latter-day pentecostal manifestation indeed fulfilled Joel's prophecy. Visions and spiritual manifestations flowed down from the heavens as he

---

5. Joel 2:28–29.

6. Acts 2:15–16.

7. Joseph Smith–History 1:41.

8. Eliza R. Snow Smith, *Biography and Family Record of Lorenzo Snow* (Salt Lake City: Deseret News, 1884), 144–45; Joel 2:28–29.

had prophesied.[9] The Savior appeared in the temple in at least eight different visions (see chart, p. 229). The Father and the Son were seen together in four visions. In more than ten meetings, such as the two temple dedications, sacrament services, and priesthood leadership meetings, congregations experienced the presence of heavenly beings. Many Saints saw and heard manifestations such as the gift of tongues, sounds of a mighty wind, a pillar of fire resting upon the temple roof, prophesying, and voices of angels.

Benjamin Brown recorded that this pentecostal period was "even greater than at the day of Penti[cost]." He further elaborated, declaring:

> Some have seen the heavens opend & seen the savior[;] others have seen angels on the four corners of the house of the Lord with drawn swords & also stood thick on the ridge Elisha with his chariot of Fire, Peter John & James. . . . Old father Adam was seen B[ea]utiful man his hair stood back & curled most b[ea]utiful even down on his shoulders.[10]

Following are accounts of visions of Deity in the Kirtland Temple on four different glorious days from January to April 1836.

---

9. Joel's prophecy was fulfilled in Peter's day as well as in the Kirtland Temple, but its further fulfillment continues today. President Henry B. Eyring, in speaking to religious educators stated that Joel gave "a promise of an outpouring of the Spirit. It was quoted by Peter and by Moroni. . . . This is not poetry, nor is it allegory; it is description of reality as it will be. Some of it will happen so gradually that you may not notice it. Some has already begun across the Church and we may not have seen the blessing developing. . . .

"That scripture does not say that your sons and your daughters *may* claim the gift of prophecy by the Spirit. It says that they will. It doesn't say that your young men *may* see visions. It says that they will. And it will come because the Lord will pour out His Spirit upon all flesh. Not only will the youth you love and serve have the Spirit poured out on them, but so will the people around them and those who lead them" ("Raising Expectations," *CES Satellite Training Broadcast*, August 2004; in author's possession).

10. Benjamin Brown, in Steven C. Harper, "'A Pentecost and Endowment Indeed': Six Eyewitness Accounts of the Kirtland Temple Experience," in *Opening the Heavens: Accounts of Divine Manifestations, 1820–1844*, ed. John W. Welch and Erick B. Carlson (Provo, Utah: Brigham Young University Press; Salt Lake City: Deseret Book, 2005), 335; paragraphing altered. The events described here seem to describe happenings in the solemn assembly held March 30, 1836. However, this part of Brown's record is disjointed; therefore, it is not possible to link it to one particular meeting with certainty.

Kirtland Temple Visions of Deity

DATE IN 1836	VISION	NUMBER PRESENT	VISION OF FATHER AND SON	VISION OR APPEARANCE OF THE SAVIOR	TYPE MEETING
January 21	Joseph beholds the celestial kingdom & his family & others	16	X		Temple ordinance meeting
January 21	Joseph beholds the Twelve in foreign lands	16		X	Temple ordinance meeting
January 21	Joseph beholds the Twelve crowned in the celestial kingdom	16	X		Temple ordinance meeting
January 21	Joseph beholds the presidency in the celestial kingdom	40	X†		Temple ordinance meeting
January 28	The heavens opened and glorious visions seen by Joseph and others	100*	X		Temple ordinance and instruction meeting
January 28	Zebedee Coltrin sees the Savior on the cross	100*		X	Temple ordinance and instruction meeting
March 30	The Savior fulfills promise to appear	300*		X	Solemn assembly
April 3	The Savior stands on temple pulpit	Joseph Smith and Oliver Cowdery		X	Sacrament meeting

* Indicates the approximate number in attendance
† Although it is not explicitly stated, in Joseph Smith's other visions of the celestial kingdom, specifically the two prior this day, God the Father and Christ were present (see p. 234).

Compiled by Karl Ricks Anderson

Visions of Deity, January 21, 1836

The first recorded visions of Deity in the Kirtland Temple occurred January 21, 1836, in Joseph Smith's office on the temple's highest level. Joseph gave detailed descriptions of at least two extended visions experienced on that remarkable day. Each vision consisted of distinct parts. The occasion for each vision was the ordinance of anointing the head with oil of the First Presidency, bishoprics, and high councilors.

Vision of the Father and the Son in the Celestial Kingdom

The promised visions began as Joseph Smith was meeting with fifteen other Church leaders.[11] As the visions occurred, the Prophet introduced, for the first time in this dispensation, the ordinance of anointing with oil in a temple of the Lord. He described the start of the first vision of the day: "The heavens were opened upon us, and I beheld the celestial kingdom of God, and the glory thereof, whether in the body or out I cannot tell.

> I saw the transcendent beauty of the gate through which the heirs of that kingdom will enter, which was like unto circling flames of fire;
> Also the blazing throne of God, whereon was seated the Father and the Son.
> I saw the beautiful streets of that kingdom, which had the appearance of being paved with gold.
> I saw Father Adam and Abraham; and my father and my mother; my brother Alvin, that has long since slept.[12]

Vision of Christ and the Latter-day Twelve Apostles

In the next part of his visions of this day, Joseph saw the Savior weep over His discouraged band of Apostles. He recorded:

> I saw the 12, apostles of the Lamb, who are now upon the earth who hold the keys of this last ministry, in foreign lands,

---

11. These men were his five counselors and the presidents of the Church in Missouri, his scribe, and the bishoprics of the Church in Ohio and Missouri.

12. Doctrine & Covenants 137:1–5.

standing together in a circle much fatiegued, with their clothes tattered and feet swolen, with their eyes cast downward, and Jesus <standing> in their midst, and they did not behold him, . . . the Saviour looked upon them and wept.[13]

Twelve Apostles in the Celestial Kingdom

In the concluding scene of these visions, Joseph apparently watched until the Twelve arrived at the gate to the celestial kingdom and found Father Adam acting as gatekeeper and escort of the faithful to the throne. In recording this part of the vision, Joseph stated simply, "I finally saw the 12, in the celestial Kingdom of God."[14] Nonetheless, Heber C. Kimball remembered further details of Joseph's vision, undoubtedly told him by the Prophet:

> He (Joseph) saw until they [the Twelve] had accomplished their work, and arrived at the gate of the celestial city; there Father Adam stood and opened the gate to them, and as they entered he embraced them one by one and kissed them. He then led them to the throne of God, and then the Savior embraced each one of them and kissed them, and crowned each one of them in the presence of God. He saw that they all had beautiful heads of hair and all looked alike. The impression this vision left on Brother Joseph's mind was of so acute a nature, that he never could refrain from weeping while rehearsing it.[15]

---

13. Jessee, Ashurst-McGee, and Jensen, *Journals*, 1:168.

14. Jessee, Ashurst-McGee, and Jensen, *Journals*, 1:168.

15. Heber C. Kimball, in Orson F. Whitney, *Life of Heber C. Kimball* (Salt Lake City: Bookcraft, 1945), 93–94. It is assumed that this account relates to the January 21 visions for the following reasons: (1) Accounts of both Joseph and Heber refer to the gate through which the faithful enter the celestial kingdom. (2) This vision is the final scene of Joseph's extended vision. In Heber's account he said this scene was preceded by Joseph seeing the Twelve "in a far distant land . . . their clothes all ragged, and their knees and feet sore. They formed into a circle, and all stood with their eyes fixed upon the

Vision of Christ with the High Councils
of Kirtland and Zion

Later on January 21, the high councilors of Kirtland and Zion joined the ones already in the meeting, which increased attendance to forty brethren. These brethren also participated in visions of Deity that day. Joseph recorded:

> The vision of heaven . . . <was> opened to these also, some of them saw the face of the Saviour, and others were ministered unto by holy angels, and the spirit of propesey and revelation was poured out in mighty power, and loud hosanahs and glory to God in the highest, saluted the heavens for we all communed with the h[e]avenly hosts.[16]

According to Joseph, "Some of them saw the face of the Savior." This probably indicates that at least three[17] other Church leaders besides Joseph became eyewitnesses to Christ's existence and leadership of the Church.[18]

---

ground. The Savior appeared and stood in their midst and wept over them" (Heber C. Kimball, in Whitney, *Life of Heber C. Kimball,* 93). (3) Joseph sees the throne of God. (4) Christ is present at the throne. (5) Adam is part of the vision. In recording this vision in his journal, Joseph Smith also recorded seeing Michael (*Personal Writings of Joseph Smith,* comp. Dean C. Jessee, rev. ed. [Salt Lake City: Deseret Book, 2002], 175). Doctrine & Covenants 137 follows the current edition of the *History of the Church* (2:380), which simplifies Joseph Smith's journal by eliminating "and Michael" after Abraham. Perhaps this was done because the editors knew that Michael was another name for Adam. Heber C. Kimball's account gives Adam, or Michael, the double roles of gatekeeper and the one who escorts the faithful to the throne. This double role may account for his double mention in the Prophet's report of the vision.

16. Jessee, Ashurst-McGee, and Jensen, *Journals,* 1:170; Doctrine & Covenants 137.

17. Although it is not known how many leaders saw the Savior, Joseph's use of the word *some* would probably indicate more than two.

18. Newel Knight, a member of the high council in Zion, may have been one who saw the Savior in this meeting. He is a witness of Christ because he saw both the Father and the Son in a vision in June 1830 in Fayette, New York (*History of the Church,* 1:85). He is not listed as a witness in this book, however, because no record exists of his bearing witness of this vision in Kirtland.

Vision of the Presidency in the Celestial Kingdom

During this final meeting of leaders that now included the high councilors of Kirtland and Zion, Joseph Smith beheld his third vision of the celestial kingdom that day. This time he saw many of those forty brethren, including the presidency, in that celestial setting. He stated: "I saw in my vision all of the presidency in the Celistial Kingdom of God, and, many others who were present."[19] In each of his two other visions of the celestial kingdom that day, the Prophet had seen the Father and the Son and also men who were assisting Joseph in leading the Church, many of whom were present in the meetings. In the first of those visions, Joseph saw God's throne, the Father and the Son, and others, including his father, who had just anointed him. In the next vision, he saw the Twelve being embraced by the Savior in the presence of the Father. In the third vision, he sees the presidency there with other leaders who are with him in the meeting. Although he didn't state it directly, it is probable that this final vision also included the Father and Son, because that was the pattern set in the two other visions.

Apparently because of the sacred nature of the visions, Oliver Cowdery, who was present at the meeting, did not record many details. He leaves us wishing for more details, however, with what he did write: "The glorious scene is too great to be described in this book, therefore, I only say, that the heavens were opened to many, and great and marvelous things were shown."[20]

God the Father and Christ Seen in Meeting
of Quorums, January 28, 1836

Seven days following the incredible visions of January 21, Joseph Smith and his counselors instructed high priests, seventies, and elders assembled

---

19. Jessee, Ashurst-McGee, and Jensen, *Journals*, 1:170. In recording these visions, Joseph was characteristically succinct, leaving others to fill in details such as Heber C. Kimball provided for the second vision of the day. For this third vision no additional details have surfaced.

20. Leonard J. Arrington, "Oliver Cowdery's Kirtland, Ohio, 'Sketch Book,'" *BYU Studies* 12, no. 4 (1972): 419.

in the Kirtland Temple. The leaders introduced to this group the ancient ordinance of anointing with oil. In addition, Joseph Smith conducted the procedure of sealing blessings given them in the anointing. During the proceedings, marvelous visions were distilled upon the priesthood quorums. In this meeting, Zebedee Coltrin saw the Savior. The Prophet recorded this and other visions: "Elder Roger Orton saw a mighty angel riding upon a horse of fire, with a flaming sword in his hand, followed by five others, encircle the house, and protect the Saints, even the Lord's anointed, from the power of Satan and a host of evil spirits, which were striving to disturb the Saints.

"President William Smith, one of the Twelve, saw the heavens opened, and the Lord's host protecting the Lord's anointed.

"President Zebedee Coltrin, one of the seven presidents of the Seventy, saw the Savior extended before him, as upon the cross, and a little after, crowned with glory upon his head above the b[r]ightness of the sun."[21]

Harrison Burgess added that Joseph Smith also saw the Savior. In his autobiography, Harrison vividly recalled that in the middle of the meeting, "Joseph exclaimed aloud, 'I behold the Saviour, the Son of God.'"[22] He recorded the following:

The Lord blessed His people abundantly in that Temple with the Spirit of prophecy, the ministering of angels, visions, etc. I will here relate a vision which was shown to me. It was near the close of the endowments. I was in a

---

21. *History of the Church,* 2:386–87; Ashurst-McGee, and Jensen, *Journals,* 1:174–75.

22. Harrison Burgess, Autobiography, in *Windows: A Mormon Family,* comp. and ed. Kenneth Glyn Hales (Tucson, Ariz.: Skyline Printing, 1985), 102–3. The account Harrison recorded does not specify a date for the meeting he described; however, a careful comparison of the events correlates with the January 28 meeting. No other meeting during this period comes close. Both Joseph Smith (*History of the Church,* 2:386) and Harrison identify the meeting location as the attic of the temple. Both indicate that Roger Orton saw a vision of heavenly horses in the meeting. Both say Hyrum Smith was present. Both indicate that the Melchizedek Priesthood quorums were present. Both refer to endowments or anointings given in the meeting. Both describe a heavenly atmosphere that surrounded them. Both specifically mention that instruction was received in the meeting.

meeting for instruction in the upper part of the Temple, with about a hundred of the High Priests, Seventies and Elders. The Saints felt to shout "Hosannah!" and the Spirit of God rested upon me in mighty power and I beheld the room lighted up with a peculiar light such as I had never seen before. It was soft and clear and the room looked to me as though it had neither roof nor floor to the building and I beheld the Prophet Joseph and Hyrum Smith and Roger Orton enveloped in the light: Joseph exclaimed aloud, "I behold the Savior, the Son of God." Hyrum said, "I behold the angels of heaven." Brother Orton exclaimed, "I behold the chariots of Israel."[23]

Two journal accounts lead to a conclusion that both the Father and the Son appeared in vision in this meeting. In an 1879 Sunday meeting, Harrison supplemented his journal account by adding that Joseph Smith also saw God the Father at that time. Charles Lowell Walker, one of the Church's foremost diary keepers, heard Harrison say that Joseph saw both the Father and the Son. Charles then carefully recorded Harrison's words in his journal entry:

> Br Harrison Burgess spoke of the first Endowments given in the Kirtland Temple and that all the quorums met at one time in the Attic; Joseph and Hyrum met with them. He said that all at once there was a Heavenly and Divine Atmosphere surrounded them, and it seemed as if the rafters and Beams were all gone and Joseph gazing up said, I See the Son of God sitting at the right hand of the Father. Hyrum at the same instant said,

---

23. Harrison Burgess, "Sketch of a Well-Spent Life," in *Labors in the Vineyard* in *Classic Experiences and Adventures* (Salt Lake City: Bookcraft, 1969), 67; *History of the Church*, 2:387.

I behold the Angels of Heaven, and Roger Orton said, I see the Horses and Chariots of Heaven.[24]

Although Joseph omitted in his journal account that he saw a vision of Deity, he did record that he saw "a glorious vision."[25] In his journal Harrison concluded that all present experienced the power of God. He wrote, "All who were in the room felt the power of God to that degree that many prophesied, and the power of God was made manifest, . . . the remembrance of which I shall never forget while I live upon the earth."[26]

Another account attests to both the Father and the Son appearing, probably on this day. David Patten, a member of the Quorum of the Twelve Apostles, also attended. David visited Abraham Smoot, a recent convert, in Kentucky within weeks of the temple dedication and told him about seeing God the Father and Jesus Christ in vision. Wilford Woodruff recorded his account:

He [Abraham Smoot] had Been with Elder Patten & his wife for several days. Br Smoot related the news to me from Br Patten which was glorious in the first degree. He gave me an account of the endowment at Kirtland Ohio. The heavens Was opened unto them. Angels & Jesus Christ was seen of them sitting at the right hand of the father.[27]

24. *Diary of Charles Lowell Walker*, ed. A. Karl Larson and Katharine Miles Larson, 2 vols. (Logan: Utah State University Press, 1980), 2:483. Harrison Burgess does not give the date of this meeting, but because its details correlate with Joseph Smith's account of the January 28 meeting, we can conclude that Harrison's recollection was from the same meeting (see 234n22).

25. *History of the Church*, 2:387; Jessee, Ashurst-McGee, and Jensen, *Journals*, 1:175.

26. Burgess, *Windows*, 102–3.

27. Wilford Woodruff, *Wilford Woodruff's Journal, 1833–1898*, ed. Scott G. Kenney, typescript, 9 vols. (Midvale, Utah: Signature Books, 1983–85), 1:67. David Patten does not specify the date of the vision; however, the account seems to correlate more closely with January 28 than with any other meeting because David and the others of the Twelve were not present on January 21, when Joseph saw both the Father and the Son, but David and other members of the Twelve were present on January 28.

Joseph Smith described how the impact of the vision stayed with him during the night: "After these quorums were dismissed, I retired to my home, filled with the Spirit, and my soul cried hosanna to God and the Lamb, through the silent watches of the night; and while my eyes were closed in sleep, the visions of the Lord were sweet unto me, and His glory was round about me. Praise the Lord."[28]

Divine Presence Felt in Dedicatory Services, March 27, 1836

Many journals testifying of heavenly manifestations on the day the temple was dedicated made reference to a divine presence. In what may have been a reference to Deity, Nancy Tracy recorded that "the heavenly influence rested down upon that house. . . . Heavenly Beings appeared to many. . . . It was heaven on earth."[29]

Eliza R. Snow stated that "an abiding holy heavenly influence was realized."[30] In another account she wrote that the whole congregation felt the presence of divinity: "The ceremonies of that dedication may be rehearsed, but no mortal language can describe the heavenly manifestations of that memorable day. Angels appeared to some, while a sense of divine presence was realized by all present, and each heart was filled with 'joy inexpressible and full of glory.'"[31]

Therefore, if we assume that the word "them" includes David Patten, this vision probably occurred January 28. The word also implies that more witnesses saw the Father and the Son in the vision.

28. *History of the Church*, 2:387; Jessee, Ashurst-McGee, and Jensen, *Journals*, 1:175.

29. Nancy Naomi Alexander Tracy, Autobiography, typescript, 9–10, L. Tom Perry Special Collections, Harold B. Lee Library, Brigham Young University, Provo, Utah; hereafter cited as BYU Special Collections.

30. *Eliza R. Snow, an Immortal: Selected Writings of Eliza R. Snow*, ed. Nicholas G. Morgan Sr. (Salt Lake City: Nicholas G. Morgan Sr. Foundation, 1957), 63.

31. Edward W. Tullidge, *The Women of Mormondom* (New York: Tullidge & Crandall, 1877; repr., Salt Lake City: n.p., 1975), 95.

It is generally assumed that the Savior appeared during the dedication of the Kirtland Temple, but no eyewitness accounts can be verified. One possible reference to an appearance of the Savior comes from a family tradition that cannot be documented with certainty.[32] Two other references to the Savior's appearance exist, but they are also problematic.[33]

Other spiritual manifestations were evident. Participants such as Benjamin Brown testified: "There the Spirit of the Lord, as on the day of Pentecost, was profusely poured out. . . .

"We had a most glorious and never-to-be-forgotten time. Angels were

---

32. An Alpheus Cutler family tradition claims that Alpheus "saw the Lord descending on a long strip, which resembled a carpet." While this account may be accurate, the documentation is far from first-hand and therefore not included (Danny L. Jorgenson, *Differing Visions: Dissenters in Mormon History*, ed. Roger D. Launius and Linda Thatcher [Urbana and Chicago, Ill.: University of Illinois Press, 1994], 160).

33. Two secondary sources, Edward Partridge and George A. Smith, recorded that Frederick G. Williams saw the Savior at the dedication. Edward Partridge wrote, "Doct. F. G. Williams saw an angel or rather the savior" (Journal and Other Writings of Edward Partridge, typescript, Church History Library, The Church of Jesus Christ of Latter-day Saints, Salt Lake City, Utah, 11; hereafter cited as Church History Library.) Statements by Joseph Smith, Oliver Cowdery, Truman O. Angell, and Stephen Post indicate that Frederick G. Williams saw an angel (*History of the Church*, 2:427; *Messenger and Advocate* 2, no. 6 [March 1836]: 281; "Truman Angell Autobiography," *Our Pioneer Heritage*, comp. Kate B. Carter, 20 vols. [Salt Lake City: Daughters of Utah Pioneers, 1958–77], 10:198; Stephen Post, Papers [March 27–31, 1836], in *Opening the Heavens*, 351). Had the angel been Christ, Joseph and Oliver would have recognized Him and probably mentioned it. Moreover, Joseph Smith identified the angel as "the Angel Peter" (Carter, "Truman Angell Autobiography," 10:198). George A. Smith said, "President Frederick G. Williams . . . bore testimony that the Savior, dressed in his vesture without seam, came into the stand and accepted of the dedication of the house" (in *Journal of Discourses*, 26 vols. [London: Latter-day Saints' Book Depot, 1854–86], 11:10). But in a contradictory statement, Joseph Smith said, "The Personage who had appeared in the morning was the Angel Peter come to accept the dedication" (Carter, "Truman Angell Autobiography," 10:198). In reference to the George A. Smith account, it should be noted that the Savior did come "into the stand" (or pulpit area) and accept the dedication of the temple one week later, on April 3, 1836 (D&C 110:7). It seems unlikely that the Savior would appear twice to accept the dedication. It should also be noted that Frederick did not record that he saw the Savior at the dedication. Scholars believe that these accounts are probably confused with either the appearance of the Apostle Peter at the dedication or with another appearance of Christ (Lyndon W. Cook, "The Apostle Peter and the Kirtland Temple," *BYU Studies* 15, no. 4 [1975]: 550–52).

seen by numbers present."[34] A heavenly messenger who Joseph Smith said was Peter and who had "come to accept the dedication" was seen entering the temple and sat between Frederick G. Williams and Joseph Smith Sr.[35] It seems that on the day of dedication, the Savior sent Peter, the presiding Apostle of the prior dispensation, to visibly accept the dedication. Then, a week later, Christ Himself appeared.

The Pentecost Continues in Priesthood Meeting, March 27, 1836

At a priesthood meeting held in the temple the evening of the temple dedication, additional pentecostal manifestations were given to the Saints. Benjamin Brown recorded:

> Sunday Evening . . . Joseph spoke . . . & told them the day of Penticost was continued the . . . Brethren began to . . . prophesy many prophesied in the name of the Lord then began speaking in tongues and it filled as it were the whole house, perhaps there were forty speaking at once Cloven tongues of fire was seen to sit on many of them an hand was seen laid upon one when he spake in tongues . . . many Visions seen, one saw a [pillar] or cloud rest down upon the house bright as when the sun shines on a cloud like as gold, two others saw three personages hovering in the room with bright keys in their hands, and also a bright chain in their hands. . . .

---

34. Benjamin Brown, Testimonies for the Truth: A Record of Manifestations of the Power of God, Miraculous and Providential, Witnessed in the Travels and Experience of Benjamin Brown, High Priest in the Church of Jesus Christ of Latter-day Saints, Pastor of the London, Reading, Kent, and Essex Conferences (Liverpool: S. W. Richards, 1853), 6.

35. Carter, "Truman Angell Autobiography," 10:198; Truman O. Angell, Journal 5, typescript, BYU Special Collections; Heber C. Kimball 1801–1868, Journal Excerpts (1833–1837), Church History Library; Heber C. Kimball, in Whitney, *Life of Heber C. Kimball,* 91.

... The west end of the House was illuminated by a light
from heaven seen on the outside by many. ...

Father Stephens saw ... two rows of Angels through the
House, at another time the glory of God came down on the
Elders from the head down half way.[36]

Joseph Smith recorded the events of this evening meeting. He made a
note about personally beholding a pillar of fire, writing:

All the congregation simultaneously arose, being moved
upon by an invisible power; many began to speak in tongues
and prophesy; others saw glorious visions; and I beheld the
Temple was filled with angels, which fact I declared to the
congregation. The people of the neighborhood came running together (hearing an unusual sound within, and seeing a
bright light like a pillar of fire resting upon the Temple), and
were astonished at what was taking place.[37]

Oliver Cowdery, present on the evening of the dedication, saw the glory
of God descend upon the temple. He recorded:

In the evening I met with the officers of the church in
the Lord's house. The Spirit was poured out—I saw the glory
of God, like a great cloud, come down and rest upon the
house, and fill the same like a mighty rushing wind. I also
saw cloven tongues, like as of fire rest upon many, (for there
were 316 present,) while they spake with other tongues and
prophesied.[38]

36. Benjamin Brown, Harper, in Welch and Carlson, *Opening the Heavens,* 336–37.

37. *History of the Church,* 2:428.

38. Arrington, "Oliver Cowdery's 'Sketch Book,'" 426.

On the day of dedication, the Lord indeed rewarded His valiant people by opening the heavens.[39] These Saints, in addition to building the Kirtland Temple, had sanctified their lives so that "the Son of Man might have a place to manifest himself to his people."[40]

The Savior Appears at the Solemn Assembly in the Kirtland Temple, March 30, 1836

Joseph Smith, upon convening the long-awaited solemn assembly, said, "The presidency, the 12, the seventies, the high . . . councils, the Bishops and their entire quorums, the Elders, and all the official members in this stake of Zion amounting to about 300 met in the temple of the Lord."[41] Heber C. Kimball remembered the procedure followed in the solemn assembly:

> When the Prophet Joseph had finished the endowments of the First Presidency, the Twelve and the Presiding Bishops, the First Presidency proceeded to lay hands upon each one of them to seal and confirm the anointing; and at the close of each blessing the whole of the quorums responded to it with a loud shout of Hosanna! Hosanna! etc.
>
> While these things were being attended to the beloved disciple John was seen in our midst by the Prophet Joseph, Oliver Cowdery and others. After this all the quorums arose in order, together with the three Presidencies; and the Twelve

---

39. Accounts for the two meetings on dedication day indicate that the Savior might have been present, although unseen, as indicated in chapter 9 regarding a meeting with the Smith family attended by Mary Elizabeth Lightner in 1831 (see pp. 172–73 herein). In that meeting, Joseph Smith announced, "The Savior has been in your midst. . . . [But] there is a veil over your eyes for you could not endure to look upon Him" (Mary Elizabeth Rollins Lightner, typescript, April 14, 1905, 1, BYU Special Collections). That could account for the outward manifestations and sense of the divine reported on dedication day.

40. Doctrine & Covenants 109:5.

41. Jessee, Ashurst-McGee, and Jensen, *Journals,* 1:213.

then presented themselves separately and individually before the First Presidency, with hands uplifted towards heaven, and asked of God whatever they felt to desire; and after each individual petition the whole of the quorums answered aloud Amen! Hosanna! Hosanna! Hosanna! To God and the Lamb, forever and ever, amen and amen.

. . . As a reward for their preparation, the Prophet promised, "All who are prepared, and are sufficiently pure to abide the presence of the Savior, will see Him in the solemn assembly."[42]

The reward came to those who were prepared. The Savior appeared to some of the priesthood as described by Joseph:

> The brethren continued exhorting, prophesying, and speaking in tongues until five o'clock in the morning. The Savior made His appearance to some, while angels ministered to others, and it was a Pentecost and an endowment indeed, long to be remembered, for the sound shall go forth from this place into all the world, and the occurrences of this day shall be handed down upon the pages of sacred history, to all generations; as the day of Pentecost, so shall this day be numbered and celebrated as a year of jubilee, and time of rejoicing to the Saints of the Most High God.[43]

Benjamin Brown recorded additional details of these and other spiritual manifestations in a letter to his wife. He mentioned two brethren who saw Christ. Although he wrote without punctuation and in seemingly

---

42. *History of the Church,* 2:310; Karen Lynn Davidson, David J. Whittaker, Mark Ashurst-McGee, and Richard L. Jensen, eds., *Histories, 1832–1844,* vol. 1 of the Histories series of *The Joseph Smith Papers,* edited by Dean C. Jessee, Ronald K. Esplin, and Richard Lyman Bushman (Salt Lake City: Church Historian's Press, 2012), 1:123.

43. *History of the Church,* 2:432–33; Jessee, Ashurst-McGee, and Jensen, *Journals,* 1:215–16.

disjointed thoughts, he provides a more complete account. He wrote: "Many Prop[h]esys [were] given & speaking in tongues . . . two corums continued all night in the House the twelve guarded it the Heavens was opened two saw the savior some saw chariots and other thing[s] one lay about half an hour & saw from Eternity to Eternity many Miracilous Experiences told Many Visions told."[44]

Vision of Christ, Moses, Elias, and Elijah, April 3, 1836

The pinnacle of all the holy events transpiring in Kirtland and possibly even in the history of the young latter-day Church was reached with the supernal visions of this day. The Savior Jesus Christ—followed by Moses, Elias, and Elijah—stood before Joseph Smith and Oliver Cowdery to instruct them and to bestow on them long-awaited priesthood keys and authority to carry out the missions of the Church. Joseph's journal relates that as he and Oliver rose from prayer, Christ stood before them in His full glory. After testifying of Himself and His resurrection, He acknowledged His acceptance of His house, the temple. He then promised to appear again to His faithful servants. Joseph testified:

We saw the Lord standing upon the breastwork of the

---

44. Benjamin Brown, Harper, in *Opening the Heavens,* 337. Benjamin Brown attributes these events to a meeting on March 29, 1836, but the events he describes seem more compatible with a March 30, 1836, meeting. Some problems exist in his account, however. Benjamin says the Twelve guarded the temple, but the Twelve were not present on March 29 to guard the temple. He first dates the meeting on April 29 and then changes it to March 29. If he confused the month, he could have confused the day, especially in light of the fact that his letter is somewhat disjointed at the end. Benjamin would not have been in attendance on March 29. The March 30 meeting is more in line with Joseph's account because he makes reference to greater spiritual manifestations and pentecostal events on March 30 than he does on March 29 (*History of the Church,* 2:428–33). Because the March 29 meeting continued all night, Benjamin could have begun his entry with the March 29 meeting and then continued it into the March 30 meeting. Therefore, it is likely these events took place March 30, not March 29.

pulpit, before us. . . . His eyes were as a flame of fire; the hair of his head was white like the pure snow; his countenance shone above the brightness of the sun; and his voice was as the sound of the rushing of great waters, even the voice of Jehovah, saying: I am the first and the last; I am he who liveth, I am he who was slain; I am your advocate with the Father. . . . I have accepted this house. . . . I will appear unto my servants, and speak unto them with mine own voice, if my people will keep my commandments, and do not pollute this holy house.[45]

Joseph and Oliver related this vision to other early leaders. In turn, William W. Phelps told his wife of the vision, saying, "On Sunday, April 3, the twelve held meeting and administered the sacrament. It was a glorious time. The curtains were dropt in the afternoon. And there was a manifestation of the Lord to Br Joseph and Oliver, [by] which they [learned] thus the great & terrible day of the Lord as mentioned by Mal[a]chi, was near, even at the doors."[46]

Lorenzo Snow remembered the testimonies of Joseph and Oliver almost fifty years later. He said, "Those who saw Him testify to this fact."[47] He made particular reference to his association with Joseph and Oliver and to their vision. He said, "There were two persons [Joseph Smith and Oliver Cowdery] with whom I was very well acquainted who saw [Christ] . . . in the Temple in Kirtland, Ohio."[48] Lorenzo was so well acquainted with the vision that he gave these details: "They were sitting side by side, as my brethren are sitting here on this stand, and the Son of God appeared to them." Lorenzo

45. Doctrine & Covenants 110:2–4, 7–8.

46. William W. Phelps, Journal, April 1836 (letter 27), 3, William Wines Phelps (1792–1872) Papers, Vault MSS 810, BYU Special Collections.

47. Lorenzo Snow, in *Journal of Discourses*, 23:342.

48. Snow, in *Journal of Discourses*, 23:291.

had obviously heard them relate the vision in 1836. He knew which pulpit Christ stood upon. He later said, "I have preached from that pulpit many times."[49] In relating his feelings in his journal, he tells of the first time he preached from the pulpit:

> No language can describe my feelings when, for the first time, I stood up in one of those pulpits to address an audience—a pulpit on the breastwork of which, only a short time before, this holy Personage stood—*'his hair as white as pure snow, his eyes as a flame of fire'*—where also Moses, Elias and Elijah came and committed the keys of their dispensations to Joseph Smith.[50]

The appearance of these divine heavenly visitors was even stamped on the memory of children. Mary Ann Stearnes Winters, a stalwart Utah pioneer, always remembered how, when she was a child, her mother showed her the exact spot where the Savior stood. She said, "Mother took me to the stand and showed me the place on the pulpit where the Savior had stood when He appeared to the Prophet, and where afterwards Moses and Elias came and delivered the keys for the gathering of the Saints (Israel), and the redemption of the dead."[51]

Seemingly, the non-LDS community was aware of the Savior's visit. One week after this vision of Christ, Lucius Parsons, a local resident, wrote of it to his sister: "They report that the Savior appeared personally with angels and endowed the Elders with powers to work Miracles."[52]

---

49. Lorenzo Snow, discourse at the Brigham City Tabernacle, March 6, 1887, reported by John Burroughs, in *Collected Discourses: Delivered by Wilford Woodruff, His Two Counselors, the Twelve Apostles, and Others*, comp. and ed. Brian H. Stuy, 5 vols. (Burbank, Calif.: B. H. S. Publishing, 1987–92), 1:28.

50. Snow Smith, *Biography and Family Record*, 11–12.

51. *Relief Society Magazine* 3, no. 8 (August 1916), 432.

52. Lucius Pomeroy Parsons to Pamelia Parsons, April 10, 1836, Church History Library, in Harper, in

Orson Pratt, who no doubt was present on April 3, 1836, concluded that this vision of Christ, Moses, Elias, and Elijah in itself rewarded the Saints for all they had endured in building the temple. He said:

> Then you see that even this one revelation, which God gave in that Temple, paid the people for the toil they had endured in erecting it. What a satisfaction it was to them to know that angels administered in that Temple! What a satisfaction it was for them to go into that Temple and have the heavens opened to them so that they could gaze on the glory of God! What a satisfaction it was for them to know that the Lord accepted, as His own, the house which they had built according to the pattern which He had given! And what a satisfaction it was for them to know that they loved God by keeping His commandments![53]

The Voice of God

Other manifestations experienced by the early Saints in the Kirtland Temple were preserved. For example, Warren Snow testified: "I have seen the power of God manifested.... I remember when receiving my endowments in the Temple at Kirtland, I heard the voice of God as plain as I hear my own, and this testimony I have borne for thirty-one years."[54]

Opening the Heavens, 329. Parson's letter does not identify in which meeting the Savior appeared. He wrote in the letter that the manifestation occurred "behind the curtains." He dated the time for the meeting as being "of late" and around the time of the solemn assembly (March 30, 1836). It is concluded that it was the April 3 meeting because this was the only vision of Christ in the Kirtland Temple that occurred behind the dropped curtains with angels (likely a reference to Moses, Elias, and Elijah).

53. Orson Pratt, in *Journal of Discourses,* 13:359.

54. *Millennial Star* 26 (January 23, 1864): 51.

That We Might Know Jesus Christ

Through visions, appearances, manifestations, and an infusion of glory, the Lord bestowed His divine love upon His new Saints. With His voice from the heavens, He defined the path to be taken for His children to return and dwell with Him forever. When the accounts of the visions are read through spiritual eyes, a sense of overwhelming love seems to draw us closer to the Savior. From the Kirtland Temple, there comes an assurance that the crucified Savior truly did rise from the tomb. As He declared to Joseph and Oliver, He was slain, was resurrected, bears our sins, and truly is our advocate with the Father.[55]

55. Doctrine & Covenants 110:4–5.

CHAPTER 13

CHRIST FULFILLS THE
PROMISED ENDOWMENT

The first elders of my church should receive their endowment from on high in my house . . . in the land of Kirtland. . . . let those be chosen that are worthy.
—DOCTRINE & COVENANTS 105:33, 35

The Kirtland Temple endowment was central to the Lord's purpose for bringing His Saints to Kirtland. Understanding varies, however, regarding what the Lord meant when He promised such a blessing. The one thing historians seem to agree on is that the Kirtland endowment included a great spiritual outpouring—a pentecost. By tracing the thread of this promised endowment through the Kirtland period, it becomes evident that this great spiritual outpouring was not *the* endowment but only an outward manifestation that accompanied it.

The endowment as known today was not completed in the Kirtland Temple. But initial ordinances were introduced that constituted what the Kirtland Saints referred to as the "endowment."[1] The Kirtland Temple endowment consisted of sacred ordinances that required significant personal

---

1. The term *endowment* as used in this chapter refers to ordinances performed in the Kirtland Temple. They were referred to scripturally and by 1830s Saints essentially as "an endowment" or "the endowment." They are not what Saints today refer to as "the endowment," which has grown to include

and physical preparation. After the final ordinance of the endowment was administered, Moses, Elias, and Elijah appeared to Joseph Smith and Oliver Cowdery. These ancient revered prophets bestowed priesthood keys upon them that gave the Lord's authorization for the elders to disseminate the gospel to "foreign lands," where Latter-day Saints everywhere would eventually build temples and "greatly rejoice" as they conducted sacred temple ordinances that were begun in the Kirtland Temple.[2]

Missionaries repeatedly had been sent to other states and nearby areas of Canada before 1836, but they could not and did not go throughout the world until after they had received the endowment of power promised them by the Lord. The endowment at Kirtland was accompanied by the same great manifestations of the Spirit that were present on the New Testament day of Pentecost.

Semantics becomes an obstacle in understanding the Kirtland endowment. In a general sense, any outpouring of the spirit, granting of a blessing, or even bestowing of priesthood offices could be viewed as an endowment. The meaning of the word *endow* is "to enrich or furnish with any gift, quality or faculty."[3] As an example of its general usage, prayers are often petitions to the Lord to endow us with power or spirit to carry out assignments.

However, as will be explained, the Lord did not consider this broad meaning to be the promised Kirtland endowment. This endowment consisted of more than great spiritual outpourings or even priesthood ordinations. To better understand the Kirtland endowment from a historical and revelatory perspective, we will trace its thread through scripture

---

expanded instruction, among other things. The Kirtland ordinances of endowment might be more generally included today under the category of initiatory ordinances.

2. Doctrine & Covenants 110:9–10.

3. Noah Webster, *American Dictionary of the English Language* (1828; repr., San Francisco: Foundation for American Christian Education, 1980), s.v. "endow."

and the journals of those who received it. This thread ran from 1831 to 1836.

On January 2, 1831, the Lord promised the faithful that He would bestow an endowment in Kirtland. He commanded the Saints living in New York and Pennsylvania to sell, rent, or simply leave their farms to go to Kirtland. He made promises to them as follows: "Go to the Ohio; and there I will give unto you my law; and there you shall be endowed with power from on high; and from thence, whosoever I will shall go forth among all nations . . . for Israel shall be saved. . . . and when men are endowed with power from on high and sent forth, all these things shall be gathered unto the bosom of the church."[4]

Three days after this revelation, the Lord reinforced His determination to send missionaries to the world from Kirtland, saying, "From thence [Kirtland] men shall go forth into all nations."[5]

The Lord identifies three purposes for going to Ohio and implies that a sequence of events will follow, which is later borne out: 1) He will give His law, 2) He will there endow His elders with power from on high, and 3) He will send them from Kirtland unto all nations as soon as they receive their endowment.[6]

In February 1831 the Lord began to lay out requirements for personal worthiness that the elders had to meet before they could receive the promised endowment. He said, "Purge ye out the iniquity which is among you. . . . Sanctify yourselves and ye shall be endowed with power."[7] Later, instructions gradually became more specific, and requirements were tightened for receiving the promised endowment.

Two years later, in June 1833, the Lord laid out an imposing physical requirement. He said: "You should build a house, in the which house I design

---

4. Doctrine & Covenants 38:32–33, 38.

5. Doctrine & Covenants 39:15.

6. Doctrine & Covenants 38:32–33.

7. Doctrine & Covenants 43:11, 16.

to endow those whom I have chosen with power from on high; . . . therefore I command you to tarry, even as mine apostles at Jerusalem."[8] Four conclusions can be drawn from this scripture:

1. The Saints must build the Kirtland Temple, where Christ would endow them.

2. The Savior would choose those who would receive the endowment.

3. The Saints had not yet received the endowment.

4. Christ's latter-day Apostles were to wait (tarry) to be endowed with power from on high as His Apostles in Jerusalem waited for the day of Pentecost before they went to preach the gospel to the world.

Nearly one year later, on May 6, 1834, Church leaders Sidney Rigdon, Oliver Cowdery, and Bishop Newel K. Whitney further emphasized that the endowment must be administered in the Kirtland Temple before the gospel could go to the world. They wrote in a letter, "If the house is not built the Elders will not be endowed with power, and if they are not they can never go to the nations with the everlasting gospel."[9]

Almost seven weeks later, on June 22, 1834, as Zion's Camp was being disbanded in Missouri, the Lord again emphasized that the endowment would come in the Kirtland Temple. He said, "The first elders of my church should receive their endowment from on high in my house . . . in the land of Kirtland. . . . The time has come for a day of choosing; and let those be

8. Doctrine & Covenants 95:8–9. Christ told the earlier Twelve, "Tarry ye in the city of Jerusalem, until ye be endued with power from on high" (Luke 24:49). The fulfillment of this earlier promise came on the day of Pentecost with a great outpouring of spiritual gifts and manifestations.

9. Sidney Rigdon, Newel K. Whitney, and Oliver Cowdery, May 6, 1834, in Stanley R. Gunn, *Oliver Cowdery: Second Elder and Scribe* (Salt Lake City: Bookcraft, 1962), 101.

chosen that are worthy. And it shall be manifest unto my servant, by the voice of the Spirit."[10]

In this scripture the Lord calls this promise of being endowed with power from on high an "endowment." He reemphasized personal preparation. He also restricted the endowment to those who are worthy. Finally, He commissioned Joseph Smith to designate those who were to receive the promised endowment.

The first recorded choosing came the following day, on June 23, 1834. Fifteen brethren were selected specifically by name. Recorded in the meeting minutes, each was "called and chosen" to go to Kirtland from Missouri and receive their "endowment with power from on high."[11]

Another essential step in the command to "tarry, even as mine apostles at Jerusalem" was the choosing of the latter-day Twelve Apostles, who were called and ordained in February 1835.[12] Efforts to prepare for the endowment now intensified. At this point more frequent mention of the endowment is made in minutes and journals, and instruction expanded. Through Oliver Cowdery, the First Presidency gave the newly ordained Twelve their apostolic charge, which included the endowment. Oliver firmly stated, "Remember you are not to go to other nations, till you receive your endowment. Tarry at Kirtland, until you are endowed with power from on high."[13]

---

10. Doctrine & Covenants 105:33, 35–36.

11. *The Far West Record,* ed. Donald Q. Cannon and Lyndon W. Cook (Salt Lake City: Deseret Book, 1983), 68–69. Those called were Edward Partridge, William W. Phelps, Isaac Morley, John Corrill, John Whitmer, David Whitmer, Algernon Sidney Gilbert, Peter Whitmer Jr., Simeon Carter, Newel Knight, Parley P. Pratt, Christian Whitmer, Solomon Hancock, Thomas B. Marsh, and Lyman Wight.

12. Those called were Thomas B. Marsh, David W. Patten, Brigham Young, Heber C. Kimball, Orson Hyde, William E. McLellin, Parley P. Pratt, Luke S. Johnson, William Smith, Orson Pratt, John F. Boynton, and Lyman E. Johnson.

13. Kirtland Council Minute Book, typescript by Lyndon W. Cook, 1978, Church History Library, The Church of Jesus Christ of Latter-day Saints, Salt Lake City, Utah, 162; hereafter cited as Church History Library.

On November 3, 1835, the Lord specified requirements for personal worthiness. He revealed to the Twelve that "all [must] humble themselves before me, before they will be accounted worthy to receive an endowment to go forth in my name unto all nations."[14] Nine days later, Joseph called The Twelve together to give more detailed instructions. He said:

> The endowment you are so anxious about you cannot comprehend now . . . we must be clean evry whit . . . do not watch for iniquity in each other if you do you will not get an endowment for God will not bestow it on such; but if we are faithful . . . I will venture to prophesy that we shall get a . . . blessing that will be worth remembering if we should live as long as John the Revelator, our blessings will be such as we have not realized before, nor in this generation. . . . You need an endowment brethren in order that you may be prepared and able to over come all things.[15]

Some of the Twelve, however, struggled to prepare to meet the requirements. Orson Hyde, about December 15, 1835, wrote Joseph a bitter letter about being refused credit at the Church store when it was given to others. After reading it, Joseph recorded the following prayer:

> I pray Thee, my heavenly Father, in the name of Jesus of Nazareth, that he may be delivered from the power of the destroyer, that his faith fail not in this hour of temptation, and prepare him, and all the Elders, to receive an endowment in Thy house, even according to Thine own order from time to

---

14. *The Papers of Joseph Smith*, ed. Dean C. Jessee, 2 vols. (Salt Lake City: Deseret Book, 1992), 2:64.

15. Jessee, *Papers of Joseph Smith*, 2:77.

time, as Thou seest them worthy to be called into Thy solemn assembly.[16]

About this time, William Smith, the Prophet's brother, wanted to resign his office as an Apostle, partly because of the staggering preparation he needed to make to become worthy. He wrote:

> I was called to an account, by the Twelve, yesterday, for my conduct. . . . I told them that on reflection upon the many difficulties that I had had with the Church, and the much disgrace I had brought upon myself in consequence of these things, and also that my health would not permit me to go to school to make any preparations for the endowment.[17]

On January 13, 1836, Sidney Rigdon taught elements of the endowment to Church leaders.[18] On January 16 the First Presidency met in a special council meeting with the Twelve to reconcile dissension. The Twelve expressed their intention "that they might act in perfect unison and harmony . . . and be prepared for the endowment."[19]

---

16. Joseph Smith, *History of The Church of Jesus Christ of Latter-day Saints,* ed. B. H. Roberts, 7 vols., 2d ed. rev. (Salt Lake City: The Church of Jesus Christ of Latter-day Saints, 1932–51), 2:334; Dean C. Jessee, Mark Ashurst-McGee, and Richard L. Jensen, eds., *Journals, 1832–1839,* vol. 1 of the Journals series of *The Joseph Smith Papers,* edited by Dean C. Jessee, Ronald K. Esplin, and Richard Lyman Bushman (Salt Lake City: Church Historian's Press, 2008), 1:123.

17. *History of the Church,* 2:339; Karen Lynn Davidson, David J. Whittaker, Mark Ashurst-McGee, and Richard L. Jensen, eds., *Histories, 1832–1844,* vol. 1 of the Histories series of *The Joseph Smith Papers,* edited by Dean C. Jessee, Ronald K. Esplin, and Richard Lyman Bushman (Salt Lake City: Church Historian's Press, 2012), 1:152.

18. *History of the Church,* 2:368; Jessee, Ashurst-McGee, and Jensen, *Journals,* 1:151.

19. *History of the Church,* 2:373; Jessee, Ashurst-McGee, and Jensen, *Journals,* 1:157.

The Solemn Assembly

On November 3, 1835, the Lord commanded the Twelve to "prepare their hearts for the solemn assembly."[20] Nine days later Joseph told them that they had to be worthy as well as prepared. He said, "Strive to be prepared in your hearts, be faithful in all things, that when we meet in the solemn assembly . . . we must be clean every whit."[21] In December, Joseph prayed for the Twelve, asking that the Lord would see "them worthy to be called into Thy solemn assembly."[22] It seems that the task of instructing and preparing Church leaders and members weighed heavily on Joseph's mind. In January the beleaguered Prophet recorded, "I returned to my house, being weary with continual anxiety and labor, in putting all the authorities in order, and in striving to purify them for the solemn assembly, according to the commandment of the Lord."[23] The Lord then gradually revealed to Joseph those whom He would invite to attend the solemn assembly. Joseph said, "God shall name out" those who would be invited to attend.[24]

On January 21 an ordinance of endowment, anointing with oil, was introduced in Joseph's upper office in the temple. On January 24, Joseph records that he "met the Presidency . . . and counseled on the subject of endowment, and the preparation for the solemn assembly, which is to be called when the house of the Lord is finished."[25] It seems that at this point, attention turned beyond the upcoming dedication of the temple to the solemn assembly, which was to be held three days after the dedication. The solemn assembly was a unique meeting that originated in Old Testament times. In the

---

20. *History of the Church,* 2:301; Jessee, Ashurst-McGee, and Jensen, *Journals,* 1:83.

21. *History of the Church,* 2:309; Jessee, Ashurst-McGee, and Jensen, *Journals,* 1:98.

22. *History of the Church,* 2:334; Jessee, Ashurst-McGee, and Jensen, *Journals,* 1:123.

23. *History of the Church,* 2:388; Jessee, Ashurst-McGee, and Jensen, *Journals,* 1:178.

24. *History of the Church,* 2:309; Jessee, Ashurst-McGee, and Jensen, *Journals,* 1:98.

25. *History of the Church,* 2:385; Jessee, Ashurst-McGee, and Jensen, *Journals,* 1:172.

Kirtland solemn assembly, the sacrament was distributed, the ordinance of washing of feet was administered, and Joseph instructed the priesthood as to their duties. It also marked the greatest outpouring of the Spirit, greater than in any previous meeting.

The solemn assembly, which the Lord commanded Joseph to hold, was more important than is commonly recognized. The solemn assembly had been the focal point of blessings promised since 1832, when the Lord commanded Joseph to build the Kirtland Temple. In that revelation he was told, "Tarry ye, tarry ye in this place, and call a solemn assembly."[26] In the Kirtland Temple's dedicatory prayer, Joseph was inspired to pray for a fulfillment of the Lord's promise in the solemn assembly.[27]

On March 30, the Prophet convened the long-awaited solemn assembly. In this meeting the ordinance of washing of feet was the last ordinance of endowment for the chosen and worthy elders then in Kirtland. Leaders were specifically chosen to attend. The attendees were "the Presidency, the Twelve, the Seventies, the High Council, the Bishops and their entire quorums, the Elders and all the official members in this stake of Zion, amounting to about three hundred."[28]

Stephen Post, one who was chosen, recorded:

> Wednesday 30th [March 1836] . . . the ordained members met in the house of the Lord to attend to the last ordinance of the endowment. . . . This ordinance is administered to none but those who are clean. . . . I did not expect much to receive the ordinance as I had not labored much in the vineyard. . . . However, when we came together, the word of the Lord was that we all

---

26. Doctrine & Covenants 88:70; other scriptural references also speak of the solemn assembly, including Doctrine & Covenants 88:117; 95:7; 109:6, 10.

27. Doctrine & Covenants 109:6, 10.

28. *History of the Church*, 2:430; Jessee, Ashurst-McGee, and Jensen, *Journals*, 1:213.

should receive the ordinance. Oh the goodness and condescension of God.[29]

Probably more spiritual outpourings occurred in this meeting than in any other recorded meeting in Kirtland. Joseph Smith likened it to the original Day of Pentecost after Christ's ascension in Jerusalem. He elaborated, saying:

> The brethren continued exhorting, prophesying, and speaking in tongues until five o'clock in the morning. The Savior made His appearance to some, while angels ministered to others, and it was a Pentecost and an endowment indeed, long to be remembered, for the sound shall go forth from this place into all the world, and the occurrences of this day shall be handed down upon the pages of sacred history, to all generations; as the day of Pentecost, so shall this day be numbered and celebrated as a year of jubilee, and time of rejoicing to the Saints of the Most High God.[30]

The promised bestowal of the final ordinance of the washing of feet was completed in this meeting, as stated by Joseph Smith: "I then observed to the quorums, that I had now completed the organization of the Church, and we had passed through all the necessary ceremonies, that I had given them all the instruction they needed, and that they now were at liberty, after obtaining their licenses, to go forth and build up the Kingdom of God."[31]

After administering the ordinance in the solemn assembly on March 30, 1836, Joseph then declared, "I made the following remarks: that the

29. Diary of Stephen Post, Holograph, Church History Library, 5.

30. *History of the Church,* 2:432–33; Jessee, Ashurst-McGee, and Jensen, *Journals,* 1:215–16.

31. *History of the Church,* 2:432; Jessee, Ashurst-McGee, and Jensen, *Journals,* 1:215.

time that we were required to tarry in Kirtland to be endowed, would be fulfilled in a few days, and then the Elders would go forth."[32]

Four days later, the Lord confirmed that the endowment had indeed been given. He declared, "The hearts of thousands and tens of thousands shall greatly rejoice in consequence of . . . the endowment with which my servants have already been endowed . . . in this House."[33]

The original promise of the endowment in 1831 was that after they were endowed with power from on high, they would go "among all nations."[34] However, one last critical requirement remained before the elders could be sent to all nations. This consisted of Moses conferring priesthood keys upon Church leaders so they could gather Israel "from the four parts of the earth."[35] The significance of Moses' visit to the Kirtland Temple on April 3, 1836, probably had not yet been fully understood. From a missionary context, the Lord would not authorize the Prophet to send missionaries throughout the earth until after Moses had appeared and given the keys to gather Israel.

Those "few days" mentioned by Joseph Smith were marked forever on April 3, 1836. Christ, Moses, Elias, and Elijah appeared in the temple and bestowed priesthood keys upon Joseph and Oliver. Thus began the divinely appointed responsibilities of Christ's restored Church of gathering Israel through missionary work and enabling the salvation of the dead by building temples and performing vicarious ordinances. Finally the promise made in New York, that Israel should be saved, was formally initiated. The Kirtland endowment was given. Moses, particularly, gave the keys to gather Israel from the four parts of the earth. This initial missionary effort was the

---

32. *History of the Church,* 2:431; Jessee, Ashurst-McGee, and Jensen, *Journals,* 1:214.

33. Jessee, Ashurst-McGee, and Jensen, *Journals,* 1:222. This wording is as it appears in the original record as published in Jessee, Ashurst-McGee, and Jensen, *Journals,* 1:222 (photograph on 220). The language makes clear that the endowment had been given before April 3, 1836, adding the word "already" to the text found in Doctrine & Covenants 110:9.

34. Doctrine & Covenants 38:33.

35. Doctrine & Covenants 110:11.

beginning of the vast dispersion of the latter-day gospel to all nations, kindred, tongues, and people.

First, the promised endowment consisted of ordinances.[36] Second, the endowment consisted of power derived from ordinances. In September 1832 the Lord instructed the Church, "In the ordinances [of the priesthood], the power of godliness is manifest."[37]

Historically it is clear that those who received the Kirtland endowment understood that, in fact, it consisted of sacred ordinances. The following quotations illustrate that understanding:

George A. Smith: "I passed through the ordinances of endowment and received much instruction and many manifestations of the spirit."[38]

Heber C. Kimball: "I attended the dedication of the House of the Lord . . . and participated in all the blessings and ordinances of endowment which were then administered."[39]

Wilford Woodruff: "The day had now arived for preperations for the solumn assembly the Annointing & the endowment. . . . I was absent at that time [in 1836] my day is now come & my time at hand for those blessings & I shall record the events of each day of the endowment for the benefit of the generation to come."[40]

Joel Johnson: "I also received my endowments in the House of the Lord . . . by ordinations, washings, anointings, sealings, etc."[41]

---

36. Ordinances performed in the Kirtland Temple or "attic story of the printing office" adjacent to the temple included a washing ordinance, an anointing of the head with oil, a sealing of the anointing, and a washing of the feet (*History of the Church*, 2:379, 386, 430; Wilford Woodruff, *Wilford Woodruff's Journal, 1833–1898*, ed. Scott G. Kenney, typescript, 9 vols. [Midvale, Utah: Signature Books, 1983–85], 1:130).

37. Doctrine & Covenants 84:20.

38. George A. Smith, "My Journal," *Instructor* 81, no. 11 (1946): 514.

39. "Synopsis of the History of Heber Chase Kimball," *Millennial Star* 26 (September 3, 1864): 569.

40. Woodruff, *Journal*, 1:128.

41. Joel Hills Johnson, Autobiography (1802–1868), typescript, Church History Library, 5.

Stephen Post: "The last ordinance of the endowment . . . [was] the ordinance of the washing of feet."[42]

Truman O. Angell Jr.: "I immediately commenced working upon the House of the Lord, known as the Kirtland Temple, and continued until its dedication, previous to which I had received my first Endowments, which were conducted in the upper chambers or attic, this part of the house having been finished and prepared for use."[43]

Newel Knight: "I arrived in safety in Kirtland, in the Spring of 1835, and commenced labor on the temple, where I continued to work until it was finished, and ready for the endowments. . . .

"I remained in Kirtland until the temple was finished and dedicated. I then received my anointings."[44]

William Draper: "The following winter [1835–36] . . . I received much good . . . instructions preparatory to the endowment, when the temple was finished. . . . During the meetings and endowment . . . I received the ordinances and blessings which were many and great."[45]

Oliver Huntington: "In the [winter] of 1837 father . . . underwent a partial endowment and passed through the . . . ordinances of washing and anointing."[46]

It is also clear from accounts that the Saints in Kirtland understood the ordinances of the Kirtland endowment to be a restoration of Old and New Testament ordinances. Following are representative quotations:

42. Diary of Stephen Post, 5.

43. "Truman Angell Autobiography," in *Our Pioneer Heritage*, comp. Kate B. Carter, 20 vols. (Salt Lake City: Daughters of Utah Pioneers, 1958–77), 10:197.

44. "Newel Knight's Journal," in *Scraps of Biography* in *Classic Experiences and Adventures* (Salt Lake City: Bookcraft, 1969), 94.

45. Carter, "William Draper—Defender of the Faith," 15:67.

46. Oliver Huntington, Autobiography, 29–30, L. Tom Perry Special Collections, Harold B. Lee Library, Provo, Utah; hereafter cited as BYU Special Collections.

Oliver Cowdery: "Those named in the first room were anointed with the same kind of oil and in the man[ner] that were Moses and Aaron, and those who stood before the Lord in ancient days."[47]

Erastus Snow: "All the several authorities and quorums of the Church . . . received the holy anointing like . . . Aaron, David and the holy men of old."[48]

Stephen Post: "Now having attended through the endowment, I could form an idea of the endowment anciently for God's ordinances change not."[49]

Ebenezer Robinson: "We rejoiced greatly, and felt to 'praise the name of the Lord of hosts, because he was restoring to the children of men in these days the ancient order of things, and opening the way for the gathering of Israel.'"[50]

Heber C. Kimball: "This order of things [anointing and washing of feet] is similar to that which was attended to by the Savior, amongst His disciples, previous to His ascension."[51]

Perhaps the most beloved hymn from the Kirtland years reflected the Saints desire to receive the ordinances. The original fourth verse of the hymn "The Spirit of God" contained the following words:

> *We'll wash, and be wash'd, and with oil be anointed*
> *Withal not omitting the washing of feet:*

47. Leonard J. Arrington, "Oliver Cowdery's Kirtland, Ohio, 'Sketch Book,'" *BYU Studies* 12, no. 4 (1972): 419.

48. Erastus Snow, "A Journal or Sketch of the Life of Erastus Snow," typescript, 5, BYU Special Collections.

49. Diary of Stephen Post, 5.

50. Ebenezer Robinson, *The Return* 1, no. 6 (June 1889), 90–91.

51. Heber C. Kimball, in Orson F. Whitney, *Life of Heber C. Kimball* (Salt Lake City: Bookcraft, 1945), 92–93.

For he that receiveth his PENNY appointed,
Must surely be clean at the harvest of wheat.[52]

Journals of 1836 and 1837 indicated characteristics of the initial endowment that are seen in temple practice today:

Each recipient received the endowment individually. For example, George A. Smith, Daniel Tyler, Artemus Millet, Harrison Burgess, Zerah Pulsipher, Joel Johnson, and Truman O. Angel refer to the Kirtland Temple ordinances as "my endowment" or "my endowments."

The endowment was apparently not bestowed on the same individual twice. Wilford Woodruff was absent in 1836. He records that ordinances were repeated in 1837 "for those that were not endowed . . . in the spring of 1836."[53]

Missionaries received their endowment and then left on their missions. George A Smith, Truman O. Angel, and Artemus Millet were among those missionaries.

Receiving the endowment required personal preparation and worthiness. W. W. Phelps wrote to his wife, Sally, of this preparation, saying, "We are preparing [to receive an endowment] to make ourselves clean, by first cleansing our hearts, forsaking our sins, forgiving every body, all we ever had against them . . . and by Keeping all the commandments. As we come nearer to God we see our imperfections and nothingness plainer and plainer."[54]

Approaching the Lord in His temple meant being dressed in a way appropriate to entering into His presence. W. W. Phelps made special mention of

---

52. *A Collection of Sacred Hymns, for the Church of the Latter Day Saints,* sel. Emma Smith (Kirtland, Ohio: F. G. Williams & Co., 1835), 120–21. These verses were sung at the 1836 temple dedication. The title recorded in *History of the Church* was "Hosanna Hymn."

53. Woodruff, *Journal,* 1:128.

54. William W. Phelps, Journal, January [17], 1836, 110, William Wines Phelps (1792–1872) Papers, Vault MSS 810, BYU Special Collections.

this to Sally. He related, "We are preparing . . . by . . . putting on clean decent clothes."[55]

Many other journals made general reference to the endowment. Some, such as journals by Benjamin Brown, Zerah Pulsipher, William Hyde, and Truman O. Angel, referred to the Kirtland endowment as a "first" endowment.

The Kirtland endowment was indeed a powerful fulfillment of the Lord's promise in gathering His Saints there; however, it should not be confused with the expanded endowment given in Nauvoo. Orson Pratt explained:

> The Lord begins little by little; he does not reveal everything all at once. He gave the pattern of these things in Kirtland, Ohio, as the beginning; but there were not rooms for the washings, no rooms such as we have now, and such as were prepared in the Nauvoo Temple; and in other respects, there was something added to the Nauvoo Temple. Why; Because we had greater experience, and were prepared for greater things. There was no font in the basement story of the Kirtland Temple, for baptismal purposes in behalf of the dead? Why not! Because that principle was not revealed.[56]

Brigham Young confirmed that the Kirtland endowment was preparatory to the Nauvoo endowment. He said, "Those first Elders . . . received a portion of their first endowments, or we might say more clearly, some of the first, or introductory, or initiatory ordinances, preparatory to an endowment."[57]

55. Phelps, Journal, 110.

56. Orson Pratt, in Journal of Discourses, 26 vols. (London: Latter-day Saints' Book Depot, 1854–86), 19:19.

57. Brigham Young, in Journal of Discourses, 2:31.

Nevertheless, we must be careful not to minimize the Kirtland endowment. It was central to the purpose of the Church's gathering in Kirtland and its expansion to the world. It was central to the purpose for building the Kirtland Temple. Kirtland Saints compared the ordinances of that endowment to sacred ordinances conducted in ancient times. From the Kirtland endowment sprang temple ordinances and instruction central to subsequent temple practices. Today, building upon keys and ordinances given in the Kirtland Temple, millions of people receive the fulness of the temple endowment and its accompanying sacred ordinances. Today, because of the "beginning of the blessing . . . poured out" in the Kirtland Temple, temples are proliferating throughout the world.[58]

---

58. Doctrine & Covenants 110:10.

CHAPTER 14

CHRIST RAISES AN ENSIGN AND BEGINS A LONG-AWAITED GATHERING

From [Kirtland], whosoever I will shall go forth among all nations
. . . for Israel shall be saved, and I will lead them.
—DOCTRINE & COVENANTS 38:33

On April 3, 1836, the Lord Jesus Christ stood on the pulpit of the Kirtland Temple and lifted His long-prophesied ensign of gathering His children for all people to see. He fulfilled many prophecies that day, including Isaiah's assurance that Christ "shall set up an ensign for the nations, and shall assemble the outcasts of Israel . . . from the four corners of the earth."[1] In one sense, the Lord raised the Kirtland Temple itself as an ensign. From its elevated pulpits that April day, the Savior declared, "The fame of this house shall spread to foreign lands."[2] Four days before Christ's visit, Joseph prophesied that this message of restoration would "go forth from [the Kirtland Temple] into all the world."[3]

---

1. Isaiah 11:12.

2. Doctrine & Covenants 110:10.

3. Joseph Smith, *History of The Church of Jesus Christ of Latter-day Saints*, ed. B. H. Roberts, 7 vols., 2d ed. rev. (Salt Lake City: The Church of Jesus Christ of Latter-day Saints, 1932–51), 2:433; Dean C. Jessee, Mark Ashurst-McGee, and Richard L. Jensen, eds., *Journals, 1832–1839*, vol. 1 of the

In His unprecedented visit, Christ brought with Him three celestial companions—Moses, Elias, and Elijah, two of whom Christians, Muslims, and Jews hail as prophets. On this day, these revered prophets set in motion the fulfillment of the Abrahamic covenant. That covenant is particularly recognizable to those of all three major faiths, who are the "seed" of Abraham. Abraham also appeared in the Kirtland Temple,[4] and he wrote the book of Abraham, which Joseph Smith translated in 1835. Abraham's appearance and his writings are often overlooked as an ensign to the Muslim and Jewish peoples, who count him as their father and a great prophet. In fact, the news of these four divine visitors to the first latter-day temple should have been hailed with rejoicing and headlines throughout the world to those of all faiths.

Completing the Lord's Four-Phase Plan

On April 3, 1836, the Lord set in motion the final phase of His plan to save each of His children.[5] It appears that after the Flood, the Lord enacted this four-phase plan. The *first phase* probably began at the time of the Tower of Babel when He began to establish the Gentile nations.[6] Ancient scripture

---

Journals series of *The Joseph Smith Papers,* edited by Dean C. Jessee, Ronald K. Esplin, and Richard Lyman Bushman (Salt Lake City: Church Historian's Press, 2008), 1:216.

4. Doctrine & Covenants 137:5.

5. In the context of the Old Testament, the terminology "Christ" and "the Lord" are used synonymously. Bruce R. McConkie wrote, "Jehovah-Christ is the God of Israel. . . . when he, as a resurrected person, invited the Nephites to feel the prints of the nails in his hands and in his feet, he did it so that they may know that he was the God of Israel . . . and had been 'slain for the sins of the world' (3 Ne. 11:14). As Israel's God, it is clear that he and not the Father spoke to all the ancient prophets—to Moses, Isaiah, Malachi, to all who were called as guides and lights to the Lord's ancient peoples. He it was who gave the Law of Moses and in him it was fulfilled (3 Ne. 15:1–10). In fact, the whole Old Testament is most explicit that the Deity in whose name the ancient prophets spoke was Jehovah, not Elohim" (*The Promised Messiah* [Salt Lake City: Deseret Book, 1978], 122).

6. The term *Gentile* is generally used to denote all nations and people not of the house of Israel; however, the earliest usage of the word in the King James Bible occurred before the house of Israel was established and dates from the same general time period as the Tower of Babel. Nimrod, the great-grandson of Noah, is often credited as being the builder of the Tower of Babel. According to the biblical account, his cousins, who were sons of Japeth and, like Nimrod, great-grandsons of Noah,

documents how the Lord confounded the language of His disobedient children. This resulted in the inability of the people to understand one another's speech and in the scattering of the people throughout the world. The Lord documented His plan by declaring, "I the Lord, will scatter them abroad . . . upon all the face of the land, and unto every quarter of the earth."[7]

The *second phase* of the plan was to establish the house of Israel hundreds of years later through Abraham, Isaac, and Jacob, whose name was changed to Israel. The children of Israel are also known as the covenant people because the Lord made covenants with their patriarchs Abraham, Isaac, and Jacob, as well as patriarchs as far back as Adam.[8] The Lord covenanted with Abraham to give him a land inheritance and make him a "father of many nations."[9] Christ also made an "everlasting covenant" that He would always be God to Abraham and his posterity.[10] He promised the children of Israel, "I will redeem you . . . And I will take you to me for a people, and I will be to you a God."[11] He covenanted that Abraham's posterity would be as innumerable as the "stars of heaven"[12] or "sand upon the

---

divided "the isles of the Gentiles . . . in their lands; every one after his tongue, after their families, in their nations" (Genesis 10:5). It is therefore assumed that the Gentile nations emerged after the confusion of tongues.

7. JST, Genesis 11:5.

8. It should be noted that from the beginning, the Lord established a pattern of making covenants with patriarchs and peoples. Professor George S. Tate discussed these covenants: "God's covenant relationship with mankind began with Adam and Eve. Texts in the Pearl of Great Price show that Adam and Eve were the first after the Fall to enter into a covenant relationship with God—through sacrifice, baptism (Moses 6:64–66), and receiving the priesthood and ordinances associated with the temple: 'Thus all things were confirmed unto Adam, by an holy ordinance' (Moses 5:59; see also 4:4–5, 8, 10–12). Adam and Eve were promised a savior and were instructed to be obedient, to be repentant, and to do all things in the name of the Son of God (Moses 5:6–8)" ("Covenants in Biblical Times," in *Encyclopedia of Mormonism*, ed. Daniel H. Ludlow et al., 4 vols. [New York: Macmillan, 1992], 1:334.)

9. Genesis 17:4; see also 15:18; 17:8.

10. Genesis 17:7.

11. Exodus 6:6–7.

12. Exodus 32:13.

seashore."[13] Abraham and his posterity were also to be blessed to hold the priesthood.[14] And Abraham's name was to be remembered throughout the earth, which would result in the gospel and the priesthood being taken to all people so that they could receive salvation and eternal life:

> I will make . . . thy name great among all nations, and
> . . . thy seed . . . shall bear [the] Priesthood unto all nations; . . .
> and in thy seed . . . (that is to say, the literal seed, or the seed
> of the body) shall all the families of the earth be blessed, even
> with the blessings of the Gospel, which are the blessings of
> salvation, even of life eternal.[15]

The *third phase* of His plan began in 722 B.C. when the Lord began to disperse the millions of His chosen Israel throughout the Gentile nations. The ten tribes, who lived in the Northern Kingdom, were taken captive at that time into Assyria. From there, the main body was taken to non-disclosed locations in the "land of the north."[16] However, great numbers were apparently left behind.[17] Others after about 600 B.C., such as Lehi and Ishmael, populated other lands. After this time the remaining Israelites in the Southern Kingdom, primarily of Judah, were scattered throughout

---

13. Doctrine & Covenants 132:30.

14. Abraham 1:3–4, 18.

15. Abraham 2:9, 11.

16. Doctrine & Covenants 110:11.

17. Esdras, or Ezra, an authoritative and oft-quoted apocryphal writer is cited by Apostle James E. Talmage as having given "evidence that many remained in the land of their captivity" (*Articles of Faith* [Salt Lake City: Deseret Book, 1981], 295). Apostle Bruce R McConkie quotes a source that theorizes that others dropped out on the journey north by asking the question, "Is it altogether improbable that in that long journey of one and a half years, as Esdras states it, from Media the land of their captivity to the frozen north, some of the backsliding Israel rebelled, turned aside from the main body, forgot their God, by and by mingled with the Gentiles and became the leaven to leaven with the promised seed all the nations of the earth?" (George Reynolds, *Are We of Israel?* 3d ed. [Salt Lake City: Deseret Sunday School Union, 1916], 10, in Bruce R. McConkie, *Mormon Doctrine*, 2d ed. [Salt Lake City: Bookcraft, 1966], 457).

many nations. The Lord informed holy prophets of His plan to scatter Israel long before it happened. He also caused them to record His words in holy writ. The following scriptures are representative of what numerous prophets recorded in the Bible and Book of Mormon:

- "I shall scatter them among the nations, and disperse them in the countries."[18]
- "I will scatter you among the heathen."[19]
- "I will sift the house of Israel among all nations."[20]
- "The Lord shall cause thee to be . . . removed into all the kingdoms of the earth."[21]
- "The Lord shall scatter thee among all people, from the one end of the earth even unto the other."[22]
- "The house of Israel, sooner or later, will be scattered upon all the face of the earth."[23]

The Lord apparently effected this dispersion and scattering to ultimately be a spiritual blessing and salvation to all Gentile nations. President Joseph Fielding Smith, a latter-day prophet and student of the scriptures, pointed out that this scattering enabled the bloodline of Abraham to be assimilated into Gentile nations:

> The house of Israel [was] scattered among the Gentiles to be a blessing to the Gentile nations and make them of the blood of Israel through the gospel. The scattering of Israel among the nations was not intended merely as a

18. Ezekiel 12:15.

19. Leviticus 26:33.

20. Amos 9:9.

21. Deuteronomy 28:25.

22. Deuteronomy 28:64.

23. 1 Nephi 22:3.

punishment, but as the leaven which would leaven the Gentile nations and make them of the blood of Abraham, according to the promises given to Abraham.[24]

President Smith also used the Book of Mormon allegory of the olive trees to explain the scattering of Israel:

> The interpretation of this parable . . . is a story of the scattering of Israel and the mixing of the blood of Israel with the wild olive trees, or Gentile peoples, in all parts of the world. Therefore we find in China, Japan, India, and in all other countries that are inhabited by the Gentiles that the blood of Israel was scattered, or 'grafted,' among them. Therefore in this day of gathering the Lord is fulfilling his purposes and is calling back into the fold of the True Shepherd, the children of Abraham.[25]

Hugh Nibley, a respected Latter-day Saint scholar of ancient history, explained the effect of the scattering in more colorful language:

> Abraham's seed [is] sown among all the nations of the earth. What we have here is this long, fitful motion and mixing and separation and collision and ebb and flow and breaking and joining and scattering—springing there, expanding here, withering there. Absorbed, rejected, leavening the whole lump, like yeast—this constant churning around that makes all of the blood of Israel.[26]

---

24. Joseph Fielding Smith, *Answers to Gospel Questions*, comp. Joseph Fielding Smith Jr., 5 vols. (Salt Lake City: Deseret Book, 1957–66), 1:141.

25. Smith, *Answers to Gospel Questions*, 4:40–41.

26. Hugh W. Nibley, "Lecture 24: Jacob 3–4," in *Teachings of the Book of Mormon: Semester 1* (lectures presented to an honors Book of Mormon class at Brigham Young University, 1988–90); available online at maxwellinstitute.byu.edu.

In astounding fulfillment of ancient covenants and promises, it appears that Abraham's bloodline is now found in almost all people on earth. His posterity is indeed innumerable. Elder Bruce R. McConkie explained the religious significance of integrating the bloodline of Israel with that of all other nations and people. He said that this bloodline could be called "believing blood" because it brought with it a tendency to recognize truth and accept the gospel. He wrote:

> In general, the Lord sends to earth in the lineage of Jacob those spirits who in pre-existence developed an especial talent for spirituality and for recognizing truth. Those born in this lineage, having the blood of Israel in their veins and finding it easy to accept the gospel, are said to have *believing blood.*
>
> Since much of Israel has been scattered among the Gentile nations, it follows that millions of people have mixed blood, blood that is part Israel and part Gentile. [27]

Christ Fulfills Ancient Covenants

In the Kirtland Temple, on April 3, 1836, Christ personally launched the fulfillment of the *fourth and final phase* of His plan. On that long-awaited day, He fulfilled some of His most deeply rooted covenants that He entered into with Abraham and ancient Israel. It seems that the Savior would have had great joy and desire to fulfill His age-old covenants. In His own words, Christ discussed some specific covenants that He had made and was about to fulfill:

---

27. Elder Bruce R. McConkie defined "believing blood" as follows: "This is a figurative expression commonly used to designate the aptitude and inclination of certain persons to accept and believe the principles of revealed religion" (*Mormon Doctrine*, 81).

- "I remember my covenant with Jacob . . . Isaac, and . . . Abraham."[28]
- "And then will I remember my covenant which I have made unto my people, O house of Israel, and I will bring my gospel unto them."[29]
- "I sware unto your fathers . . . I will never break my covenant with you."[30]
- "I will remember my covenant unto you, O house of Israel."[31]

Now, after about twenty-five hundred years of integrating Israel's bloodline throughout the world, Christ was finally ready to send His messengers out to gather in His covenant people. Christ documented this final phase of His plan long in advance. Following are only a few of His promises:

"I will gather the remnant of my flock out of all countries whither I have driven them, and will bring them again to their folds; and they shall be fruitful and increase. And I will set up shepherds over them which shall feed them: and they shall fear no more, nor be dismayed, neither shall they be lacking, saith the Lord."[32]

"I will bring thy seed from the east, and gather thee from the west; I will say to the north, Give up; and to the south, Keep not back: bring my sons from far, and my daughters from the ends of the earth; even every one that is called by my name."[33]

---

28. Leviticus 26:42.

29. 3 Nephi 16:11.

30. Judges 2:1.

31. 3 Nephi 16:12.

32. Jeremiah 23:3–4.

33. Isaiah 43:5–7.

"I will gather them out of all countries, whither I have driven them. . . . And they shall be my people, and I will be their God."[34]

April 3, 1836, was certainly a high and holy day!

Parley P. Pratt, in another area of the temple that day, described the significance of the long-awaited gathering empowered by sacred events that transpired on April 3, 1836. In the hymn "The Morning Breaks," Parley highlights visits by Christ and angelic messengers. He tells of the latter-day gathering of both Israel and the Gentile nations. Since 1840, the Church has frequently placed this hymn first in Church hymnals:

> *The morning breaks, the shadows flee;*
> *Lo, Zion's standard is unfurled!*
> *The glory bursting from afar . . .*
> *Wide o'er the nations soon will shine.*
> *The Gentile fulness now comes in;*
> *And Israel's blessings are at hand. . . .*
> *Jehovah speaks! Let earth give ear,*
> *And Gentile nations turn and live . . .*
> *Angels from heaven and truth from earth*
> *Have met, and both have record borne;*
> *Thus Zion's light is bursting forth*
> *To bring her ransomed children home.*[35]

---

34. Jeremiah 32:37–38.

35. Taken from the hymn "The Morning Breaks," written by Parley P. Pratt and published in 1840 on the cover of the first issue of the Church's first periodical in England, entitled *The Star* (see B. H. Roberts, *A Comprehensive History of the Church, Century One,* 6 vols. [Salt Lake City: The Church of Jesus Christ of Latter-day Saints, 1930], 2:87). It has often appeared as the first hymn in Church hymnals (including the 1985 *Hymns of The Church of Jesus Christ of Latter-day Saints*) since it appeared first in the Manchester, England, hymnal entitled *A Collection of Sacred Hymns for the Church of Jesus Christ of Latter-day Saints in Europe* in 1840. In the hymn, Parley tells of visits by angels and Christ and highlights the latter-day gathering of Israel.

Christ Instructs Joseph Smith in His Mission

Christ announced His plan to gather Israel as early as 1823 when Moroni told Joseph Smith that Moroni himself was "sent to bring the joyful tidings that the covenant which God made with ancient Israel was at hand."[36] In 1829, Joseph learned from the title page of the Book of Mormon that its purpose was "to show unto the remnant of the house of Israel . . . that they may know the covenants of the Lord, that they are not cast off forever."[37] In 1831, the Lord told Joseph that the gathering of Israel would commence in Kirtland, "And from thence [Kirtland], whosoever I will shall go forth among all nations . . . for Israel shall be saved, and I will lead them."[38]

Joseph Smith obviously felt the heavy weight of the enormity of his task to gather Israel. This is evidenced in 1833, when he anxiously requested a New York newspaper to publish the news that the long anticipated time was finally at hand. He boldly stated:

> The time has at last arrived when the God of Abraham, of Isaac, and of Jacob, has set his hand again the second time to recover the remnants of his people, which have been left from Assyria, and from Egypt, and from Pathros, and from Cush, and from Elam, and from Shinar, and from Hamath, and from the islands of the sea, and with them to bring in the fulness of the Gentiles, and establish that covenant with them, which was promised.[39]

When Joseph discovered that the editor had published only part of his letter, he pleaded for the full text to be printed. Joseph's need to inform the world is evidenced by an uncharacteristic threatening tone of a second letter:

---

36. *History of the Church,* 4:537.

37. Title Page of the Book of Mormon.

38. Doctrine & Covenants 38:33.

39. *History of the Church,* 1:313.

DEAR SIR:—I was somewhat disappointed on receiving my paper with only a part of my letter inserted in it. The letter which I wrote you for publication, I wrote by the commandment of God, and I am quite anxious to have it all laid before the public. . . .

. . . I now say unto you, that if you wish to clear your garments from the blood of your readers, I exhort you to publish that letter entire; but if not, the sin be upon your head. Accept, sir the good wishes and tender regard of your unworthy servant,

Joseph Smith, Jun.[40]

Although the Prophet clearly understood his responsibility to gather Israel, he also knew that Israel's gathering could not commence until the Kirtland Temple was completed. In 1832, missionaries who would be sent out into the world were told to wait until the temple was built. The Lord declared, "Tarry ye, tarry ye in this place [Kirtland]. . . . and establish a house, even . . . a house of God."[41] In 1834, Church leaders warned, "If the house is not built the Elders . . . can never go to the nations with the everlasting gospel."[42] In 1835, the Kirtland Temple, the place where the Twelve Apostles would receive their endowment, was still under construction. They were told, "Remember you are not to go to other nations, till you receive your endowment. Tarry at Kirtland."[43] Thus, the Kirtland Temple became the key link in the chain of the gathering. A primary purpose for the temple was to

---

40. *History of the Church,* 1:326; "History of Joseph Smith," *Millennial Star* 14, no. 24 (August 7, 1852): 374.

41. Doctrine & Covenants 88:70, 119.

42. Sidney Rigdon, Newel K. Whitney, and Oliver Cowdery, May 6, 1834, in Oliver Cowdery letter book, letter numbers 45–46, in Stanley R. Gunn, *Oliver Cowdery: Second Elder and Scribe* (Salt Lake City: Bookcraft, 1962), 101.

43. Given in the Apostolic Charge administered by Oliver Cowdery, in Kirtland Council Minute Book, typescript by Lyndon W. Cook, 1978, Church History Library, The Church of Jesus Christ of Latter-day Saints, Salt Lake City, Utah, 162.

receive final keys and authority. Moses couldn't return the keys of gathering Israel until the temple was completed. President Joseph Fielding Smith explained that missionaries needed to be endowed and prepared in the temple: "The Lord commanded the Saints to build a temple [the Kirtland Temple] in which he could reveal the keys of authority and where the apostles could be endowed and prepared to prune his vineyard for the last time."[44]

The Visitation of Moses

Moses, the prophet who parted the Red Sea, spoke with God on Sinai and revealed commandments whereby Christians and Jews gauge their conduct—stood in glory before Joseph Smith and Oliver Cowdery in the Kirtland Temple. How must Joseph and Oliver have felt to face such a powerful and revered prophet? Few experiences could have been as glorious to them as they stood at Moses' feet. Moses, God's anointed prophet who gathered Israel the first time from Egypt, now transferred the authority to gather and lead Israel again in the latter days.

As Moses received the authority and commission anciently to "bring forth my people the children of Israel out of Egypt," Joseph received the authority and a similar commission to be a latter-day Moses—to gather the Lord's people, the children of Israel, out of all parts of the earth in the latter days.[45] Of this experience, Joseph and Oliver wrote: "The heavens were again opened unto us; and Moses appeared before us, and committed unto us the keys of the gathering of Israel from the four parts of the earth, and the leading of the ten tribes from the land of the north."[46]

Joseph Smith understood his role in the gathering of Israel. Earlier, on January 21, 1836, he was given an assignment paralleling the Lord's mandate to Moses. Joseph was anointed and blessed by his father "to lead Israel

---

44. Joseph Fielding Smith, *Doctrines of Salvation,* comp. Bruce R. McConkie, 3 vols. (Salt Lake City: Bookcraft, 1954–56), 2:234.

45. Exodus 3:10; 2 Nephi 3:9, 11, 13, 15, 16.

46. Doctrine & Covenants 110:11.

in the latter days, even as Moses led him in days of old."⁴⁷ Joseph acknowledged his designated role, saying, "I have the honor . . . to be your leader & lawyier as Moses to the Children of Israel."⁴⁸

As a direct consequence of Moses appearing in the temple, Orson Hyde was commissioned in 1840 to go to Jerusalem. On October 24, 1841, Elder Hyde dedicated that land where about twenty-five thousand Jews then lived, for the return of scattered Israel. In the God-given dedicatory prayer for the Kirtland Temple, Joseph prayed that "Jerusalem, from this hour, may begin to be redeemed; and the yoke of bondage may begin to be broken off from the house of David; and the children of Judah may begin to return to the lands which thou didst give to Abraham, their father."⁴⁹ When Moses appeared in Kirtland in 1836, it was unthinkable that the Jewish people could return to their homeland. By the year 2012, more than three million Jews had returned to Israel.⁵⁰

Part of Moses' keys of gathering extends to the return of the lost ten tribes. Little is known about them. Christ, concerned about all of latter-day Israel, didn't forget them. The Lord told Joseph Smith that the lost tribes are "in the north countries."⁵¹ The Lord says that they will come in remembrance before him and come to Zion "filled with songs of everlasting joy."⁵² They will "fall down and be crowned with glory" under the hands of the children of Ephraim.⁵³

47. *History of the Church,* 2:380; Jessee, Ashurst-McGee, and Jensen, *Journals,* 1:167.

48. Wilford Woodruff, in *The Words of Joseph Smith*, comp. and ed. Andrew F. Ehat and Lyndon W. Cook (Provo, Utah: Brigham Young University Religious Studies Center, 1980), 221.

49. Doctrine & Covenants 109:62–64.

50. Between the years 1948 and 2012 the total number of people who immigrated to Israel was 3,092,729 ("Immigration to Israel," Jewish Virtual Library, accessed June 28, 2012, https://www .jewishvirtuallibrary.org/jsource/Immigration/Immigration_to_Israel.html).

51. Doctrine & Covenants 133:26.

52. Doctrine & Covenants 133:33.

53. Doctrine & Covenants 133:32.

The Lord made clear that the gathering would begin from the Kirtland Temple. In the dedicatory prayer, the Lord inspired Joseph Smith to pray:

> And from this place they may bear exceedingly great and glorious tidings, in truth, unto the ends of the earth, that they may know that this is thy work, and that thou hast put forth thy hand, to fulfil that which thou hast spoken by the mouths of the prophets, concerning the last days. . . .
>
> . . . thou hast a great love for the children of Jacob [Israel], who have been scattered. . . .
>
> We therefore ask thee to have mercy upon the children of Jacob. . . .
>
> And cause that the remnants of Jacob . . . be converted . . . to the fulness of the everlasting gospel. . . .
>
> And may all the scattered remnants of Israel, who have been driven to the ends of the earth, come to a knowledge of the truth.[54]

On Sunday, March 27, the "House of God," the Kirtland Temple, was dedicated. The solemn assembly was held three days later on March 30. At that time, the final Kirtland endowment ordinance was bestowed on leaders and missionaries who would take the message to the world. During that sacred meeting, just four days prior to Moses' visit, Joseph announced, "The time that we were required to tarry in Kirtland . . . would be fulfilled in a few days, and then the elders would go forth."[55] Joseph then told the assembled missionaries that they could obtain their licenses.[56] On

---

54. Doctrine & Covenants 109:23–67.

55. *History of the Church,* 2:431; Jessee, Ashurst-McGee, and Jensen, *Journals,* 1:214.

56. *History of the Church,* 2:432; Jessee, Ashurst-McGee, and Jensen, *Journals,* 1:215.

April 3, Christ formally accepted the Temple.[57] Immediately afterward, Moses came to bring keys to initiate the gathering of Israel. Church members today associate the keys of Moses with a mission of the Church to "Preach My Gospel."

No longer were these latter-day gatherers to be restrained. During the week that Moses returned with the keys, Joseph sent missionaries out with this instruction: "Let the redemption of Zion be our object." Joseph continued by saying of the elders, "They now were at liberty, after obtaining their licenses, to go forth and build up the Kingdom of God."[58] Is it coincidence that Moses returned during Passover, a Jewish holy day that began thousands of years earlier when Moses led and guided the children of Israel out of Egypt?

The Lord Initiates Events for the Gospel to Go to Europe

Immediately after Moses returned the keys of gathering Israel, the Lord set events in motion for the gospel to go to England. This chain of events started with the visit of Heber C. Kimball and others to Parley Pratt's home in Kirtland. Heber, who would sail across the Atlantic a year later as leader of the first missionary contingent to go to Europe, gave a priesthood blessing to Parley and his wife, Thankful. Heber prophesied that Parley would fulfill a mission to Canada and plant seeds there that would result in a bounteous harvest of English converts.

In an inspired prophecy, Heber said:

> Arise . . . and go forth in the ministry, nothing doubting. Take no thoughts for your debts, nor the necessaries of life, for the Lord will supply you with abundant means for all things.

---

57. Doctrine & Covenants 110:7.

58. *History of the Church,* 2:432; Jessee, Ashurst-McGee, and Jensen, *Journals,* 1:215–16.

Thou shalt go to Upper Canada, even to the city of Toronto, . . . and there thou shalt find a people prepared for
the fulness of the gospel, and they shall receive thee, and
. . . the Church . . . shall spread thence into the regions round
about, and many shall be brought to the knowledge of the
truth . . . and from the things growing out of this mission,
shall the fulness of the gospel spread into England, and cause
a great work to be done in that land.[59]

Just two days following Moses' visit, Parley left Kirtland and set his
course for the city of Toronto, where the Lord would lead him to connections He had already put in place to begin the work in England. As Parley
reached Hamilton, Canada, on Lake Ontario, the Lord, true to the inspired
prophecy, extended His helping hand. To reach Toronto faster, Parley desired to take a ship, which would take only two hours. Traveling on the lake
was far more favorable than days of laborious trudging through the mud of
Canada's spring thaw. Alone and without the two dollars required for passage to Toronto, Parley described his situation:

I was an entire stranger in Hamilton, and also in the
province; and money I had none. Under these circumstances I pondered what I should do. I had many times received answers to prayer in such matters; but now it seemed
hard to exercise faith, because I was among strangers and
entirely unknown. The Spirit seemed to whisper to me to
try the Lord, and see if anything was too hard for him, that
I might know and trust Him under all circumstances. I
retired to a secret place in a forest and prayed to the Lord
for money to enable me to cross the lake. I then entered

59. Parley P. Pratt, *Autobiography of Parley P. Pratt*, ed. Parley P. Pratt Jr. (Salt Lake City: Deseret Book, 1985), 110.

Hamilton and commenced to chat with some of the people. I had not tarried many minutes before I was accosted by a stranger, who inquired my name and where I was going. He also asked me if I did not want some money. I said yes. He then gave me ten dollars and a letter of introduction to John Taylor, of Toronto.[60]

After arriving in Toronto on April 19, Parley proceeded immediately to John Taylor's home with his letter of introduction. Parley met with immediate success in the area. He held a series of meetings, performed a miracle, and received referrals to a family named Fielding and others who had relatives and friends in England. Parley baptized the Taylors; Joseph Fielding; Joseph's sisters, Mary (who would later marry Hyrum Smith) and Mercy; and many others. He also organized a branch of the Church near Toronto. In addition to Joseph Fielding, three other brethren with connections in England were baptized—John Goodson, Isaac Russell, and John Snyder. These four would later join the first missionary complement of seven elders sent to England under the direction of Heber C. Kimball.

The first missionary contacts in England came through letters written by Parley's converts. John Taylor said, "I was the first person that wrote a letter to England on the subject of the Gospel; I did it at the request of Brother Fielding, who got me to write for him to a brother and brother-in-law of his who were ministers in England."[61]

Joseph, Mary, and Mercy Fielding also wrote letters proclaiming the truth of the restored gospel to their brother, James Fielding, and to their brother-in-law, Timothy Matthews, both leaders of congregations in England. James read their letters over the pulpit to his congregation. Other converts wrote similar letters of testimony to friends and family in England.

---

60. Pratt, *Autobiography*, 113–14.

61. John Taylor, in *Journal of Discourse*, 26 vols. (London: Latter-day Saints' Book Depot, 1854–86), 23:31.

According to Parley, "Several of the Saints in Canada were English, who had friends in England. Letters had already been sent to them with information of the rise of the Church, and of its principles. Several of the Canadian Elders felt a desire to go on a mission to their friends in that country."[62]

These letters later proved to be influential in paving the way for the first missionaries in England to receive a warm welcome. The two clerics, James Fielding and Timothy Matthews, turned their pulpits over to the missionaries. Heber C. Kimball wrote, "The greater portion of their members received our testimony, obeyed the ordinances we taught, and are now rejoicing in the blessings of the new and everlasting covenant."[63] Neither man accepted baptism, but they enabled the gospel to be firmly established in England.

John Taylor concluded in 1836 that Parley's mission "was the means . . . of sending the Gospel to England."[64] Parley's mission to Canada also proved to be the first step in sending the gospel to the world.

The Lord's preparation in Canada resulted in the first baptisms abroad in England in 1837. Missionaries who were endowed with ordinances, spiritual manifestations, and power were finally commissioned under the full keys of gathering bestowed by Moses. They then left under the direction of the latter-day Moses, Joseph Smith. To the seven-year-old Church, this meant that missionaries, who had limited their activity to the United States and Canada, could now proselyte throughout the earth.

The Keys of Moses and of Peter, James, and John

In 1829, Peter, James, and John ordained Joseph Smith and Oliver Cowdery to the Melchizedek Priesthood and confirmed them to be Apostles and especial witnesses of Christ. With this ordination came the

---

62. Pratt, *Autobiography*, 143.

63. Heber C. Kimball, in Orson F. Whitney, *Life of Heber C. Kimball* (Salt Lake City: Bookcraft, 1945), 149.

64. Taylor, in *Journal of Discourses*, 23:31.

keys of Christ's kingdom and its final gospel dispensation.[65] Under that authority, missionaries preached the gospel in the United States and Canada and began to build up the Church. The Lord, however, restrained missionaries from going abroad until Moses returned with his keys to gather Israel. The difference between the keys of 1829 and 1836 are not fully understood, but we do know that Moses' keys broadly pertained to gathering Israel from the four parts of the earth. Those of Peter, James, and John were used to initiate missionary work in Canada and the United States.

Joseph Fielding Smith, drawing a distinction between the keys to preach and the keys to gather, taught: "The keys or power to go forth and proclaim the gospel was restored to Joseph Smith and Oliver Cowdery when Peter, James, and John conferred upon them the Melchizedek Priesthood before the organization of the Church."[66] He said, "Moses was sent to restore the keys of the gathering, not the preaching of the gospel. It was after people were converted that the spirit of gathering entered their souls."[67]

Elder Bruce R. McConkie used the phrase "full gathering" to explain the meaning of Moses' keys and powers:

> By the 3rd of April in 1836 many thousands had come out of the Egypt of the world into a promised land of gospel peace. And then the heavens were rent, the Great God sent Moses back to confer keys and powers upon mortals, and the way was prepared for the full gathering that would make the first flight out of Egypt seem as nothing.[68]

---

65. Doctrine & Covenants 27:12–13.

66. Smith, *Answers to Gospel Questions*, 1:131.

67. Smith, *Answers to Gospel Questions*, 3:153.

68. Bruce R. McConkie, *The Millennial Messiah* (Salt Lake City: Deseret Book, 1982), 202.

"An Ensign to the Nations"

Finally, a prophecy revealed in an upstairs room of Newel K. Whitney's simple frontier store became an ensign from Kirtland to all nations. The Lord declared: "For it shall come to pass in that day, that every man shall hear the fulness of the gospel in his own tongue, and in his own language, through those who are ordained unto this power, by the administration of the Comforter, shed forth upon them for the revelation of Jesus Christ."[69]

The Lord made it immediately clear in Ohio that He was concerned with all people: "The voice of the Lord is unto all men. . . . all that will hear may hear. . . . I the Lord am willing to make these things known unto all flesh; For I am no respecter of persons."[70] Joseph Smith taught that those who are not of Israel but accept the gospel and receive the Holy Ghost are literally changed and chosen to receive all blessings promised to the obedient in Israel.[71]

Six years after Moses' visit to the Kirtland Temple, Joseph Smith reported the progress of the Church in a letter to a Chicago newspaper. He stated that a principle purpose of the Church was "the literal gathering of Israel and . . . the restoration of the Ten Tribes."[72] He noted that the worldwide gathering was well under way: "The Elders of this Church [have] gone forth. . . . into England, Ireland, Scotland, and Wales, where . . . over five thousand joined . . . [and] there are numbers now joining in every land." He further stated, "Our missionaries are going forth to different nations . . . Germany, Palestine, New Holland, Australia, the East Indies, and other places.[73]

---

69. Doctrine & Covenants 90:11.

70. Doctrine & Covenants 1:2, 11, 34, 35.

71. Joseph Smith, *Teachings of the Prophet Joseph Smith,* sel. Joseph Fielding Smith (Salt Lake City: Deseret Book, 1976), 149–50.

72. Articles of Faith 1:10; *History of the Church,* 4:541.

73. *History of the Church,* 4:540.

The Prophet then declared the Church's commitment and determination to see the gathering of Israel completed:

> The Standard of Truth has been erected; no unhallowed hand can stop the work from progressing; persecutions may rage, mobs may combine, armies may assemble, calumny may defame, but the truth of God will go forth boldly, nobly, and independent, till it has penetrated every continent, visited every clime, swept every country, and sounded in every ear, till the purposes of God shall be accomplished, and the Great Jehovah shall say the work is done.[74]

The gospel of Jesus Christ as empowered in Kirtland would never be stopped.

---

74. *History of the Church*, 4:540.

CHAPTER 15

CHRIST RETURNS KEYS
FOR FULL SALVATION

Let the dead speak forth anthems of eternal praise to the King Immanuel,
who hath ordained . . . that which would enable us to redeem them.

—JOSEPH SMITH, DOCTRINE & COVENANTS 128:22

"Jesus Christ miraculously returns to earth and brings the ancient prophets Moses, Elias, and Elijah with Him!" If the news media of 1836 had covered this epic event in the Kirtland Temple on April 3, this is how they might have reported it. Had they understood the full implication of this heavenly manifestation, they might have announced, "Christ's visit on April 3, 1836, provided the latter-day opportunity for full salvation to all of God's children."[1]

---

1. Temple ordinance work for the living and vicarious work for the dead are requirements for full salvation (Joseph Smith, *History of The Church of Jesus Christ of Latter-day Saints,* ed. B. H. Roberts, 7 vols., 2d ed. rev. [Salt Lake City: The Church of Jesus Christ of Latter-day Saints, 1932–51], 6:184). Basic and possibly higher ordinances were performed in the patriarchal ages as well as in the Christian era on more than one continent, but latter-day keys for sealings of generations will potentially affect people of all ages. This statement assumes that full salvation depends in part on generational sealings being one day completed back to Adam. Joseph Smith taught, "We [the children] without them [the fathers] cannot be made perfect; neither can they without us be made perfect. . . . for it is necessary in the ushering in of the dispensation of the fulness of times . . . that a whole and complete and perfect union, and welding together of dispensations . . . should take place, and be revealed from the days of Adam even to the present time" (D&C 128:18). Of course, not all of the dead to whom the gospel is preached will accept it. Ordinances conducted for the dead will be effective only for those who accept them in the spirit world.

Before Christ's April 3, 1836, visit, full salvation was a promise, not a reality, except for those He empowered through His priesthood in earlier times. For almost eighteen hundred years no knowledge or authority existed to conduct temple ordinances. On April 3, 1836, the Savior fulfilled the promise by sending Elias and Elijah to deliver priesthood keys and authority to the Church.

Joseph Smith taught that the fulness of salvation comes only in temples through Elijah's keys. He encouraged Church members to submit to "all the ordinances . . . and sealing powers" for themselves and for their dead progenitors. He was concerned that members of the Church would be "*divided, broken up, and scattered,* before we get our salvation secure." Joseph connected full salvation to Elijah's keys, stating: "The question is frequently asked 'Can we not be saved without going through with all those ordinances, &c.?' I would answer, No, not the fullness of salvation."[2]

Redemption, salvation, and *exaltation* are words that keep recurring in prophecy, tradition, and scripture. The power to fully attain redemption, salvation, and exaltation for all mankind was fulfilled on that landmark day, April 3, 1836. Jewish tradition for thousands of years created an expectation that the Messiah, the son of David, would come with Elijah to "redeem us."[3] So they did. In fact, the timing of their visit to the Kirtland Temple came in the Jewish calendar month of Nisan, known as "the month of redemption."

President Joseph Fielding Smith explained that Christ came with Moses, Elias, and Elijah on April 3, 1836, to bring complete salvation and exaltation. He said that they revealed "the authorities which make it possible to bring to pass the complete salvation and exaltation of all who are willing to obey the gospel. Today, through the restoration of these keys every ordinance and power has been given to the Church which is essential to the fulness of celestial exaltation."[4]

---

2. *History of the Church,* 6:184; Wilford Woodruff Journal, January 21, 1844, "Documents," Joseph Smith Resource Center, josephsmith.net.

3. "Elijah," Jewish Virtual Library, a comprehensive online Jewish encyclopedia, http://www .jewishvirtuallibrary.org/jsource/biography/Elijah.html; accessed March 1, 2012.

4. Joseph Fielding Smith, *Church History and Modern Revelation,* 2 vols. (Salt Lake City: Deseret Book, 1953), 2:47.

"Even As Many As Will"

In the three days of Christ's atonement, death, and resurrection in A.D. 33, He *unconditionally* broke the bands of death for all mankind. He *conditionally* atoned for individual sin and extended complete salvation and exaltation to all who would *accept* His gospel and *submit* to ordinances such as baptism, temple ordinances, and sealings. This conditional aspect of the Atonement is reflected in the words of Christ's promise to Adam: "As thou hast fallen thou mayest be redeemed, and all mankind, even as many as will."[5]

Before the birth of Christ, many died without receiving baptism and other sacred ordinances. Those who did receive them were probably limited in number. In the time between Christ's resurrection and His return to the Kirtland Temple, some ordinances of salvation were completed. Peter and the other ancient Apostles undoubtedly administered baptisms and probably other temple ordinances,[6] including baptisms for the dead, but the actual numbers of those who received such ordinances would also have been limited.[7] The authority to perform temple ordinances vanished with the death of the Apostles.[8] Therefore, ordinances to fully extend the conditional part of Christ's atonement to individuals had essentially been held in abeyance for virtually all mankind on both sides of the veil until keys and authority were returned on April 3, 1836.

During those almost 1,800 years, believers were sustained by the reality of Christ's suffering for sin and the promise of the Atonement. Many of these believers sacrificed and even laid down their lives during dark times to preserve

---

5. Moses 5:9.

6. Regarding temple ordinances being performed by Peter and the ancient apostles, President Joseph Fielding Smith said, "We do know that in that day they baptized for the dead. What was there to prevent them from giving endowments? Truly it would not be done in the temple at Jerusalem, for that had fallen into apostate hands. But they could, and most likely did, give endowments to the other apostles and many others in some secluded spot or on some mountain" (Joseph Fielding Smith, *Doctrines of Salvation*, comp. Bruce R. McConkie, 3 vols. [Salt Lake City: Bookcraft, 1954–56], 2:165).

7. 1 Corinthians 15:29.

8. John the Baptist restored authority to baptize the living in May 1829, but keys bestowed on April 3, 1836 by Elijah authorized baptisms for the dead and other sealing ordinances for the living *and* the dead.

the Bible, religious freedom, and faith in the Savior. Many fulfilled missions to prepare for and enable the latter-day Restoration. Despite all that the believers did, however, saving ordinances were still required for their full redemption.

Wilford Woodruff, who received initial temple ordinances in the Kirtland Temple, learned that deceased individuals yearn to receive redemptive temple ordinances. Signers of the Declaration of Independence personally visited him. They requested redemption that could only come through keys restored in the Kirtland Temple. President Woodruff said that as they stood before him in the St. George Temple, they wanted to know "why we did not redeem them."[9] As a result of their visit, he wrote:

> I feel to say little else to the Latter-day Saints wherever and whenever I have the opportunity of speaking to them, than to call upon them to build these Temples now under way, to hurry them up to completion. The dead will be after you, they will seek after you as they have after us in St. George. They called upon us, knowing that we held the keys and power to redeem them. . . .
>
> . . . The spirits of the dead gathered around me. . . . Said they, "You have had the use of the Endowment House for a number of years, and yet nothing has ever been done for us. We laid the foundation of the government you now enjoy, and we never apostatized from it, but we remained true to it and were faithful to God." . . . they waited on me for two days and two nights. . . . I straightway went into the baptismal font.[10]

When Elias and Elijah appeared in the Kirtland Temple, Jesus Christ provided keys for the conditional part of His atonement to be extended to all who had not yet met its conditions.

---

9. Wilford Woodruff, in *Journal of Discourses,* 26 vols. (London: Latter-day Saints' Book Depot, 1854–86), 19:229.

10. Woodruff, in *Journal of Discourses,* 19:229.

Through these priesthood keys and authority, He unlocked the door for any of His children (past, present, or future) who would accept vicarious ordinances of salvation. Christ showed His love by empowering the latter-day Church with the means of full salvation and exaltation. Many but not all of the billions who have lived will accept these potential blessings. Because of Elijah, billions of the dead could now accept the plan of salvation and the authorized ordinances. Required ordinances for exaltation, such as baptism for the dead and celestial marriage and sealings for both the living and the dead, could now be performed. Most important, all could now have the opportunity to accept the full effect of the Savior's atonement.

Redemption of All Mankind

The promise of Christ to Adam was that "all mankind, even as many as will" could be redeemed.[11] The phrase "all mankind" represents a staggering number of people. It is estimated that the world's population on April 3, 1836, was more than one billion people. Statisticians estimate that about ninety billion people had lived and died by that time.[12] Therefore, when Elijah repeated Malachi's prophecy that the hearts of the children would turn to the fathers, there could have been as many as ninety times more fathers (ancestors) who had passed into the spirit world than there were children on earth. Billions had probably accepted the gospel in the spirit world and were eagerly awaiting Elijah's return with keys to "redeem them."[13] An immense gathering in the spirit world probably celebrated the restoration of Elijah's keys on April 3, 1836.

Billions Could Now Rejoice

Temple work for the dead, authorized through Elijah's keys, must have been a surprising concept to the early Saints. Joseph Smith called the power

---

11. Moses 5:9.

12. Carl Haub, "How Many People Have Ever Lived on Earth?" Population Reference Bureau, accessed March 1, 2012, www.prb.org/Articles/2002/HowManyPeopleHaveEverLivedonEarth.aspx.

13. Doctrine & Covenants 128:22.

by which it was done "very bold doctrine."[14] In helping the Saints to comprehend temple work for the dead, Joseph said, "It is no more incredible that God should *save* the dead, than that he should *raise* the dead."[15]

On April 3, 1836, authorized temple work began on a scale unparalleled in all history on both sides of the veil.[16] We cannot even envision the great desire and anticipation of those who wait on the other side of the veil for us to complete their temple work. Many had waited for thousands of years for Christ to introduce Elijah to Joseph Smith and Oliver Cowdery, thereby opening the door for their redemption. These two latter-day Apostles were reserved for this time and place to use these keys and initiate the great work of building temples and performing ordinances "for the redemption of the dead, and the sealing of the children to their parents."[17] God promised all of His children "before the world was" that in the latter days, temples would be built in which redeeming ordinances would be performed for the salvation of the dead.[18]

Saviors on Mount Zion

April 3, 1836, opened the latter-day gate through which all must pass to receive saving temple ordinances and covenants for themselves or vicariously for the dead. Based upon gospel obedience, all mankind may receive exaltation in the celestial kingdom and a continuance of marriage beyond the grave with unending eternal offspring.

---

14. Doctrine & Covenants 128:9.

15. *History of the Church,* 4:425; *Times and Seasons* 1–2 (October 15, 1841): 577.

16. Vicarious work for the dead was practiced in only one earlier dispensation. It took Christ's atonement to enable work for the dead to proceed, as President Joseph Fielding Smith stated: "There could be no baptisms or endowments or any other work for the dead before the death of Jesus Christ. He it was who carried the message of the gospel to the dead and bridged the gulf spoken of in the parable of the rich man and Lazarus. He it was who, in fulfillment of the prophets, opened the door of the prison house and permitted the prisoners to come free. Until that time the dead were waiting for their salvation or redemption, which should come through the blood of Christ" (*Doctrines of Salvation,* 2:164–165). Peter and the other Apostles initiated baptisms for the dead and probably other temple ordinances as well (see 1 Corinthians 15:29).

17. Doctrine & Covenants 138:48.

18. Doctrine & Covenants 128:22, 24; 138:53–56.

Christ made it possible to bless our ancestors with vicarious service in a way similar to how He blessed us through His vicarious suffering. In so doing, we participate with Him in ensuring the opportunity for exaltation for our ancestors if they accept the ordinances performed for them. Our ancestors cannot do this work for themselves. Joseph Smith adapted the phrase "Saviors on Mount Zion"[19] to describe us in our efforts to perform redeeming temple ordinances for the dead. He challenged us to "come up as Saviors on mount Zion." He said we do this by "going forth & receiving all the ordinances . . . & sealing powers . . . in behalf of all our Progenitors who are dead & redeem them that they may Come forth in the first resurrection & be exhalted."[20]

Keys of Elias

As Elias appeared on April 3, 1836, Joseph Smith said he "committed the dispensation of the gospel of Abraham, saying that in us and our seed all generations after us should be blessed."[21] Elder Bruce R. McConkie connected "the gospel of Abraham" to the Abrahamic covenant, stating:

Elias brings back "the gospel of Abraham," the great Abrahamic covenant whereby the faithful receive promises of eternal increase, promises that through celestial marriage their eternal posterity shall be as numerous as the sands upon the seashore or as the stars in heaven for multitude. Elias gives the promise . . . that in modern men and in their seed all generations shall be blessed. And we are now offering the blessings of Abraham, Isaac, and Jacob to all who will receive them.[22]

---

19. See Obadiah 1:21.

20. Wilford Woodruff, in *The Words of Joseph Smith,* comp. and ed. Andrew F. Ehat and Lyndon W. Cook (Provo, Utah: Brigham Young University Religious Studies Center, 1980), 318.

21. Doctrine & Covenants 110:12.

22. Bruce R. McConkie, "The Keys of the Kingdom," *Ensign,* May 1983, 22.

On another occasion, Elder McConkie expanded understanding of the temple nature of these keys of Elias: "The gospel of Abraham was one of celestial marriage . . . ; it was a gospel or commission to provide a lineage for the elect portion of the preexistent spirits, a gospel to provide a household in eternity for those who live the fulness of the celestial law."[23]

There is a connection with the keys of the three messengers—Moses, Elias, and Elijah. Elder Russell M. Nelson highlighted this connection in a general conference talk on the gathering of Israel. He pointed out that Church members "help to gather the elect of the Lord on both sides of the veil." He pointed out that the gathering of Israel in the spirit world "requires earthly efforts of others. We gather pedigree charts, create family group sheets, and do temple work vicariously to gather individuals unto the Lord and into their families."[24]

The question is often asked, "Who was Elias who appeared on April 3, 1836?" His identity has not been made known, but we can conclude that Elias was a prophet who held the keys of authority to the dispensation in which Abraham lived.[25] It might be deduced from scripture and Joseph Smith's statements that Elias is Noah.[26] President Joseph Fielding Smith stated that "Elias was Noah, who came and restored his keys."[27]

Keys of Elijah

Joseph Smith defined the keys Elijah restored. He said, "The . . . power & calling of Elijah is that ye have power to . . . perform all the ordinances

---

23. Bruce R. McConkie, *Mormon Doctrine*, 2d ed. (Salt Lake City: Bookcraft, 1966), 219–20.

24. Russell M. Nelson, "The Gathering of Scattered Israel," *Ensign*, November 2006, 80–81.

25. McConkie, *Mormon Doctrine*, 219.

26. Joseph Smith said that "Noah . . . is Gabriel" (*History of the Church*, 3:386). Luke said that Gabriel is the angel who appeared to Zacharias and told him that he would have a son (Luke 1:19). The Lord said that the angel who visited Zacharias was Elias (D&C 27:7). Therefore it appears scripturally that Elias, Gabriel, and Noah may be the same person.

27. Joseph Fielding Smith, in Conference Report, April 1960, 72.

belonging to the Kingdom of God even unto the sealing of the hearts of the fathers unto the children & the hearts of the children unto the fathers even those who are in heaven."[28]

Elijah's keys pertain mainly to the temples, but President Joseph Fielding Smith enlarged upon his keys by informing the Church that "Elijah restored to this Church . . . the keys of the sealing power; and that sealing power puts the stamp of approval upon every ordinance that is done in this Church and more particularly those that are performed in the temples of the Lord."[29]

Elder McConkie clarified this stamp of approval on ordinances for the living even further, stating in general conference:

> Elijah brings back the keys of the sealing power, the power that enables men now living, as it was with Peter of old, to bind on the earth below and have their acts sealed everlastingly in the heavens above.
>
> . . . Because Elijah came, the baptisms we perform on earth will have efficacy, virtue, and force in eternity. In literal reality they give us membership in the earthly kingdom which is the Church, and in the heavenly kingdom which is the celestial realm where God and Christ are.[30]

Elijah's Visit Fulfills Ancient Prophecy

One of the Lord's best-known scriptural promises was that Elijah would return. Malachi was the first prophet to make that prophecy hundreds of years before Christ's birth. He recorded the Lord's words: "Behold, I will send you Elijah the prophet before the coming of the great and dreadful

---

28. Wilford Woodruff, in Ehat and Cook, *Words of Joseph Smith*, 329.

29. Joseph Fielding Smith, in Conference Report, April 1948, 135; Smith, *Doctrines of Salvation*, 3:129.

30. McConkie, "Keys of the Kingdom," 22.

day of the LORD: And he shall turn the heart of the fathers to the children, and the heart of the children to their fathers, lest I come and smite the earth with a curse."[31]

The Lord has since repeated this promise in each successive book of scripture. Christ repeated Malachi's prophecy verbatim to the Nephites during His visit to the Americas because they had no record of Malachi. He next commanded the Nephites to record the words. Then, to give the prophecy added emphasis, He said that even He was given a specific directive to tell them, "The Father commanded that I should give [Malachi's promise of Elijah's return] unto you; for it was wisdom in him that they should be given unto future generations."[32]

In his appearance to Joseph Smith, Moroni repeated the Lord's promise to Malachi as he instructed Joseph three times during the night of September 23, 1823.[33] In the Doctrine and Covenants, Malachi's promise is proclaimed five times.[34] The Lord fulfilled all of these words of prophecy when Elijah appeared in the Kirtland Temple on April 3, 1836.

Elijah returned at Passover season with keys and power to redeem the dead. Redemption is central to the theme of the Passover. The Lord gave a promise to the children of Israel who were in bondage, saying, "I will redeem you."[35] Under keys delivered by Elijah in the Kirtland Temple, we administer vicarious temple ordinances to redeem the dead from a type of bondage. President Joseph F. Smith, who saw the spirits of the dead for whom these redeeming keys were given, taught that ordinances would redeem the "captives who were bound."[36] He came to understand that Elijah's keys were

---

31. Malachi 4:5–6.

32. 3 Nephi 26:2.

33. Joseph Smith–History 1:39.

34. Doctrine & Covenants 2; 27:9; 110:13–16; 128:17–18; 138:46–47.

35. Exodus 6:6.

36. Doctrine & Covenants 138:22–24, 31–33, 54.

given for "the redemption of the dead. . . . [and that the] dead had looked upon the long absence of their spirits from their bodies as a bondage."[37]

Orson Pratt, who attended the endowment meetings in the Kirtland Temple, explained that Elijah brought not only the keys of temple work but also the understanding of it:

> He [Elijah] appeared in his glorious majesty, and there revealed the keys unto the servants of the Lord which should restore this union between the fathers and the children— something that we did not understand anything about, until the angel Elijah revealed it unto us. . . . that work [of redeeming ancestors] we could not commence until Elijah the Prophet was sent from heaven.[38]

The Spirit of Elijah

Joseph Smith coined the phrase "spirit of Elijah" to describe the interest and desire to "redeem our dead."[39] The "spirit of Elijah" descended on the earth with Elijah's visit. It is a universal power that inspires people to research ancestors and perform vicarious temple work. Many who are driven to research family history attest that this unseen power operates upon all people. Elder McConkie pointed out that "genealogical research . . . was born on the third day of April in 1836."[40] Interest in family history research began in the Church and, it seems, in the world as well with the visit of Elijah in 1836. Even government bodies and scientists catch this spirit. For example, a bill to mandate the registration of births, marriages, and deaths was introduced in England in 1836 and became law in 1837. This became critical to family

---

37. Doctrine & Covenants 138:48, 50.

38. Orson Pratt, in *Journal of Discourses*, 13:358–59.

39. *History of the Church*, 6:252.

40. Bruce R. McConkie, *The Millennial Messiah* (Salt Lake City: Deseret Book, 1982), 402.

history research. The first American patent for photography, upon which much of our body of family history data depends, was issued in 1840. President Joseph Fielding Smith said: "The first organized effort to collect and file genealogies of the common people was made shortly after the coming of Elijah. This was the formation of *The New England Historic and Genealogical Society*. In 1844, this society was incorporated. Its chief purpose is to gather and publish data in relation to American Families."[41]

Perspectives on Redemption of the Dead

Joseph Smith, who in premortality was given his mission to build temples and perform ordinances therein, received and taught revelation upon revelation to help us understand that our focus needs to turn to our dead. The subject of vicarious work for the dead was on the Prophet's mind "more than most any other subject that was given to him."[42] He taught that baptism for the dead is the "most glorious of all subjects belonging to the everlasting gospel."[43] He stated, "The greatest responsibility that God has laid upon us [is] to seek after our dead."[44]

Brigham Young, who participated in many of the visions in the Kirtland Temple, said, "What do you suppose the fathers would say if they could speak from the dead? Would they not say: 'We have lain here thousands of years in this prison house, bound and fettered in the association of the filthy and corrupt.' If they had the power the very thunders of heaven would resound in our ears."[45]

---

41. Joseph Fielding Smith, *The Way to Perfection* (Salt Lake City: Deseret Book, 1975), 168.

42. Wilford Woodruff, in Conference Report, April 1894; *Collected Discourses: Delivered by Wilford Woodruff, His Two Counselors, the Twelve Apostles, and Others*, comp. and ed. Brian H. Stuy, 5 vols. (Burbank, Calif.: B. H. S. Publishing, 1987–92), 4:6.

43. Doctrine & Covenants 128:17.

44. Thomas Bullock Report, April 7, 1844 (2) (Sunday Afternoon), in Ehat and Cook, *Words of Joseph Smith*, 353.

45. Matthias F. Cowley, *Wilford Woodruff: History of His Life and Labors* (Salt Lake City: Bookcraft, 1964), 494.

President Wilford Woodruff, who heard angels' voices in the Kirtland Temple and was obviously moved upon by the spirit of Elijah, said,

> I wish . . . that the veil was lifted off the face of the Latter-day Saints; I wish we could see and know the things of God as they do who are laboring . . . in the spirit world; for if this were so, this whole people, with very few, if any, exceptions, would lose all interest in the riches of the world, and . . . their whole desires and labors would be directed to redeem their dead, to perform faithfully the work and mission given us on earth.[46]

Elder John A. Widtsoe, an Apostle, described Elijah's authorization of work for the dead as the doctrinal "keystone" in our gospel arch:

> The beginning and the end of the Gospel is written, from one point of view, in Section 2 of the Book of Doctrine and Covenants. If I read this section correctly, [temple work for the dead] is the keystone of the wonderful Gospel arch. If this center stone is weakened, and falls out, the whole arch falls into a heap of unorganized doctrinal blocks.[47]

"The Fame of This House"

From the small and simple beginning in Kirtland, temple work for the living and the dead is literally spreading throughout the earth in fulfillment of Christ's prophecy. On April 3, 1836, the Savior declared as He accepted the Kirtland Temple, "The fame of this house shall spread to foreign lands;

---

46. Woodruff, in *Journal of Discourses,* 21:302.

47. John A Widtsoe, "Temple Worship," in *Utah Genealogical and Historical Magazine,* 12 (April 1921): 64.

and this is the beginning of the blessing which shall be poured out upon the heads of my people."[48]

Since 1836 untold missionaries have spread the fame of the Kirtland Temple throughout the world as they have testified of Elijah's return and the importance of temple work for the living and the dead. In 1856, Brigham Young prophesied, "There will have to be not only one temple but thousands of them, and thousands and tens of thousands of men and women will go into those temples and officiate for people who have lived as far back as the Lord shall reveal."[49] In 1877, President Wilford Woodruff foresaw the millennial time when "temples will appear all over . . . North and South America . . . Europe and elsewhere."[50] In 1975, President Spencer W. Kimball sought to prepare the Church for a time "when the temples will be used around the clock and throughout the year."[51]

Even now temples are being taken to members throughout the world. The pace of temple building quickens as Christ's glorious coming approaches. The Church greatly increased the pace in 1997, when President Gordon B. Hinckley announced that temple building would be accelerated with the construction of smaller temples near members of the Church throughout the world.[52]

It becomes apparent to a student of sacred events, then, that April 3, 1836, was a joyous day of latter-day Christology in the Kirtland Temple. It introduced again the profound and grand redeeming temple ordinances and sealings for both the worthy living and dead. At the same time, it liberated the obedient who were waiting in spirit prison for their blessed release. The

---

48. Doctrine & Covenants 110:10.

49. Brigham Young, in *Journal of Discourses*, 3:372.

50. Woodruff, in *Journal of Discourses*, 19:230.

51. Spencer W. Kimball, in J. M. Heslop, "Greater Need Brings Temple's Renovation," *Church News*, April 19, 1975, 3.

52. Gordon B. Hinckley, "Some Thoughts on Temples, Retention of Converts, and Missionary Service," *Ensign*, November 1997, 49.

atonement of Jesus Christ did reach down through the ages and beyond the veil to encompass all who would accept it.

Is it any wonder that on April 3, 1836—the very day Elijah and Elias returned keys to earth—that the Savior would repeatedly encourage the Saints to rejoice? He declared: "Lift up your heads and *rejoice*. Let the hearts of your brethren *rejoice,* and let the hearts of all my people *rejoice*. . . . the hearts of thousands and tens of thousands shall greatly *rejoice*. . . . and this is the beginning of the blessing which shall be poured out."[53]

Is it any wonder that after baptisms for the dead and other ordinances were finally being performed that Joseph Smith would be exuberant? He exclaimed: "Let the dead speak forth anthems of eternal praise. . . . Let the mountains shout for joy. . . . Let all the sons of God shout for joy! . . . Let us present in his holy temple . . . a book containing the records of our dead."[54]

Is it any wonder that in the Kirtland Temple angels joined with Saints singing praises to God? Joseph reported, "Angels mingled their voices with ours, while their presence was in our midst, and unceasing praises swelled our bosoms."[55]

Christ did come with Moses, Elias, and Elijah to Kirtland!

---

53. Doctrine & Covenants 110:5–6, 9, 10; emphasis added.

54. Doctrine & Covenants 128:22–24.

55. *History of the Church,* 2:383; Dean C. Jessee, Mark Ashurst-McGee, and Richard L. Jensen, eds., *Journals, 1832–1839,* vol. 1 of the Journals series of *The Joseph Smith Papers,* edited by Dean C. Jessee, Ronald K. Esplin, and Richard Lyman Bushman (Salt Lake City: Church Historian's Press, 2008), 1:172.

CHAPTER 16

APRIL 3, 1836:
A MOTHER LODE OF
CHRISTOLOGY

Prophets, priests, and kings . . . have looked forward with joyful
anticipation to [our] day. . . . [It is] a work that God and angels have
contemplated with delight, for generations past.

—*TIMES AND SEASONS*

On April 3, 1836, Christ came to the Kirtland Temple and declared, "I
am he who liveth, I am he who was slain."[1] President Joseph Fielding Smith
pointed out the significance of this visit when he said, "[Christ's] coming to
the Kirtland Temple carries great weight and is far more significant than
some among us have thought it to be."[2]

April 3, 1836, was a religiously symbolic day that centered on Christ
fulfilling ancient prophecy, prayers, promises, and religious tradition. The
day lies at the heart of the Savior's redemptive mission. On no other day—
to date—in the final dispensation is such a mother lode of Christology to
be found.[3] He displayed forceful evidence of His literal resurrection as He

---

1. Doctrine & Covenants 110:4.

2. Joseph Fielding Smith, *Church History and Modern Revelation*, 2 vols. (Salt Lake City: Deseret
Book, 1953), 2:47–48.

3. Dictionaries define *Christology* as the theological study of the person and deeds of Jesus. It is
also the study of how the human (Christ was part mortal) and the divine (Christ was part God)

stood on the sacred pulpits of the Kirtland Temple. As part of His mission, He opened the door of full salvation to untold billions of God's children as keys and authority were bestowed for temple sealings and ordinance work for the living and the dead.[4] The events He initiated that day potentially affected everyone who has ever lived or will ever live on the earth.[5]

A Dispensational Highpoint

April 3, 1836, might be considered a pinnacle of the Restoration. Every instruction and organizational step Joseph received, beginning in the Sacred Grove, prepared the Church for this day. Keys bestowed on this day have empowered the Church's divinely appointed responsibilities, including unparalleled efforts to proclaim the gospel and redeem the dead.

April 3, 1836, is the date Jesus Christ and heavenly messengers heralded eight of the most-sought-after events for people of all faiths and especially for the children of Israel scattered across the face of the earth. This was the day Christ—

- Brought Moses to commence the latter-day gathering of Israel, thus unleashing an unprecedented worldwide missionary force.

- Brought Elijah and Elias to authorize temple sealings and

---

coexist in one person. This study is usually broken into three subtopics: (1) incarnation—Christ is the son of man and the Son of God; (2) resurrection; (3) salvation and deliverance ("Christology," Answers.com; *The American Heritage Dictionary of the English Language*, 4th ed. [Boston: Houghton Mifflin, 2004]; www.answers.com/topic/christology, accessed February 29, 2012; see chapter 5, pp. 95–125, herein for a discussion of Christ's teaching of His incarnation). Evidence of Christ's resurrection is reflected repeatedly through visions in Kirtland. No vision, however, defines His resurrection more clearly than the one given on April 3, 1836. The largest implementation of Christ's conditional mission may have begun through keys and authority bestowed upon Joseph Smith and Oliver Cowdery that day.

4. Joseph Smith, *History of The Church of Jesus Christ of Latter-day Saints*, ed. B. H. Roberts, 7 vols., 2d ed. rev. (Salt Lake City: The Church of Jesus Christ of Latter-day Saints, 1932–51), 6:184.

5. This statement assumes that full salvation depends in part on generational sealings being completed back to Adam (see chapter 15, pp. 289–303, herein).

saving ordinances, thus providing for the redemption of innumerable obedient souls, both living and dead.

- Came to a dedicated temple for the first time in thousands of years to fulfill ancient prophecy.[6]

- Fulfilled Old and New Testament religious symbolism.

- Initiated the fulfillment of His promises and covenants with Israel.

- Brought to pass the convergence of past gospel dispensations into this last dispensation by a "welding together of dispensations."[7]

- Answered ages of Jewish prayers, songs, and observances for the return of heavenly messengers.

- Signified through the combined events of the day that His "coming in the clouds of heaven, with power and great glory" was finally at hand.[8]

Christ Comes to His Dedicated Temple

Christ fulfilled a well-known Old Testament prophecy as He appeared in the Kirtland Temple on April 3, 1836. Malachi prophesied, "The Lord whom ye seek, shall suddenly come to his temple . . . behold, he shall come, saith the Lord of hosts."[9] Indicating that this prophecy has been fulfilled, President Joseph Fielding Smith said: "May it not be the case that this predicted coming has already taken place in [His] wonderful manifestation in

---

6. See Malachi 3:1; 3 Nephi 24:1; Doctrine & Covenants 36:8; 133:2.

7. Doctrine & Covenants 128:18.

8. Joseph Smith–Matthew 1:36; Malachi 4:5–6; JST, Mark 13:42; JST, Matthew 17:13–14. Elijah would be a recognizable signal that the Lord's return in glory was imminent.

9. Malachi 3:1.

the Kirtland Temple? The Savior came suddenly to this temple. He accepted the house and made promises of great blessings."[10]

Some interpret Malachi's prophecy as an allusion to the time when Christ comes in glory. Elder Bruce R. McConkie, however, explains, "This sudden latter-day appearance in the temple does not have reference to his appearance at the great and dreadful day, for that coming will be when he sets his foot upon the Mount of Olivet in the midst of the final great war."[11]

Symbolically Significant

The date of April 3, 1836, is highly symbolic, for it is deeply rooted in religious history. By choosing a date with such deep religious symbolism and biblical parallels, the Lord seemingly placed a stamp of authenticity on the events of that day. April 3, 1836, fell on the sixteenth day of the Jewish month of Nisan—the heart of that Hebrew calendar month (also known as Abib in Old Testament times). The Jewish month of Nisan is sacred to the Jews. It is called in Jewish tradition the "month of redemption." The Talmud, the official book of Jewish law, states, "In Nisan our ancestors were redeemed from Egypt, and in the same month we shall again be redeemed."[12]

The few days surrounding the sixteenth of Nisan are arguably the most significant dates in ecclesial history. Throughout the millennia the Lord has chosen those days of Nisan for His most sacred religious historical events. Elder McConkie points out that events falling in the middle of the Jewish month of Nisan are symbolic and designed for us to focus our attention on salvation: "Everything connected with . . . Nisan 14 through 21, is so dramatic, so filled with symbolism, so designed to center the attention of the Lord's people in the great and eternal truths of salvation that even today,

---

10. Smith, *Church History and Modern Revelation*, 2:47.

11. Bruce R. McConkie, *Mormon Doctrine*, 2d ed. (Salt Lake City: Bookcraft, 1966), 693–94.

12. *Babylonian Talmud*, trans. and ed. Michael L. Rodkinson, 10 vols. (Boston: The Talmud Society, 1918), 3:16.

. . . we are still prone to use its happenings to teach various related truths and principles."[13]

At least six significant religious events occurred on or about this date in history:

1. The ancient Passover and Moses' leading Israel out of Egypt.[14]

2. The children of Israel were brought to the promised land.[15]

3. Christ's birth.

4. The beginning of Christ's earthly ministry.

5. Christ's atonement, crucifixion, and resurrection.

6. The formal founding of Christ's latter-day Church on April 6, 1830.[16]

Promises Fulfilled

As Joseph Smith offered his inspired prayer of dedication on the Kirtland Temple, he said, "Holy Father, we ask thee . . . that we may be found worthy, in thy sight, to secure a fulfilment of the promises which thou hast made unto us."[17]

His answer came quickly. One week later, Christ, Moses, Elias, and Elijah each stood in succession before the Prophet and Oliver Cowdery in fulfillment of the Lord's promises. It is probable that the scope of both the promises and their fulfillment are broader and deeper than most people

---

13. Bruce R. McConkie, *From Bethlehem to Calvary*, The Mortal Messiah series, 4 vols. (Salt Lake City: Deseret Book, 1982), 1:165.

14. Numbers 33:3.

15. Joshua 5:10–12.

16. April 6, 1830, fell on the thirteenth day of Nisan.

17. Doctrine & Covenants 109:10–11.

realize. Listed below are promises selected from a great number of scriptures. Some references have been shortened to highlight key promises:

- "I will redeem you [Israel]."[18]
- "In thee [Abraham] and in thy seed shall all the families of the earth be blessed."[19]
- "I will bring you into the bond of the covenant."[20]
- "He shall set up an ensign for the nations."[21]
- "The Lord . . . shall suddenly come to his temple."[22]
- "I will send you Elijah the prophet before the coming of the great and dreadful day of the Lord."[23]
- "Ye shall be gathered one by one, O ye children of Israel."[24]
- "I will gather them out of all countries, whither I have driven them . . . And they shall be my people, and I will be their God."[25]
- "I will bring them from the north country, and gather them from the coasts of the earth."[26]
- "I shall gather in, from their long dispersion, my people, O house of Israel."[27]

---

18. Exodus 6:6.
19. Genesis 28:14.
20. Ezekiel 20:37.
21. Isaiah 11:12.
22. Malachi 3:1; Doctrine & Covenants 36:8.
23. Malachi 4:5.
24. Isaiah 27:12.
25. Jeremiah 32:37–38.
26. Jeremiah 31:8.
27. 3 Nephi 21:1.

- "I will send for many fishers ... and they shall fish them."[28]
- "I [will] send for many hunters, and they shall hunt them from every mountain, and from every hill, and out of the holes of the rocks."[29]

Past Dispensations Flow into the Last Dispensation

The cumulative keys of past dispensations were needed to fully engage the work of the dispensation of the fulness of times. Just as Peter, James, and John ascended the Mount of Transfiguration to receive their dispensational keys and authority from Moses and Elijah, so did Joseph and Oliver receive the same keys as they ascended their latter-day mount, the elevated pulpits of the Kirtland Temple.[30]

Christ, with Moses, Elias, and Elijah, completed the chain of dispensational keys by bestowing the final keys upon Joseph and Oliver. Elijah, at the conclusion of their visit, said, "Therefore, the keys of this dispensation are committed into your hands."[31] Perhaps the prophet of each past dispensation visited Joseph and Oliver in the Kirtland Temple to bestow their dispensational keys.[32] President Joseph Fielding Smith, tenth president of the

---

28. Jeremiah 16:16.

29. Jeremiah 16:16.

30. Just as on the Mount of Transfiguration, a two-part purpose was fulfilled in Kirtland in our latter-day echo of the meridian-day events on the Mount of Transfiguration. It came in two parts. First, the bestowal of the keys of the First Presidency and second, the bestowal of the keys of missionary work and sealing powers. In the final step of organizing the First Presidency, the Prophet Joseph had already conferred keys on his counselors, Sidney Rigdon and Frederick G. Williams, in the Newel K. Whitney store schoolroom. Now Joseph and Oliver would receive the sealing keys (*The Words of Joseph Smith*, comp. and ed. Andrew F. Ehat and Lyndon W. Cook [Provo, Utah: Brigham Young University Religious Studies Center, 1980], 9).

31. Doctrine & Covenants 110:16.

32. It is known that Adam, Abraham, Moses, Elias (who may have been Noah), Elijah, and Peter, James, and John appeared in vision to Joseph Smith in the Kirtland Temple. It's interesting to note that Peter, James, John, and Elijah all held symbolic keys in their hands when they were seen. At an 1881 conference in Manti, Apostle Erastus Snow "spoke of the heavenly vision in the Hallowed Temple

Church, alluded to this when he stated, "It is possible that there may have been others whose coming [to the Kirtland Temple] was not recorded."[33] In reference to this possibility, he further wrote, "How many other messengers came at that time we do not know."[34]

In a memorial service to honor the Prophet Joseph, President Joseph F. Smith, sixth president of the Church, concluded, "No man yet that ever lived upon the earth had all the keys of the gospel and of the dispensations bestowed upon him as were bestowed upon the Prophet Joseph Smith in the temple at Kirtland."[35]

Priesthood authority to conduct Church affairs was first conveyed in 1829 when John the Baptist and later Peter, James, and John gave authorization to act in God's name to Joseph and Oliver. However, the full restoration was not complete until all the prophets of past dispensations also conveyed their keys and authority to Joseph and Oliver. Elder McConkie said, "It took all of them to bring to pass the restoration of all the keys and powers and authorities needed to save and exalt man."[36]

President Joseph Fielding Smith added: "Peter, James, and John gave Joseph Smith and Oliver Cowdery the Melchizedek Priesthood, but in the restoration of all things it became necessary for the prophets who held

---

at Kirtland, of Peter, James, and John and Elijah being Seen in the Holy of Holies with golden keys in their hands, in the Arch of the Temple" (*Diary of Charles Lowell Walker*, ed. Karl Larson and Katherine Miles Larson, 2 vols. [Logan: Utah State University Press, 1980], 2:563). Benjamin Brown recorded that during one meeting during dedication week, "two others saw three personages . . . in the room with bright keys in their hands" (in Steven C. Harper, "Kirtland Temple Experience," in *Opening the Heavens: Accounts of Divine Manifestations, 1820–1844*, ed. John W. Welch and Erick B. Carlson [Provo, Utah: Brigham Young University Press, 2005], 336).

33. Smith, *Church History and Modern Revelation*, 2:42; *History of the Church*, 3:74.

34. Smith, *Church History and Modern Revelation*, 1:237; *History of the Church*, 2:10.

35. Joseph F. Smith, December 23, 1894, in *Collected Discourses: Delivered by Wilford Woodruff, His Two Counselors, the Twelve Apostles, and Others*, comp. and ed. Brian H. Stuy, 5 vols. (Burbank, Calif.: B. H. S. Publishing, 1987–92), 5:29–30.

36. Bruce R. McConkie, *The Millennial Messiah* (Salt Lake City: Deseret Book, 1982), 120.

the keys of dispensations in the past to come to Joseph Smith and Oliver Cowdery and restore their keys and authorities."[37]

Reflecting on Elijah's keys, the Prophet Joseph Smith said, "It is necessary in the ushering in of the dispensation of the fulness of times . . . [that a] welding together of dispensations, and keys, and powers, and glories should take place, and be revealed from the days of Adam even to the present time."[38]

The Prophet Joseph explained that various prophets from Adam to the present came to him, "all declaring their dispensation, their rights, their keys, their honors, their majesty and glory, and the power of their priesthood."[39] On another occasion, he stated simply, "There has been a chain of authority and power from Adam down to the present time."[40]

Building the Kirtland Temple was essential for the return of keys necessary for the latter-day work. The "welding together of dispensations" had to wait until the Saints finished the temple. The completed and dedicated temple was needed for these keys to be restored, as explained by President Joseph Fielding Smith:

> These keys, according to divine decree, were to be restored within the walls of a sacred temple built to the name of the Lord. It is only in case of expediency, when there is no such house, that keys of authority are bestowed upon men. . . .
>
> The main purpose for [the Kirtland] temple was to have a house where the Lord could come and where he could send his servants with the keys of their dispensations.[41]

---

37. Joseph Fielding Smith, *Answers to Gospel Questions*, comp. Joseph Fielding Smith Jr., 5 vols. (Salt Lake City: Deseret Book, 1957–66), 2:43.

38. Doctrine & Covenants 128:18.

39. Doctrine & Covenants 128:21.

40. *History of the Church*, 4:425; *Times and Seasons* 1–2 (October 15, 1841): 577.

41. Smith, *Church History and Modern Revelation*, 2:42; Doctrine & Covenants 124:28–41.

President Smith likened the passing down of keys to a mighty river that receives pure waters from all past dispensations. He wrote, "All the authority and keys of priesthood of the past . . . flow into the most glorious and greatest of dispensations, like clear streams flowing into a mighty river."[42] He later emphasized this idea by saying, "All other dispensations flow into it."[43]

Millennia of Jewish Prayers, Songs, and Observances Answered

Not only was the return of Elijah a direct answer to the temple dedicatory prayer but it was also an answer to millennia of Jewish prayers, songs, and observances. For more than two thousand years, faithful Jews have prayed for the return of their revered prophet Elijah. Aharon Wiener, a noted Hebrew scholar, explains that Jews yet pray daily and weekly for Elijah's return. Daily, when grace is offered after meals, they say, "May God in His mercy send us the prophet Elijah." Weekly, in benedictions after public Sabbath reading, they say, "Let us rejoice, O Lord, through your servant, the prophet Elijah . . . may he come soon and rejoice our heart."[44]

Evidence that Elijah's return was expected is found in the New Testament when John the Baptist was asked, "Art thou Elias [Elijah]?"[45] Some also thought that the Savior might be Elijah.[46] At some point, this yearning and anticipation was incorporated into Jewish traditions during the Feast of the Passover. As a result, for countless years millions of faithful Jewish families have eagerly anticipated Elijah's return at Passover. The

---

42. Joseph Fielding Smith, *Doctrines of Salvation,* comp. Bruce R. McConkie, 3 vols. (Salt Lake City: Bookcraft, 1954–56), 1:168.

43. Smith, *Doctrines of Salvation,* 3:126.

44. Aharon Wiener, *The Prophet Elijah in the Development of Judaism: A Depth-Psychological Study* (Boston: Routledge & Kegan Paul, 1978), 132–33.

45. John 1:21. Elias is the New Testament (Greek) form of Elijah.

46. Matthew 16:14.

faithful symbolically and routinely set a chair and table setting for Elijah at their Passover meal. They also pour a cup of wine for him and leave the door open a crack so that he may enter. Rabbi Steven G. Yisrael Sager, speaking of Elijah's return at Passover, emphasizes the significance of this Jewish tradition. "We open the door and expect to find him there. We expect nothing less of Elijah than to reveal, to explain and to redeem—us."[47]

Jewish prayers and rituals anticipating Elijah are also vocalized in song. Aharon Wiener cites an example—a song that even foreshadows a tradition that he will return with the Messiah: "Elijah songs are sung in many Jewish homes. The best known, included in all traditional prayer books. . . . expresses the hope that he will soon proclaim the redemption. The refrain of this song is: 'The prophet Elijah, the Tishbite from Gilead, may he come to us soon with the son of David, the Messiah.'"[48]

Even the Passover date is significant to Jewish tradition. Legends, beginning in the Talmud, indicate that "Israel's redemption in future days will happen on the fifteenth of Nisan, the night of Israel's redemption from Egypt, for thus did Moses say, 'In this night God protected Israel against the Angels of Destruction, and in this night He will also redeem the generations of the future.'"[49]

Parallels and Symbolism Connecting Events on April 3, 1836

April 3, 1836, was no ordinary calendar date. It was a day replete with correspondences. It fell on a Sunday. It was Easter. It was a holy day of Passover. It was one of two Seder (Passover meal) days celebrated throughout the Jewish

---

47. Steven G. Yisrael Sager, "Stories of Elijah the Prophet from Talmud and Midrash," 5, accessed February 29, 2012, www.betheldurham.org/docs/Elijah_stories.pdf.

48. Wiener, *Prophet Elijah*, 133–34.

49. Louis Ginzberg, *The Legends of the Jews*, trans. Henrietta Szold, 7 vols. (Philadelphia: Jewish Publications Society of America, 1909–38), 2:373.

world.[50] It seems that Christ, when He appeared in the Kirtland Temple, desired to establish evidence, both symbolic and literal, for Jews and Christians to see.

Jewish Symbolism

- In a symbolic message to Israel, the Lord was identified as "Jehovah."[51]
- In the prayer dedicating the Kirtland Temple, He identified Himself as "the Lamb."[52] The heart of the Passover was the lamb whose blood redeemed the children of Israel and freed them from bondage.
- He identified Himself as "he who was slain."[53] This was another reference to the lamb that was slain, whose blood on the doorposts during the first Passover protected them.

Christian Symbolism

- The Lord declared His crucifixion as He announced, "I am he who was slain."[54]
- He declared His resurrection as He announced, "I am he who liveth."[55]
- He identified Himself as your "advocate with the Father." Christians would remember that John, the ancient Apostle, gave Christ this same title.[56]
- His hair, eyes, countenance, and voice were described

---

50. Stephen D. Ricks, "The Appearance of Elijah and Moses in the Kirtland Temple and the Jewish Passover," *BYU Studies* 23, no. 4 (Fall 1983): 483–86.

51. Doctrine & Covenants 110:3.

52. Doctrine & Covenants 109:79.

53. Doctrine & Covenants 110:4.

54. Doctrine & Covenants 110:4.

55. Doctrine & Covenants 110:4.

56. Doctrine & Covenants 110:4; 1 John 2:1.

much the same as John the Revelator described Christ almost two millennia before.[57]

Jews and Christians the world over with "eyes to see" and "ears to hear" could recognize that the Lord of the Old and New Testaments was resurrected and had personally returned to fulfill His promises to them.[58]

Ceremonial Day of the Passover Seder

On April 3, 1836, in conservative and orthodox Jewish homes in the Western Hemisphere, families united and conducted an ancient ritual that included eating of the second Passover meal or Seder.[59] The Seder symbolizes the ancient Passover. The Seder also formally ritualizes Elijah's long-promised return to bring redemption. Little did they know that the house that Elijah would enter would be the Lord's house in Kirtland, Ohio. Little did they know that the year would be 1836. Little did they know that he would bring keys and authority to redeem the generations through temples.

Kirtland's Five-Year Window Closes April 3, 1836

The Lord established a timetable in advance for the Kirtland years. In 1831, He disclosed that His purposes for Kirtland would be completed by 1836. He told Joseph that the Saints were to remain in Kirtland "for the space of five years."[60] In June 1833 the Lord severely chastised the Saints for delaying construction of the Kirtland Temple after He had commanded them to build it. He called it a "very grievous sin."[61] To have the events of April 3, 1836, meet His deadline, it is no wonder that He chastised Joseph Smith so severely. He had a deadline to meet. Much work needed to be done

---

57. Revelation 1:14–16.

58. Ezekiel 12:2; Isaiah 53:7; Revelation 5:6, 9, 12.

59. Ricks, "Elijah and Moses," 483–86.

60. Doctrine & Covenants 64:21.

61. Doctrine & Covenants 95:3.

in a short time. Apparently, the Lord set these dates well in advance just as He had set other key dates in religious history. Consider what was accomplished in those formative years of the Church:

- The temple was completed and dedicated.
- Initial ordinances of endowment were revealed and administered.
- Christ fulfilled ancient prophecy.
- Missionaries were issued licenses to officially represent the Church and gather children of Israel from the four parts of the earth.
- The keys for the fulfillment of the ancient Abrahamic covenant began functioning.
- Joseph came to understand many principles of eternal marriage.[62]
- The Prophet received authority to perform sealings and temple ordinances for the living and the dead.
- The keys to preach the gospel and redeem the dead became fully invested in the Church.
- The gospel had taken root across the ocean in England.
- The Lord's purposes for Kirtland were fulfilled.

President Joseph Fielding Smith said, "There were very significant reasons why the Lord desired to retain a strong hold upon Kirtland and its vicinity for five years."[63] He observed that it was necessary for the Lord to disclose His timetable of five years because without that revelation, the Saints might have moved to Missouri, and the Kirtland Temple might not have

---

62. Doctrine & Covenants 132. The headnote indicates that the Prophet had known "the doctrines and principles" since 1831.

63. Smith, *Church History and Modern Revelation*, 1:237.

been built. He also concluded that the five years was worth the wait because the restoration of the keys of the priesthood held by ancient prophets was essential to the progress of the Church. Another writer concluded, "[The year] 1836 indeed marked both the spiritual climax of the Church as well as the beginning of the end of Kirtland as a stronghold."[64]

CONCLUSION

Christ was in Kirtland! He established His House there. These were glorious days when heaven and earth seemed as one. These were days of celestial events—events filled with great symbolism and meaning for the Church. Could any days have been more glorious in our dispensation than these?

Divine direction and manifestations were evidenced in abundance. Hundreds of angels appeared and hundreds of the Saints witnessed outward signs from the heavens. In one meeting, forty leaders "communed with the heavenly hosts."[65] In another meeting, "angels ministered" to fifty-three leaders in the temple.[66] At least fifteen ancient prophets were seen in vision.[67] God the Father manifested Himself with Jesus Christ in at least six visions. Christ was present or seen in vision on eight other occasions. Others heard Him speak. Essential keys were bestowed. In recorded history, these glorious days were possibly second only to the days of Christ's birth, ministry, atonement, and resurrection.

Events of such great magnitude as these caused Joseph Smith to exclaim:

Prophets, priests, and kings . . . have looked forward with joyful anticipation to [our] day . . . and fired with heavenly and joyful anticipations they have sung, and wrote, and prophesied of this our day;—but they died without the sight.

---

64. Lyndon W. Cook, *The Revelations of the Prophet Joseph Smith* (Salt Lake City: Deseret Book, 1985), 218.

65. *History of the Church*, 2:382.

66. *History of the Church*, 2:383.

67. Adam, Seth, Enos, Cainan, Mahalaleel, Jared, Enoch, Methuselah, Abraham, Moses, Elias, Elijah, Peter, James, and John.

... [It is] a work that God and angels have contemplated with delight, for generations past; that fired the souls of the ancient patriarchs and prophets—a work that is destined to bring about ... the renovation of the earth, the glory of God, and the salvation of the human family.[68]

Joseph Smith became acquainted with and conversed with some of these very "angels, ancient patriarchs and prophets" that day. He knew firsthand that God and angels had "contemplated" these restorations "with delight." One might ask, why did prophets, priests, and kings look forward to the latter-day work authorized and empowered in the Kirtland Temple on April 3, 1836? Could it be because promises the Lord had made to them were finally to be fulfilled? Could it be because messengers would now be sent to gather their children back into the gospel fold and provide temples through which they could accept essential vicarious ordinances and be sealed? Fathers could now be connected to the children and children to the fathers through sacred sealing ordinances for both the living and the dead. Finally, could they have been looking forward with joyful anticipation to Christ's coming, which would soon be at hand?

In response to the events of that day, Church members could rightfully and boldly declare, "We are the ... people that God has made choice of to bring about the Latter Day glory."[69]

---

68. *Times and Seasons* 3 (May 2, 1842): 776. John Taylor apparently acted as editor under Joseph Smith's name.

69. *Times and Seasons* 3 (May 2, 1842): 776.

Epilogue

In 1832 the Savior encouraged and assured His struggling Saints, many of whom had walked away from worldly possessions, friends, and family to gather to Kirtland. He told them, "Be of good cheer, for I will lead you."[1] Time and time again, Christ would visibly demonstrate His leadership, divinity, and supremacy. Elder Neal A. Maxwell said to me of this period, "There is a mother lode of Christology in Kirtland that has never been mined." As we look at Kirtland through the lens of Christ, we realize that in no other place have the visions and voice of the Savior been manifest in greater magnitude or more clearly. The number of ways He manifests Himself and the depth of His teaching are staggering.

Christ repeatedly bore first-person testimony of Himself and His atonement. He tangibly demonstrated His leadership in revelation after revelation and in vision after vision. He appeared or spoke to at least twenty-three of His servants in more than fourteen separate visions. He allowed hundreds to

_____

1. Doctrine & Covenants 78:18.

witness the secondary effects of His visions. He conversed with Joseph Smith and Sidney Rigdon for hours while presenting them with vivid scenes, beginning with the premortal existence and continuing through celestial glories.

His main focus seemed to be on His temple, which He commanded and enabled His Saints to erect. He instituted covenants and ordinances of endowment as performed anciently. He brought ancient prophets to His dedicated house to return keys and authority that would empower the work of the Church. With these keys He enabled full salvation for the living and the dead in temples. With these keys He also unleashed an unprecedented worldwide missionary force to gather scattered Israel, a divine plan instituted in ancient times. Christ fulfilled ancient prophecy and Old and New Testament religious symbolism in His temple. Through these events, He formally signified that His long-prophesied coming with power and glory was finally at hand. The Savior firmly established His divinity in the Kirtland years.

Anciently, Christ cited three indisputable measures by which His divinity was established. One was by the direct witness of John the Baptist, who saw "the Spirit descending from heaven like a dove."[2] Second was the witness of His Father.[3] The third consisted of scriptures that testified of Him.[4] All three of these measures were evidenced in Kirtland. First, more than ten witnesses testified that they saw the Savior or heard Him speak. Second, five witnesses saw the Father and the Son manifest themselves in vision together. The Father's words also witnessed of Christ more than six times. Third, hundreds of pages of scripture went to the world from Kirtland testifying of the Savior.[5] These indisputable witnesses from Kirtland thunder Christ's divinity to the world. Christ is resurrected. He leads His Church. The Redeemer and Savior of the world offers His infinite atonement to all of God's children.

---

2. John 1:32; 5:33.

3. John 5:37.

4. John 5:39.

5. As with the New Testament, meanings of ancient scripture were restored and new scriptures were given (see 95n1).

Stories That Evidence the Lord's Voice and Direction

I, the Lord, will build up Kirtland.

—Doctrine & Covenants 124:83

Just as surely as the Savior directed His work in Kirtland in the 1830s, so also has He directed recent events in Kirtland beginning in the 1970s. On January 19, 1841, the Savior prophesied His plans as He promised His Saints "I, the Lord, will build up Kirtland."[1] Nine months later, He foretold the time frame through His patriarch, Hyrum Smith, saying, "[After] many years shall pass away . . . I will send forth and build up Kirtland."[2] Referring to coming events in the Kirtland Temple, He said, "I will . . . speak unto them [my servants] with mine own voice, if my people will keep my commandments, and do not pollute this holy house."[3] Many stories demonstrate how the Lord has fulfilled these promises, but two stand out above the rest.

1. Doctrine & Covenants 124:83.

2. Joseph Smith, *History of The Church of Jesus Christ of Latter-day Saints,* ed. B. H. Roberts, 7 vols., 2d ed. rev. (Salt Lake City: The Church of Jesus Christ of Latter-day Saints, 1932–51), 4:443–44; *Times and Seasons* 3 (November 15, 1841): 589.

3. Doctrine & Covenants 110:8.

A Spiritually Powerful Sacrament Meeting

On November 6, 1993, Elder M. Russell Ballard stood in the elevated Melchizedek Priesthood pulpits of the Kirtland Temple to preside over an exceptional sacrament service. About 180 Church leaders, including General Authorities, regional representatives, mission presidents, temple presidents, and stake presidents, attended. These leaders and their wives had come together for an area training meeting. In addition to Elder Ballard, General Authorities attending the sacrament meeting were Elders Cree-L Kofford, president of the North America Northeast Area; Yoshihiko Kikuchi, counselor to Elder Kofford; and Joe J. Christensen, Marlin K. Jensen, and Rex D. Pinegar.

The Lord poured out His Spirit in this sacrament meeting in a never-to-be-forgotten way. Many present likened it to what it must have been like at the Kirtland Temple dedication in 1836. This was the first sacrament meeting in possibly 140 years that LDS Church leaders had been allowed to conduct in the Kirtland Temple. Elder Ballard and Elder Kofford blessed the sacrament. Assisted by others, including all General Authorities present, they then passed it to the congregation. People who were in that meeting have frequently made such comments as the following:

- "There was a great spiritual power that I felt in the meeting."
- "It was the most spiritual meeting I ever attended."
- "There was not a dry eye in the audience."
- "It was a meeting I will never forget."
- "I had a great spiritual experience in the meeting."
- "I received a spiritual manifestation there."
- "We heard angels singing."
- "I recorded what *I saw and heard.*"
- "Whenever I meet others who were there, we reminisce about the meeting."

- "I am one who never has this kind of experience, but I did this time."[4]

Al Walters, the representative of the Community of Christ who was present, said, "It was obvious that everyone was experiencing a great outpouring of the Spirit."[5] Elder Ballard said, "Deep spiritual feelings were felt by everyone." Elder Kofford added, "It was a tremendous spiritual experience." Elder Pinegar stated that they were so strongly affected that "we were almost unable to speak or sing, although that opportunity was afforded us." Elder Kikuchi remembered, "We [the General Authorities] sat, possibly, right beneath the spot where the Savior appeared to Joseph and Oliver."[6]

Al reported his crowning spiritual experience. Before this meeting, he had strongly objected to LDS Church leaders being given permission to administer and partake of the sacrament in the temple. His objection was based on the fact that the Community of Christ was a "closed communion" church (meaning that nonmembers were not offered the sacrament during services.)[7] He told his church leaders, "The LDS have temples of their own. Let them go to one of their temples to partake of the sacrament. Why do they come to *our* temple?" Community of Christ leaders had given formal permission, so they asked Al to support their decision. They also assigned him to attend the meeting.

As the meeting progressed, Al felt a dark cloud come over him. He even became physically ill. As the meeting progressed, the dark feeling intensified. It reached the point that his head and heart were pounding so hard that he felt he might be having a heart attack. At that point, Elder Kikuchi stood up to speak.

---

4. Karl Ricks Anderson, notes on North America Northeast Area training meeting, November 6, 1993; in author's possession.

5. Author's notes.

6. R. Scott Lloyd, "LDS Service Held in Kirtland Temple," *Church News*, December 4, 1993.

7. Community of Christ, formerly known as the Reorganized Church of Jesus Christ of Latter Day Saints, has moved away from its practice of closed communion.

Al felt the Spirit come over him. An audible voice that only he heard made three statements: "Alan, this is not your temple; this is mine. These are also my Saints. This is an acceptable use of this sacred space!"[8] Walters called this experience a "spiritual spanking" and felt that the Savior had spoken to him directly. He then humbled himself and shared with the rest the wonderful spirit of that occasion. Later Al said the Savior had completely changed his attitude.

Others in attendance were blessed with their own spiritual experiences. If journal entries of that day were to be made public, many would certify to the thinness of the veil. When the full history of Kirtland is written, the temple sacrament service of November 6, 1993, under the direction of an Apostle of the Lord and a descendant of Hyrum Smith, will undoubtedly be marked as one of its spiritual high points.

The Lord and Steve Young Move a Road

The second story is about how the Lord enabled a huge obstacle to be removed so that the Church's Historic Kirtland Village could be built. In the early 1990s the First Presidency decided that before the village could be restored, two century-old roads needed to be rerouted. These roads daily carried about twenty thousand vehicles directly through the center of the proposed village. The main intersection of these roads at the corner of the Whitney Store had four stop signs, which irritated drivers and created traffic backups. This intersection was also extremely unsafe for pedestrians.

As a longtime priesthood leader and resident of the area, I received an assignment from the Church to work with the City of Kirtland to reroute the roads. Mayor Mario Marcopoli was in favor of the road relocation, but council approval was also necessary. Mayor Marcopoli explained that he could not ensure a favorable council vote. He seemed sure that two or three council members would vote with him, but approval required a majority

---

8. Al Walters to Karl Ricks Anderson, 2012; used by permission; Anderson, journal, June 28, 1994.

vote of four of the seven council members. The mayor encouraged me to pray, saying, "You know the Man upstairs. Please talk with Him about this so that the other councilmen will vote with us." In the absence of further ideas, the mayor said, "Well, we'll just have to wait on the Lord."

About the end of May 1993, Mayor Marcopoli telephoned and said, "Thank you for arranging this with the Man upstairs." Then he suggested that I purchase a copy of the May 31, 1993, issue of *Sports Illustrated* and call him back. To my surprise, I found a photograph in the issue of star football quarterbacks Steve Young and Joe Montana. They were walking side by side on a football practice field. Each wore a pullover shirt. Joe Montana's read, "San Francisco Forty-Niners." Steve Young's shirt read, "Kirtland, Ohio, City of Faith and Beauty" and had an illustration of the Kirtland Temple in the middle of it. (The Whitney store dedication committee had given Steve the shirt nine years before when he attended the dedication of the store.) That day Steve just *happened* to wear that shirt under his football uniform, which he removed just before the photographer snapped the picture.

When I called Mayor Marcopoli back, he explained that one of the councilwomen, a teacher at a local school, discovered the photo when one of her students brought the magazine to school. She took it to the mayor and requested that he ask the Church to provide funds to purchase the photo so that it could be placed in the newly built Kirtland City Hall. The Church not only bought an enlargement of the photo but also had it framed and hung in the entryway to the council chambers. That day Steve Young became Kirtland's favorite son!

Later in the fall the 49ers traveled to Cleveland to play the Cleveland Browns. A reception was arranged for Kirtland City Council members and their families. Steve spent an hour with them. They were allowed to take individual as well as family photographs. He signed anything that was available, including clothing, napkins, and the enlarged photograph of him and Joe Montana. He then invited all to attend the Monday night football game. This experience created considerable good will with Kirtland leaders.

A few months later I appeared before the council to formally request the rerouting of roads around the Whitney store. I will never forget how council members stood when I walked into the council chambers. I actually looked behind me to see who was there, not realizing that they had stood out of respect for the Church. The council voted unanimously to allow the change of roads to proceed. I considered this an answer to prayer and a divinely designed approach to ask for the council's support. This enabled the continued growth and development of the Church's Historic Kirtland Village.

A footnote to this story confirms that the mayor also attributed the road relocation to divine intervention. Six years later, final city approval was scheduled for a vote. But animosity, not related to the Church, had developed between Mayor Marcopoli and the council. In retribution several council members announced they would vote against final road approval, which the mayor still favored. "Well," he said the day of the vote, "we may be in for some trouble tonight." Sensing my concern, the mayor then said something I should have said to him.

"Karl," he said, "don't you understand that God wants this road built? If God wants it built, how can the city council stand in the way?" He added, "One day I will have to stand before God and account for my life. I may not have a lot going for me, but I want to be able to say, 'At least I built your road in Kirtland.'" Then he concluded, "I think it will come out okay." In an action Mayor Marcopoli attributed to the Lord, the council voted six to one to finish the project.[9]

Certainly the Lord did not forget His promise: "I, the Lord, will build up Kirtland."[10]

---

9. Anderson, journal, May 31, 2001.

10. Doctrine & Covenants 124:83.

INDEX